HAYNES EXTREME Peugeot

106

The definitive guide to modifying
by **Bob Jex** & **Em Willmott**

Haynes Publishing

ISBN 978 1 84425 730 0

First printed August 2004
Reprinted March 2007

Printed by **J H Haynes & Co Ltd,**
Sparkford, Yeovil, Somerset BA22 7JJ, UK.

Tel: 01963 442030 Fax: 01963 440001
Int. tel: +44 1963 442030 Fax: +44 1963 440001
E-mail: sales@haynes.co.uk
Web site: www.haynes.co.uk

Haynes North America, Inc
861 Lawrence Drive, Newbury Park, California 91320, USA

Haynes Publishing Nordiska AB
Box 1504, 751 45 UPPSALA, Sweden

(4189 - 2AL1)

It wasn't my idea guv'nor!

1 Advice on safety procedures and precautions is contained throughout this manual, and more specifically on page 186. You are strongly recommended to note these comments, and to pay close attention to any instructions that may be given by the parts supplier.

2 J H Haynes recommends that vehicle customisation should only be undertaken by individuals with experience of vehicle mechanics; if you are unsure as to how to go about the customisation, advice should be sought from a competent and experienced individual. Any queries regarding customisation should be addressed to the product manufacturer concerned, and not to J H Haynes, nor the vehicle manufacturer.

3 The instructions in this manual are followed at the risk of the reader who remains fully and solely responsible for the safety, roadworthiness and legality of his/her vehicle. Thus J H Haynes are giving only non-specific advice in this respect.

4 When modifying a car it is important to bear in mind the legal responsibilities placed on the owners, driver and modifiers of cars, including, but not limited to, the Road Traffic Act 1988. IN PARTICULAR, IT IS AN OFFENCE TO DRIVE ON A PUBLIC ROAD A VEHICLE WHICH IS NOT INSURED OR WHICH DOES NOT COMPLY WITH THE CONSTRUCTION AND USE REGULATIONS, OR WHICH IS DANGEROUS AND MAY CAUSE INJURY TO ANY PERSON, OR WHICH DOES NOT HOLD A CURRENT MOT CERTIFICATE OR DISPLAY A VALID TAX DISC.

5 The safety of any alteration and its compliance with construction and use regulations should be checked before a modified vehicle is sold as it may be an offence to sell a vehicle which is not roadworthy.

6 Any advice provided is correct to the best of our knowledge at the time of publication, but the reader should pay particular attention to any changes of specification to the vehicles, or parts, which can occur without notice.

7 Alterations to vehicles should be disclosed to insurers and licensing authorities, and legal advice taken from the police, vehicle testing centres, or appropriate regulatory bodies.

8 The vehicle has been chosen for this project as it is one of those most widely customised by its owners, and readers should not assume that the vehicle manufacturers have given their approval to the modifications.

9 Neither J H Haynes nor the manufacturers give any warranty as to the safety of a vehicle after alterations, such as those contained in this book, have been made. J H Haynes will not accept liability for any economic loss, damage to property or death and personal injury arising from use of this manual other than in respect of injury or death resulting directly from J H Haynes' negligence.

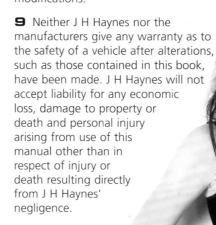

Contents

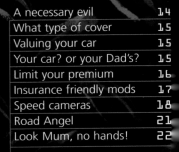

Security

04

Body styling

05

Lights & bulbs

06

Wheels & tyres

07

11

12

13

14

ICE

Engines

Exhausts

Reference

Haynes Extreme

What's that then?

Haynes Publishing have, for more than forty years, been helping people keep their cars on the roads in countries all over the world by publishing maintenance manuals. Chances are you've either got one of them yourself or you know somebody who has.

"Lights & bulbs" includes fitting high-power blue headlight bulbs, side repeaters, etc.

Before

After

Remember what it feels like on your birthday, or at Christmas, when you're faced by a pile of pressies? So do we, that gnawing feeling in your gut, what's in them? What did I get? Take that feeling and multiply it by twelve, that's how we felt when we started this project. When we decided that it was time to try something new, we couldn't wait. Because the same theories apply to modifying your car as servicing it, we reckoned we'd better get on and do it ourselves. We don't pay other people to do it for us, and we get the same dodgy instructions with kit as everybody else.

So if you've ever wondered how to fit a universal door mirror properly, smooth a tailgate or just bolt a seat in, this book is for you.

We've picked up a skip full of tips along the way, and they're all here for you to use. We haven't tried to set any trends, but we've covered every possible process we think you'll need. So where we've tinted a front door window, the same rules apply to a rear one, job done.

If you look in the magazines and want some of that, join us, 'cos so do we, and we'll show you how to get it.

Keeping it real

Modifying a car is without its problems in the 'real world', as opposed to the seemingly fantasy world of the glossy mags. For instance, it's pretty easy to spend hours fitting illegal window tints or smoked lights if you get pulled the first time you're out

afterwards. Of course, you can get pulled for all sorts of reasons (and just driving a modified car is reason enough sometimes), but keeping the car actually legal is one of the 'hidden' challenges with modifying. Throughout the book, our tips should give all the help you need to at least appear to be on the right side of the law. The annual MOT test is another favourite time for your mods to get panned, and again, we aim to give you all the help necessary to ensure at least that what you've changed doesn't lead to a fail.

Security is another major issue with a tweaked motor, and the perils of insurance cannot be taken lightly, either. We aim to give down-to-earth advice to help you keep the car in the first place, and to help you in not upsetting your insurers too much if the worst happens.

A word about fashion

In producing this book, we're aware that fashions change. What we show being fitted to our car might well be hideously out of date in 6 months time, or might not be your thing in the first place! Also, some of the stuff we've acquired from our various suppliers may no longer be available by the time you read this. We hope that, despite this, our approach of showing you step-by-step how to fit the various parts will mean that, even if the parts change slightly, the procedures we show for fitting will still be valid.

Our main project car was a 1997 Peugeot 106 1.6 XS.

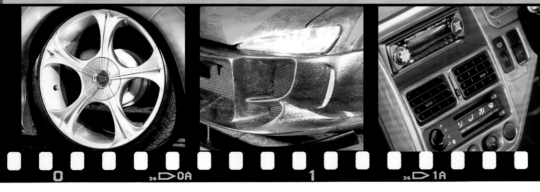

"Wheels & tyres" takes a detailed look at all the options.

"Body styling" shows you how to fit universal mirrors to full body kits.

"Interiors" includes seats, painting trim, gear knobs and loads more.

26 LJW 75

Look, it's NOT a Saxo, right

Having an identity crisis is never healthy (we've all seen "Fight Club", right?). The Peugeot 106 has one, though - people keep mistaking it for the mega-popular Citroen Saxo, especially once it's been modded. So before you start on the modifying trail with a 106, keep one thing in mind - anything which makes your car look more Saxo-like is a bad move. Individuality is what modifying's all about, and the last thing you want is to be lumped in with all those Saxo owners.

You could say that the 106 developed from another kind of crisis. When Peugeot were looking for ways to replace the huge-selling 205

in '93, they were struggling, and instead of going large, they went small, and gave us the 106. Which was based on another Citroën, the AX (no getting away from 'em, is there?). But at least the Peugeot's always been a better-looking car than its Cit equivalents, and the much-improved 106 Mk 2 which arrived in 1996 really drew a line between the two makes. Underneath, they're pretty-

much identical, which is actually good news, as it means there's a mahoosive range of kit to choose from.

If you're shopping for your first car, a 106 makes way more sense than say, a Nova - for starters, the design isn't 20+ years old. They're all affordable, there's loads of choice (including good-value sportsters like the XS and Rallye), and they're all easy (and inexpensive) to modify. Oh - and Vauxhall owners listen up here - the feisty Frenchie doesn't rust away before your eyes. Just avoid the 5-doors and diesels, and you're on your way. Choosing one instead of that S-car just means you've thought about it, instead of following the herd. We salute you.

Buyer's guide

What to buy

The main reason for buying a 106, of course, is the styling. Always better-looking than the dumpy Saxo, but with the same choice of modding parts, you're not going with the herd – and still laffing. For maximum style points, it has to be a Mk 2 106, which really made the Mk 1 look a babyface, but then we wouldn't argue against a Mk 1 Rallye in good nick. Resist the pull of the GTI, and insurance is sensible. Unlike certain small Vauxhalls and Fords, modern French cars like the 106 don't give in to the rust demon too easily.

Any bad news before you splash the cash on a 106? Well, they're not the biggest cars – any plans to carry three hefty mates around, and you'd be better off with a 306. For tall types, driving the 106 isn't a very comfortable proposition. Try the pedals for size – if you've got size 11 boots, you may find the car's almost undriveable, the pedals are so cramped. 106 5-doors are a big no-no style-wise, and there's also no excuse for buying an oil-burner.

Keeping it real

Your first important choice is whether to go for a Mk 1 or a Mk 2. This will probably be dictated by available funds, but if you can afford a Mk 2, it's worth the extra (in our humble opinion). If you're expecting masses of standard kit, you'll have to aim high in the 106 range – even the latest models struggle a little in the features department. You don't necessarily even get a 5-speed gearbox…

So what do you get, at the budget end of the range? Well, if you've opted for a Mk 1 106, you could pick yourself up a rare 1.0 litre model. And with 45 bhp, it deserves to be rare. Avoid – it's not even cheaper on insurance than the 60 bhp 1.1 litre versions.

If insurance is a problem, the 1.1 litre models are at least packing 60 bhp, and offer semi-lively performance. Mk 1 models (without the safety kit/immobiliser) fall into Group 4 or 5, while the Mk 2s are a very reasonable Group 3. Loads of special editions out there (some of which might actually feature a pop-up sunroof), but if you want any toys, you'll be after the likes of the Mk 2 XL and Zest versions.

Moving up to the 1.4 litre models (Group 5 or 6 insurance), we get a much better engine, and a few more luxuries, but again, the Mk 2 1.4 models have the most useful stuff, like electric windows, remote locking and power steering. If you don't mind dark metallic green paint, the Roland Garros special editions offer the nearest thing to a 'luxury' 106 experience. Lastly, just make sure that 1.4 you're looking at in the paper isn't a 1.4 diesel…

Insurance XS

Fancy something a little sportier? First along was the 1.4 XSi, the original top-of-the range sportster, with bodykit, sports seats, alloys

– the whole package. If you can find a pre-1993 non-cat XSi, it's worth choosing over a later model – without the catalyst, it's packing 100 bhp (94 bhp in environment-friendly form). Its baby brother, the 1.4 XS, had most of the goodies but less power (75 bhp), and a more reasonable insurance rating (Group 7 vs Group 10). The XSi grew to 1.6 litres (90 bhp) by 1994, but insurance also climbed to Group 11.

The Mk 2 XS kept the 1.6 litre 90-brake motor, but insurance dropped to Group 6! Tell me that's not a bargain – no wonder we picked one for our project car. Kit-wise, the only major omission is electric windows. Trouble is, it's a rare beast – it should've sold by the bucketload, but it only stayed in production about a year, with less than a thousand sold.

Luckily, the Mk 2 XS was succeeded in 1998 by the 1.4 Quiksilver, which if anything, is even more worthy of your spons. Alright, so it's 'only' a 1.4 engine, but it's also a GTI-lookalike, with the full bodykit and most of the toys. And – wait for it – Group 5 insurance. Surely shome mishtake? Highly sought-after, they're expensive secondhand (there had to be a catch).

Rallyes are homologation specials, built to qualify the 106 for international motorsport. What we get is a stripped-out (lightweight) car with uprated brakes and suspension, and a really hot little engine – on the Mk 1 (or series 1) we got a special 1.3 litre, 100 bhp unit, which means cheap road tax, if not insurance

(Group 9). If you can find one that's been looked after, you'll be doing very well – only 1000 made it to these shores. The Mk 2 (or series 2) Rallye carried on the line, with a tuned 1.6 litre engine which would give a GTI a good run – in fact, with its rear discs and sports trim, it's a better-value choice than the GTI. If you can find one. The later Rallye is even rarer than the original, with just a few hundred making it here. For sheer rev-the-pants-off-it driving fun, you won't beat a Rallye. It's a proper boy's toy.

Cheap insurance is for wimps

The GTI, with its snorting 16-valve 120 bhp engine, is obviously the Daddy, and definitely one for the enthusiasts. Reckoned (at one time) by no less a person than Jeremy Clarkson to be the best-handling front-wheel drive car ever, it's a serious bit of kit. If Group 13 insurance doesn't scare you off, go for it. It's the ultimate 106-sized thrill.

Diesel? Only if you must...

Awesome fuel economy's hardly very cool, and there's no getting away from the tickover rattle. There's no turbo-diesel option on the 106, so unlike its big 306 brother, you won't see many 106 diesels getting modified. The later 1.5 engine's a better bet than the 1.4 which preceded it, but neither offers anything like a fun drive. Even if funds are tight, we can't see any reason to choose one over a 1.1 litre petrol.

Don't buy a **dog**

No-one's accusing the 106 of being a girly car, but they are popular with those of the female persuasion. If you can find a one-lady-owner 106, used only as a second car, you could be in for a major bargain. Despite an apparently-lightweight build, Peugeot 106s are pretty solid, and rust is almost non-existent. So nothing ever goes wrong? Don't be silly.

Especially on sportier 106s with standard alloys, check that the spare is actually in its cradle under the back of the car, and hasn't been nicked. Many owners either carry their spare inside the boot, or leave it at home altogether, to defeat the pikeys.

Any clonking noises over bumps need investigating. The most likely culprits are the front anti-roll bar bushes (especially on sportier models, which have vertical drop links fitted). These aren't expensive to replace, but maybe the owner doesn't know that! If there's

uneven front tyre wear accompanying the noise, this could be more expensive to sort (lower arm bushes or balljoints) – get haggling.

Look round the engine (and on the owner's driveway) for any sign of oil leaks from the engine. Usually, these aren't all that serious, but if the engine's dripping with oil (or spotlessly-clean because it's just come back from the jetwash), look more carefully.

All 106s have a camshaft drivebelt (cambelt, or timing belt) which is made of reinforced rubber. The belt deteriorates with age, and for safety's sake, a new one should be fitted every 3 years or 36000 miles, especially if the engine gets a regular caning. If the belt snaps, the engine could be wrecked. Finished. Ruined. Knackered. It's not too bad a DIY job if you're confident under the hood, or budget for a garage bill around the £100 mark. Ask for a new tensioner/pulleys at the same time.

General stuff

Usually, it's far better to buy your 106 privately, as long as you know what you're doing. Dealers have to make a living, but sometimes all you'll get for the extra money is a full valet and some degree of comeback if the car's a hound. Buying privately, you get to meet the owner, gaining you valuable clues about how the car's been treated.

Everyone's nervous when buying a car, but don't ignore your 'gut feelings' at first sight, or when meeting the owner. Don't make the mistake of deciding to buy the car *before you've even seen it* - too many people make up their minds before setting out, and blindly ignore all the warning signs. Remember, there *are* other cars, and you *can* walk away! Think of a good excuse before you set out.

Take someone who 'knows a bit about cars' along with you - preferably, try and find someone who's either got a 106, or who's had one in the past.

Never buy a car in the dark, or when it's raining. If you do have to view any car in these conditions, agree not to hand over any major money until you've seen it in daylight, and when the paintwork's dry (dull, faded paint, or metallic paint that's lost its lacquer, will appear to be shiny in the rain).

Check the mileages and dates shown on the receipts and MoTs follow a pattern indicating normal use, with no gaps in the dates, and no sudden drop in the mileage between MoTs (which might suggest 'clocking'). If you're presented with a sheaf of paperwork, it's worth going through it - maybe the car's had a history of problems, or maybe it's just had some nice new parts fitted (like a clutch, starter motor or alternator, for instance).

Check the chassis number (VIN number) and engine number on the registration document and on the car. Any sign of welding near one of these numbers is suspicious - to disguise the real number, a thief will run a line of weld over the old number, grind it flat, then stamp in a new number. Other scams include cutting the section of bodywork with the numbers on from another car, then cutting and welding this section into place. The VIN plate is located under the bonnet, on the crossmember between the headlights, and it's stamped into the top edge of the driver's-side inner wing, or across the bulkhead behind the engine.

The engine number's on a metal plate riveted to the front of the engine block, or stamped onto a flat surface at the transmission end - shouldn't be difficult to spot. If the number's been removed, or if there's anything suspicious about it, you could be buying trouble.

Check the registration document (V5) very carefully - all the details should match the car. Never buy a car without seeing the V5 - accept no excuses on this point. If buying privately, make sure it's definitely the owner's name and address printed on it - if not, be very careful! If buying from a dealer, note the name and address, and try to contact the previous owner to confirm mileage, etc, before handing over more than a deposit. The car

Tricks 'n' tips

Tyres can be a giveaway to a car maintained on a shoestring - four different makes of tyre, especially cheap brands, can indicate a penny-pinching attitude which won't have done the rest of the car any favours.

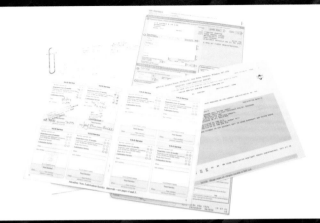

Full service history (fsh)

Is there any service history? If so, this is good, but study the service book carefully:

a *Which garage has done the servicing? Is it a proper dealer, or a backstreet bodger? Do you know the garage, and if so, would you use it?*

b *Do the mileages show a nice even progression, or are there huge gaps? Check the dates too.*

c *Does it look as if the stamps are authentic? Do the oldest ones look old, or could this 'service history' have been created last week, to make the car look good?*

d *When was the last service, and what exactly was carried out? When was the cambelt last changed? Has the owner got receipts for any of this servicing work?*

One sign of a genuine car is a good batch of old MOTs, and as many receipts as possible - even if they're for fairly irrelevant things like tyres.

shouldn't have had many previous owners - otherwise, it may mean the car is trouble, so checking its owner history is more important.

While the trim on a 106 is quite durable, it should still be obvious whether the car's been abused over a long period, or whether the mileage showing is genuine or not (shiny steering wheels, worn carpets and pedals are a good place to start checking if you're suspicious). Okay, so you may be planning to junk most of the interior at some point, but why should you pay over the odds for a tat car which the owner hasn't given a stuff about?

Although you may feel a bit stupid doing it, check simple things too, like making sure the windows and sunroof open and shut, and that all the doors and tailgate can be locked (if a lock's been replaced, ask why). Check all the basic electrical equipment - lights, front and rear wipers, heated rear window, heater fan; it's amazing how often these things are taken for granted by buyers! If your chosen 106 already has alloys fitted, does it have locking wheel bolts? Where's the key? What about the code and removal tools for the stereo?

Is the catalytic converter ('cat') working? This is a wickedly expensive part to replace - the best way to ensure at least one year's grace is to only buy a car with a full MoT (the cat is checked during the emissions test). Many 106 modifiers remove the cat altogether (by fitting a de-cat pipe), which is great for performance, but means the car's illegal to use on the road. GTIs which have lived a life on the rev limiter may have blown the cat, so get it checked if there's not a fresh MoT on it.

The VIN number is stamped across the bulkhead, behind the engine . . .

. . . and also appears on this plate under the bonnet.

Look closer

Don't take anything at face value. Even a fully-stamped service book only tells half the story of how your chosen 106 has been treated. Does the owner look bright enough to even know what a dipstick is, never mind how to check the oil level between services?

Check for signs of accident damage, especially at the front end (and even more so, on the sporty models). Ask if it's ever been in a shunt - if the seller says no, but there's paint overspray under the bonnet, what's going on? Also check for paint overspray on the window rubbers, light units and bumpers/trim. Look at the car side-on - are there any mis-matched panels? With the bonnet open, check that the headlight rear shells are the same colour - mis-matched or new-looking ones merit an explanation from the seller. Does the front number plate carry details of the supplying garage, like the back one? If not, why has a new plate been fitted?

Check the glass (and even the head and tail lights) for etched-in registration numbers - are they all the same, and does it match the car's actual registration? Later 106s have the VIN etched on the glass - does it match the logbook? A windscreen could've been innocently replaced, but new side glass indicates a break-in at least - is the car a 'stolen/recovered' (joyridden) example? Find the chassis and engine numbers, as described earlier in this Section, and satisfy yourself that they're genuine - check them against the registration document. An HPI check (or similar) is worthwhile, but even this won't tell you everything. If you're in doubt, or if the answers to your questions don't ring true, walk away. Make any excuse you like.

All Mk 2 106s at least have a keypad immobiliser as standard (this became an ignition key-type immobiliser from December 1997), but there's no harm fitting a good ultrasonic alarm on top (if it hasn't already got one). Might even be worth a bit of insurance discount. Make sure any aftermarket alarm actually works, that it looks properly installed, with no stray wires hanging out, and that you get the Thatcham certificate or other paperwork to go with it. If possible, it's worth finding out exactly how it's been wired in - if it goes wrong later, you could be stranded with no chance of disabling the system to get you home.

Model history

Note: *As usual, there's plenty of "special edition" 106 models. The majority are just the base model with different trim – not all are listed below. Don't pay over the odds for a special edition, unless it's really got some extra kit you actually want.*

October 1991 (J reg) – 106 range introduced in the UK, initially as 3-door only. 1.0 litre (45 bhp), 1.1 litre (60 bhp) and 1.4 litre (75 bhp) petrol engines, XN, XR and XT trim levels, with top-of-the-range XSi (100 bhp, sports bodykit and interior, alloys).

October 1992 (K reg) – All models now have fuel injection and catalytic converter. 1.4 litre diesel models launched. Base models now designated Graduate.

February 1993 (K reg) – 5-door models introduced.

October 1993 (L reg) – 1.4 litre XS introduced. Similar to XSi, but with 75 bhp engine.

February 1994 (L reg) – 1.3 Rallye introduced. Limited production run for competition homologation. Highly-tuned 1.3 litre multi-point injection engine (100 bhp @ 7200 rpm). Basic equipment for light weight, but with uprated suspension, sports trim / badging, red carpets and white steel wheels.

April 1994 (L reg) – 1.4 Roland Garros limited edition introduced, named after the French tennis stadium. Metallic green paint, sunroof, front fogs, sports seats, leather trim.

Performance figures

	0-60 mph	Top speed (mph)
1.0 litre	20.0	84
1.1 litre	14.2	96
1.3 Rallye	9.3	118
1.4 litre (75 bhp)	11.4	107
1.4 litre (XSi)	9.0	116
1.6 litre (90 bhp)	10.9	113
1.6 litre (Rallye)	8.8	121
1.6 litre (GTI)	7.7	124
1.4 Diesel	17.9	89
1.5 Diesel	14.3	98

August 1994 (M reg) – XSi now has 1.6 litre 90 bhp engine. Base 1.1 Graduate models get a 5-speed gearbox as standard. 1.5 litre diesel engine replaces earlier 1.4 unit. XT, XS and XSi models fitted with keypad immobiliser.

June 1995 (M reg) – Aztec limited edition models introduced – 1.4 Aztec similar to XS, but all have deep front bumper and sunroof. 1.0 litre Inca special edition also has deep front bumper.

June 1996 (N reg) – Mk 2 models introduced, with revised front and rear styling, high-level rear brake light, side impact beams and seat belt tensioners. Keypad immobiliser now fitted to all models. New XL trim level offers remote central locking, body-colour bumpers and driver's airbag. Roland Garros 1.4 litre special edition re-introduced, with sunroof, electric windows / mirrors, remote locking and rear headrests.

January 1997 (P reg) – 1.6 litre 16-valve GTI introduced, with 120 bhp. Sports bodykit, front fogs, electric windows / mirrors, driver's airbag, remote locking, power steering, ABS with all-round disc brakes, 14-inch alloys. 1.6 XL and XS models launched, with 90 bhp engine. XL has power steering, remote locking, driver's airbag. XS adds body-colour bumpers, rear spoiler, sports seats and trim.

June 1997 (P reg) – Independence 1.1 litre limited edition, with sunroof, blue dials and driver's airbag.

October 1997 (R reg) – 1.6 litre Rallye homologation special introduced, with 103 bhp. Similar to previous Rallye model, but with blue carpets and dials, and rear disc brakes.

December 1997 (R reg) – Look 1.1 litre special editions introduced. Look 2 is higher spec, with power steering, tints, body-colour bumpers / door handles, front fogs and remote locking.

April 1998 (R reg) – Zest 1.1 litre models introduced. Zest 2 has body-colour bumpers, driver's airbag – Zest 3 adds power steering, electric windows. 1.4 litre 75 bhp Quiksilver launched, with GTI bodykit, electric windows, remote locking. GTI model gains alcantara trim and rear headrests.

September 1999 (V reg) – All models now have a driver's airbag. Zest 2 and 3 gain a single CD player.

May 2000 (W reg) – Zest 2 and 3 gain remote locking and coloured dials. GTI model gains passenger airbag. Independence 1.1 litre limited edition re-introduced (basic spec).

December 2000 (X reg) – Zest 2 and 3 gain electric windows. GTI gains side airbags, spare wheel now steel instead of alloy.

May 2002 (02 reg) – Independence 1.1 litre re-introduced, with power steering, driver's airbag, body-colour bumpers.

January 2003 (52 reg) – Zen 1.1 litre replaces Zest 2, gains tilt/slide sunroof. Range now comprises 1.1 Independence, 1.1 and 1.5 diesel Zen, 1.4 Quiksilver, and 1.6 GTI.

Insurance & The Law

A necessary evil

Ah, insurance - loads of money, and all you get is a piece of paper you're not supposed to use! Of course, you must have insurance - you're illegal on the road without it, and you won't be able to get the car taxed, either. If you're ever caught driving without insurance, you'll have great trouble ever getting insurance again - insurance companies regard this offence nearly as seriously as drink-driving, so don't do it!

The way insurance companies work out premiums and assess risks is a mystery to most of us. In general, the smaller the engine you have in your 106, the less you'll pay. However, if one company's had a lot of claims on 106s in the past, the GTI factor might 'unfairly' influence the premiums of lesser 106s, too (this is why it's important to shop around). An 'insurance-friendly' XS should be a good bet for a sensible premium, but remember that insurance companies aren't stupid - if you swap in that 16-valve engine and turn your XS into a GTI-alike, they may well 'load' the premium to GTI level (and that's Group 13). Insurance is a game you can't win, but you must play.

If your annual premium seems like the national debt of a small African country (and whose isn't!), always ring as many brokers and get as many quotes as you possibly can. Yes, there's loads better ways to spend an evening/afternoon than answering the same twenty questions over and over again, but you never know what the next quote will be. A few extra minutes spent on the phone (or on the 'net) once a year may result in an extra few hundred quid in your back pocket. Well, you live in hope don't you!

With modified cars, insurance becomes even more of a problem. By putting on all the alloys, trick body kits, nice interiors, big ICE, you're making the car much more of a target for thieves (yes, ok,

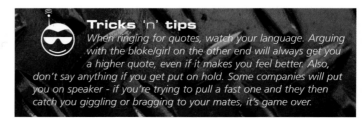

Tricks 'n' tips
When ringing for quotes, watch your language. Arguing with the bloke/girl on the other end will always get you a higher quote, even if it makes you feel better. Also, don't say anything if you get put on hold. Some companies will put you on speaker - if you're trying to pull a fast one and they then catch you giggling or bragging to your mates, it's game over.

we know you know this). The point is, the insurance companies know this too, and they don't want to be paying out for the car, plus all the money you've spent on it, should it go missing. There is a temptation 'not to tell the insurance' about the mods you've made. Let's deal with this right now. Our experience has been that, while it can be painful, honesty is best. Generally, the insurance company line is: '...thanks for telling us - we won't put the car 'up a group' (ie charge you more), but we also won't cover the extra cost of your alloy wheels/body kit/tasty seats in the event of any claim...'. This is fair enough - in other words, if your car goes missing, you get paid out, based on a standard car, minus all the goodies. If you particularly want all the extras covered, you might have a long hard search - most companies only offer 'modified for standard' policies. There are specialist insurers who are more friendly towards fully-loaded cars, but even they won't actually cover the cost of replacement goodies.

What type of cover, Sir?

For most of us, cost means there's only one option - TPF&T (third party, fire and theft). Fully-comp insurance is an unattainable dream for most people until they reach the 'magic' age of 25, but what's the real story?

Third Party only

The most basic cover you can get. Basically covers you for damage to other people's cars or property, and for personal injury claims. Virtually no cover for your own stuff, beyond what you get if you take the optional 'legal protection' cover.

Third Party, Fire and Theft

As above, with cover for fire and theft, of course! Better, but not much better. This is really only cover in the event of a 'total loss', if your car goes missing or goes up in smoke. Still no cover for your car if you stack it into a tree, or if someone breaks in and pinches your stereo (check your policy small-print).

Fully-comprehensive

In theory at least, covers you for any loss or damage. Will cover the cost of repairing or replacing your car, often with discounted windscreen cover and other benefits. If you lose control of the car on an icy road (arguably, not your fault) you get paid. If someone pinches your wheels and drops the car on the floor, you get paid - at least for the damage done to the underside, and for standard wheels and tyres. Most policies include provision of a hire car after a shunt, which is pretty useful. Some offer cheap breakdown cover packages in with the main policy. With a fully-comp policy, you can 'protect' your no-claims bonus for a small fee so you don't automatically lose all those hard-earned years' worth of discount if you prang it (generally, you can only do this on fully-comp).

All this extra cover costs, obviously, but how much? You might be surprised what the actual difference is. Think about it, anyway - it's got to be worth a couple of hundred quid more to go fully-comp, if your car's worth into four figures, surely?

Valuing your car

When your insurance pays out in the event of a total loss or write-off, they base their offer on the current market value of an identical standard model to yours (less your excess). The only way you'll get more than the average amount is to prove your 106 is in above-average nick (with photos?) or that the mileage was especially low for the year.

With this in mind, don't bother over-valuing your 106 in the hope you'll get more in the event of a claim - you won't! The only way to do this is to seek out an 'agreed-value' deal, which you can usually only get on classic-car policies (with these, the car's value is agreed in

advance between you, not worked out later by the company with you having no say in it). By over-valuing your 106, you could be increasing your premium without gaining any benefit - sound smart to you?

Equally though, don't under-value, in the hope you'll get a reduction in premium. You won't, and if there's a total loss claim, you won't get any more than your under-valued amount, no matter how loudly you complain.

Work on what you paid for the car, backed up with the sort of prices you see for similar cars in the ads (or use a secondhand car price guide). Add no more than 10% for the sake of optimism, and that's it.

Your car? Or your Dad's?

Insurance really costs when you're the wrong side of 25. Ever been tempted to tell your insurance that your full-on sorted 106 belongs to your Dad (old insurance-friendly person), then get him to insure it, with you as a named driver? Oh dear. This idea (known as 'fronting') is so old, it's grown a long white beard. And it sucks, too. First of all, insurance companies aren't stupid. They know your Dad (or your Mum, or old Uncle Bert) isn't likely to be running around in a kid's pocket-rocket, and they treat any 'named driver' application with great suspicion. Even if they do take your money, don't imagine they've been suckered. In the event of a claim, they'll look into everything very carefully, and will ask lots of awkward questions. If you get caught out in the lie, they've taken your money, and you've got no insurance - who's been suckered now?

This dubious practice also does you no favours in future years. All the time you're living the lie, you're not building up any no-claims bonus of your own - you're just delaying the pain 'til later, and without having real cover in the meantime.

'Legit' ways to limit your premium

If you do enough ringing around for quotes, you'll soon learn what the 'right answers' to some of the questions are - even if you can't actually give them (don't tell lies to your insurance company). Mind you, with a little thought, you can start to play their game and win - try these:

Volunteer to increase your excess. The 'excess' is put there to stop people claiming for piddling little amounts - when they pay out, it's always the repair/replacement cost minus whatever the 'excess' is. So, for instance, if you've got a £200 theft excess, it means you'll automatically get £200 less than the agreed value of your car, should it be stolen. Most policies have 'compulsory' excess amounts,

which you can do nothing about. By increasing excesses voluntarily, you're limiting the amount you'll get still further. Insurance companies like this, and should reduce your premium in return - but this only goes so far, so ask what the effect of different voluntary excesses will be. Don't increase your excess too far, or you'll get paid nowt if you claim!

Limit your mileage. Most companies offer a small discount if you only cover a small annual mileage. To get any meaningful reduction, the mileage has to be a lot less than 10,000 per year. Few companies, though, ever ask what the car's current mileage is - so how are they gonna know if you've gone over your self-imposed limit?

Make yourself the only driver. Pretty self-explanatory. The more people who drive your car, the greater the risk to the company, and a car's owner will always drive more carefully (it's their money that bought it) than any named driver. If you've built up 2 years' worth of no-claims, but your partner hasn't, putting them on your insurance will bump it up, due to their relative inexperience.

Get a garage - and use it. Where you park can have a big effect on your premium. Parking it on the street is the worst. Park off the road (on a driveway) when you're at home. The best thing is to have a garage of your own (don't pretend you use your Dad's garage) - see if you can rent one locally, even if it means walking a few hundred yards. If you're a student living away from home, tell your company where the car will be parked during term-time - if you're at Uni in London, this is a bigger risk than living at home 'in the country', and vice-versa.

Fit an approved alarm or immobiliser. See if you can get a list from your company of all their approved security devices, and fit whatever you can afford. Not all companies approve the same kit, so it might even be worth contacting more than one company for advice. Any device with a Thatcham or Sold Secure rating should be recognised. In some cases, the discounts offered are not that great any more - but an alarm is still a nice way to get peace of mind.

Build up your no-claims bonus. You'll only do this by owning and insuring a car in your own name, and then not making any claims. Simple really. One rather immoral (but not actually illegal) dodge is to buy an old banger, insure it cheap, then never drive it. You'll need to keep it fully road-legal (with tax, MOT) if you park it on the road. For every year you do this, you'll build up another year of NCB.

Hang onto your no-claims bonus. Obviously, the less you claim, the less your insurance will cost. If something happens to your car, don't be in too big a hurry to make a claim before you've thought it all through. How much will it cost to fix? How much is your excess? How much will your renewal premium be, next year? If you have a big enough accident which you're sure isn't your fault, ring your company, but make it quite clear you're not claiming yet - just informing them of the accident. It should be down to the other driver's insurance to pay. You don't always lose all your no-claims, either, even if it was your fault - depends how many years you've built up. Once you've got a few years, ask whether you can 'protect' your no-claims.

Avoid speed cameras and The Law. Yes, okay, easier said than done! But anything less than a clean licence is not good from the insurance perspective. One SP30 won't hurt much, but the second strike will, so take it easy. Don't get caught on traffic-light cameras, either - just one is a major no-no.

Insurance-friendly mods?

Insurers don't like any changes from standard, but some things you'll do are worse from their viewpoint than others. The guidelines below are just that - for guidance. No two companies will have the same outlook, and your own circumstances will play a big part too.

Golden Rule Number One: Before you spend huge money modifying the car, ring your insurance, and ask them how it will affect things.

Golden Rule Number Two: If in doubt, declare everything. Insurance companies are legally entitled to dispute any claim if the car is found to be non-standard in any way.

Body mods – Even a tiny rear spoiler could be classed as a 'bodykit' (yes, it's daft, but that's how it is). Anything which alters the exterior appearance should be declared. As long as the mods don't include a radical full-on bodykit, the jump in premium should be fairly small. Any genuine Peugeot add-ons (GTI spoilers, etc) might not cost at all - bonus.

Brakes – The companies view brake mods as tampering with safety-related kit, and modifying the brakes implies that you drive fast and hard. You might get away with standard-sized grooved/drilled discs and pads, but fitting bigger discs and replacement calipers will prove expensive.

Engine mods – 'Mild' mods such as induction kits and exhausts don't give much more power, so don't generally hurt. But 'chipping' your 106 will lead to drastic rises in premiums, or a complete refusal of cover. With complete engine transplants, you'll be required to give an engineer's report, and to get your wad out.

Interior mods – Don't assume that tarting up the inside won't interest the insurance company. By making any part of the car more attractive, you're also attracting the crims. Cars get trashed for parts, as often as not - and your racing seats and sexy steering wheel could be worth major money. Still, the effect on premiums shouldn't be too great, especially if you've got an approved alarm.

Lights – Change the car's appearance, and are safety-related. You'll probably get asked for lots of details, but as long as you've

kept it sensible (and legal, as far as possible), the effect on your wallet shouldn't be too harsh.

Security – Make sure you mention all security stuff - alarms, immobilisers (including mechanical devices), locking wheel nuts, large Alsatian in the back seat… But - don't over-sell the car. Tell the truth, in other words. If you've got a steering wheel lock, do you always fit it? If you didn't when your car went missing, you're in trouble. Don't say you've got a Cat 1 alarm if it really came from Argos, and don't tell them you garage the car at night if it's stuck out in the road.

Suspension – Changes the car's appearance, and is safety-related. Some enlightened companies once took the view that modded suspension helps the car corner better, so it's safer. Drops of only 30 to 40 mm shouldn't mean bigger premiums.

Wheels – Very appearance-altering, and very nickable. At least show some responsibility by fitting some locking nuts/bolts and an approved alarm. Quite likely to attract a low-to-moderate rise in premium, which still won't cover your wheels properly - you could arrange separate cover for your wheels, then at least you'll get paid. Some companies may ask for a photo of the car with the wheels on.

And finally - a new nightmare

Not telling the insurance the whole truth gets a little tricky when you make a claim. If the insurance assessor comes to check your bent/burnt/stolen-and-recovered 'standard' 106, and finds he's looking at a vehicle fitted with trick alloys/bodykit/radical interior, he's not going to turn a blind eye. Has the car got an MoT? Oh, and did you declare those points on your licence? No? You're then very much at the mercy of your insurer, especially if they can prove any mods contributed to the claim. At best, you'll have a long-drawn-out battle with your insurer to get a part-payout, and at worst they'll just refuse to get involved at all.

One more thing - *be careful what you hit*. If your insurance is declared void, they won't pay out for the repairs to the other car you smacked into, or for the lamp-post you knock down (several hundred quid, actually). And then there's the personal injury claims - if your insurance company disowns you, it'll be you who has to foot the bill. Even sprains and bruises can warrant claims, and more serious injuries can result in claims running into lots of zeroes! Without insurance cover, **you'll** have to pay. Probably for a long, long time. Think about it, and we won't see you in court.

Big Brother in a Box

Speed cameras have to be one of the most unpopular things ever. We're talking worse than exams, dentists, alcohol-free beer, and the Budget. Does anyone actually like them? Well, the makers do - they should all be living it up on a beach in the Bahamas. The people making speed camera signs are obviously lovin' it. And the Chancellor? Nuff said.

Speed, of course, is fun. The sensation of speed is the main reason we enjoy driving, and it's one of the best ways to show off your motor. There's nothing like giving your ride a good caning, being pushed back in the seat, exhaust snarling, engine singing. Sounds like fun to me - so these things are really fun cameras, then?

Like it or not, we live in a world obsessed with limiting speed. Excess speed, we're told, causes accidents and costs lives. As most of us have realised by now, excess speed really means more money for the Government. What causes accidents is driving like a tw*t. But they don't have cameras for that.

Before we get ourselves in too much trouble, we have to admit the cameras might save lives in built-up areas with lots of peds, kids and old folk about. Driving like a hooligan in those situations probably should get you a slap on the wrist for 'endangering lives'. But at night, on a dead-straight road with no traffic? We think not.

Pay attention

The best you can say about cameras is that they're a necessary evil which we all have to live with. So what's the best way of avoiding the 'bad news' letter in the post?

There is one 100% foolproof method, which is totally legal, and it's dead simple - don't ever speed. That should do the trick. Yeah, right. Back in the real world, everyone speeds some time, even if it's only by a few mph. Add a few more miles-per because you weren't really watching your speed, and then do it somewhere there's a camera (or a sneaky mobile trap you'd never spotted before), and you're nicked. Is it any wonder that clean licences are getting as rare as rocking-horse leftovers?

Even on roads you know well, the do-gooders are forever lowering the limits, so if you don't watch it, you'll be sailing through more than 10 mph over today's new limit. And that's definitely worth a few points! You've gotta concentrate, to stay clean.

Know your enemy

First of all, you've got to know what you're up against. It's the only way (short of the fantasy world of never, ever speeding) that you stand a chance. And the first thing to know is - not all cameras are the same. Some can even be beaten.

Gatso (and PEEK)

The first, the best-known, the most common, and probably the most-hated. Invented by the winner of the 1953 Monte Carlo Rally, Gatsos are the familiar large, square box in stealth grey or high-viz yellow, with a square lens and flash unit (the later, less-common PEEK cameras have two round items, set one above the other). These are radar-operated (type 24) and can only 'get' you from behind, because they use a flash to take the photo, and this would blind you if it went off with you coming towards it. These cameras, therefore, cannot in theory catch you speeding towards them (don't quote us on that). As a result of this limitation, some authorities will turn the cameras round from time to time, to catch you out.

RLCs are also Gatso-based, but they work through sensors in the road, which are active when the lights are on red. If your car passes over them in this condition, it's gotcha. Some RLCs use radar too, so if you speed through on red, you'll also get a speeding fine. Gee, thanks.

Truvelo

Oooh, nasty. The forward-facing 'gatso' is particularly unpleasant, but luckily for us, it's also more expensive than the rear-facing Gatso, so not as common. Yet. The Truvelo camera can be recognised by two round lenses side by side in the centre of its box, and one of these is a pinky-red colour (hence the 'pinkeye' nickname). The unusual pink 'lens' is actually a flash unit, fitted with a red filter to avoid blinding the driver. Because the photo's taken from the front, it's hard for the driver to claim someone else was driving, or that they 'don't know'

Gatsos have 35 mm film inside, with about 400 shots possible before the film runs out. It's obviously vital that the film is recovered from the camera, or a prosecution can't be made - these cameras get vandalised for all sorts of reasons. Some cameras are rumoured not to contain any film, so they flash without recording any evidence (that bloke down the pub could be wrong, though).

If the radar detects excess speed, the flash is triggered twice as you pass over the measured line markings on the road. From the distance you travel between the set flashes, your speed can be proved. It's anyone's guess where the trigger speed for a camera will be set, but it's almost bound to be quite a few mph over the posted limit - if it wasn't, the camera would quickly catch dozens of speeders, and run out of film. Be more wary of inner-city Gatsos, as they're probably 'emptied' more often, allowing a lower speed tolerance.

tricks 'n' tips

In a thirty limit, you're less likely to speed if you hook a lower gear than normal. Most cars will comfortably cruise through a thirty in 4th gear, but it's too easy to add speed in 4th. Try using 3rd, and the natural engine braking (and extra engine/exhaust noise) will help you keep a lid on your speed. It's not foolproof, but give it a try anyway.

who was driving (a common ploy to try and 'get off' Gatso offences). The less-visible flash gives less warning to following motorists, too. Not that we're suggesting they're out to get us. Oh no.

These babies are triggered by the car passing over piezo sensors set into the road, not radar. If you see three stripes across your path, slow the heck down.

Red Light Cameras

Intended to catch people who go through traffic lights on red. Which, you have to say, is pretty dodgy. And have you ever risked it on a single amber? If you remember your Highway Code, this means stop, the same as a red light. 'Amber-gamblers' should also beware the traffic-light cams, 'cos they'll get you one day. Unlike (a few) points for speeding, points for traffic light offences will really hurt your insurance premiums, so watch it.

SPECS

Yikes - this really is Big Bro stuff. This system uses digital cameras (no film needed), mounted high on special gantries - these are a set distance apart, and create a speed monitoring zone. When you 'enter the zone', your number plate is recorded digitally, with a date and time stamp (regardless of whether you're speeding). When you leave the zone, another camera does the same thing. Because you've travelled a known distance between the two cameras, it's possible to calculate your average speed - if you're over the limit for the stretch of road, the computer spits out a fine in your direction.

What's really worrying about this technology is that it can be used to cross-check you and your car for other offences (whether your car's taxed and MoT'd, for instance). Anything dodgy, and the next time you pass by those cameras at that time of day, you could be in for a jam-sandwich surprise. Still, it could also catch the crims making off with your motor…

Mobile or temporary speed traps

These are either Gatso, Mini-Gatso, or laser type.

The potential Gatso sites are easy enough to spot - look for three shiny strips across the road, with a sturdy grey metal post alongside, on the pavement. Mr Plod comes along, sets up his camera (which uses sensors in the road strips not radar to detect your speed), catches his daily quota of speeders, and moves on. Don't give him a short day by being one of his victims.

Mini-Gatsos are just smaller, mobile versions of the UK's least-favourite roadside 'furniture', operated out of cop-cars and anonymous white vans - to get you, you have to be driving away from them.

More sinister (and much on the increase) are the laser cameras, which are aimed at your number plate (usually the front one) and record your speed on video. Often seen mounted on tripods, on bridges overlooking busy roads, or hidden inside those white 'safety camera partnership' vans. Lasers have quite a range (1000 metres, or over half a mile), so by the time you've spotted them, they've spotted you speeding. It's up to the operator to target likely speeding vehicles - so will they pick on your maxed motor? You bet!

Achtung!
Do you live in, or regularly drive through, Northamptonshire or North Wales? We've got two words for you. Oh, dear. Northamptonshire is the area with the most cameras, and where new camera technology is often first tried out, while North Wales has one of the most active safety cam partnerships, with many roaming vans. But don't feel too bad, guys - the way it's going, the rest of us will soon catch you up.

Beating the system

No-one's condoning regular speeding, but these days, it's just too easy to get 'done' for a fairly minor speed infringement. Which hardly seems fair. There must be some way of fighting back, surely?

Cheap and legal

Don't. Ever. Speed. Simple, but not easy in the real world. Next!

Neither cheap nor legal

The James Bond option

One of 007's older cars had self-changing number plates - this may have been the inspiration for a highly-illegal speed camera dodge. Since all the detection systems rely heavily on your number plate, some skankers drive round with false plates - they might even have copied yours. Worth remembering if you ever get accused of speeding in the Outer Hebrides. Getting caught on false plates could be a £1000 fine, so is it worth the risk?

For ages now, companies have been advertising 'photo-reflective' plates (they're not illegal, but the dibble take a dim view). Most are a rip-off, but some do appear to work – on traps which flash. Speed cameras take very high-res pictures, however - even if your plates don't give you away, the coppers might i.d. your motor from its non-standard features. Money wasted, then.

Cloaking device?

The mobile laser speed trap is one of the most common, and most hated, in the UK. It sends out a laser beam which targets your front number plate. Wouldn't it be great if you could buy something to mess up its signal, so it couldn't 'lock on' ? You can - it's called a laser diffuser (sometimes marketed under the guise of a remote garage door-opener). And yes, they do work - but careful fitting is needed, and the lenses need regular cleaning. If you're caught using it for speed trap evasion, you can be done for obstruction, or perverting the course of justice - it pays to have a well-placed 'off' switch.

Gatso-beating radar 'scramblers' are said not to work, while radar jammers are an illegal transmitter - using one could see you inside for much longer than a speeding conviction.

A sound investment?

Radar detectors

These have been around for ages, and started life in the US. They're good for detecting radar-based speed cameras (most Gatsos), and any old police radar guns still in use, but that's all. Don't buy an old one (you'll get lots of false alerts if it's not meant for Euro/UK use), or a cheap one (it might not have enough range to give you a chance). *Stop press: Radar detectors and laser detectors were made illegal by the Road Safety Act 2006. At the time of writing, only GPS systems remain legal.*

GPS systems

Using Global Positioning Satellite technology, these devices are really speed camera site locators, not detectors. Using an onboard database of camera locations, they constantly monitor your car's position, and warn when you're approaching a 'danger area'. Providing you keep your dash-mounted podule updated (by downloading the latest camera/blackspot info from the maker's website), these will warn you of virtually every potential camera in the country, including Truvelo and SPECS. The only limitations are a lack of laser detection, and it won't get all the mobile sites.

You must download new info regularly, and this costs (you buy a subscription to the website). Also, if your system hasn't been in use for a while, it can take quite a few minutes for the pod to pick up the satellites it needs - during this time, you're unprotected. Don't buy secondhand units with no subscription left, as the makers sometimes can't (won't?) re-activate them.

Laser detectors

The makers say this is essential kit to combat the roaming camera van threat, but be careful. We said earlier that laser cams have a range of up to 1000 metres, but most operators don't trigger theirs until you're much, much closer than that. Which means you have far less time to react. As long as you're not the first car along, your laser detector may pick up laser 'scatter' from cars in front, but there isn't much scatter with a laser. It's said that some laser detectors will only go off if your car's already been targeted - and of course, it's too late by then.

A final word

Don't rely too heavily on even the best anti-camera technology - try and drive within the spirit, if not the letter, of the Law, with a detector as backup.

Road **Angel**

The most effective way to 'detect' a camera is to know where it is. Yeah – obviously! But with cameras still being hidden behind road signs and bridges, and increasing numbers of camera-kitted white vans, knowing where the cams are ain't easy.

A GPS locator monitors your car's position relative to known camera sites, and warns you when you're getting close. The latest offerings also warn when you're approaching schools and other areas where extra care is needed. These devices are definitely not illegal. They increase road safety, by telling you where 'accident blackspots' are – not when to brake…

tricks 'n' tips
Don't leave the mounting cradle fitted when you leave the car – it's all the clue a thief needs that there's some serious money's worth hidden in your glovebox. Even if it's not there (because you've sensibly taken it with you) you're still making it too tempting.

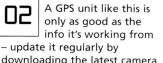

This latest Road Angel offers two main mounting options – a sticky-backed magnetic mount directly on the dash, or this rather neat screen-mounted cradle (also with a mag mount). Either way, make sure the wipers don't obscure the unit's 'view', or the laser detection function won't stand a chance.

01

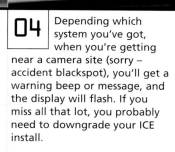

02 A GPS unit like this is only as good as the info it's working from – update it regularly by downloading the latest camera locations, or it's worse than useless. If you can use a PC well enough to download stuff from the Internet, you've got no worries.

03 Plug the unit into its lighter socket power supply (assuming it's not already taken by your phone charger or hands-free kit), then fit the unit to its bracket. First, you're greeted by a friendly message, then the unit starts searching for its satellites. While this is going on, remember that you're not protected.

04 Depending which system you've got, when you're getting near a camera site (sorry – accident blackspot), you'll get a warning beep or message, and the display will flash. If you miss all that lot, you probably need to downgrade your ICE install.

Look Mum, no hands!

As of December 2003 (okay, March 2004 really) it became illegal to hold your mobile while driving. Well, brilliant - something new to get done for. Like we were really getting short of that kind of thing. But you have to say, yipping and driving always was a pretty dodgy pastime, with driving coming off worse - if only all the UK's traffic legislation made this much sense.

Of course, the people who really benefit are the ones making hands-free car phone kits - you're looking at upwards of £50 (for a conventional kit) to get anything worth fitting. Which one do I go for? Will I have to make holes in my dash? Good questions. But we're jumping ahead - let's deal first with what the new law means in the real world.

Points of law

First, fitting a hands-free kit is merely a way of getting round part of the new legislation. They're not 'fully-legal', they're just 'not prohibited'. Even using a hands-free set-up is a distraction while you're piloting your machine, and if you start weaving about, carve up a cyclist, or run a red light, you're still likely to face

a 'driving without due care' charge, or worse. The best solution for making a call is to stop where it's safe - have voicemail enabled if you get called while you're driving.

Answering a call, even with hands-free, might not be safe in all circumstances. Let it ring. As for what you're allowed to do with the phone itself - it's just pressing the buttons (and no, this doesn't mean it's ok 2 txt). Holding the phone in any way is not permitted. Even if you're stuck in traffic, completely stationary, the engine would have to be off before you can use your mobile normally - only then could you really say you weren't 'driving'.

At the moment, getting caught using a phone on the move only carries a fixed fine. But it looks like this hasn't worked, because it's soon going to be a bigger fine, and points on the licence. Use your moby sensibly (better still, don't use it, in the car at least), or it could mean re-sitting your driving test. Paying attention now, aren'tcha?

Achtung!
Don't just pull over and screech to a stop when the phone rings. If you do this somewhere stupid, you're just as likely to get fined as you would for using the phone on the move.

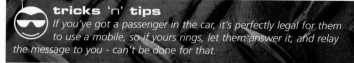

tricks 'n' tips
If you've got a passenger in the car, it's perfectly legal for them to use a mobile, so if yours rings, let them answer it, and relay the message to you - can't be done for that.

What's available?

Conventional kits

The new law has brought a whole range of new product to the market, so there's no need to settle for the old-style in-car kits, which leave holes all over your dash. Most of the latest kits have adhesive pads, and just plug into your fag lighter. The most essential item, to comply with the rules, is a phone holder or 'cradle' (holding phone bad - cradle good).

As no-one keeps the same phone for very long, it's worth looking for a kit which you can convert from one make of phone to another - by buying a different adapter lead, for instance.

Look for kits offering 'full duplex' operation - this means you can talk and listen at the same time. Just like real life. What it really means is conversations are easier and more natural - to understand fully why you need this feature, try one without it. Non-duplex kits cut out the speaker when they pick up any sound - this could be you talking (as intended), or it could just be noise inside the car. Very irritating, especially in an area where you've already got poor reception to deal with.

Some kits feature 'infra-red technology', which means you can answer/end calls by waving your hand in front of the phone. Proper hands-free operation, and great for impressing your passengers. Maybe not so good if you make lots of hand gestures while driving?

Car stereo kits

One of the newest ideas, and catching on fast. Uses a radio transmitter clipped over the phone speaker to transmit calls over a radio channel on your car stereo. When the phone rings, flick on the radio to the preset channel, speak into the phone's mike as normal, and hear your caller through your car speakers (since it's your stereo, you have easy control over call volume). They're cheap, and they appear to work, though there are potential problems with interference. Remember, this is a developing technology - it pays to buy the latest model you can find.

Bluetooth headsets

Bluetooth offers wireless operation, so get yourself a headset with mike, and you can chat away without having the phone up to your ear. Most modern handsets are Bluetooth-capable, and really new ones also have voice-activated dialling, which offers true hands-free operation in the car. Downsides? Some doubts over sound quality, and do you really want to wear a headset all the time you're driving?

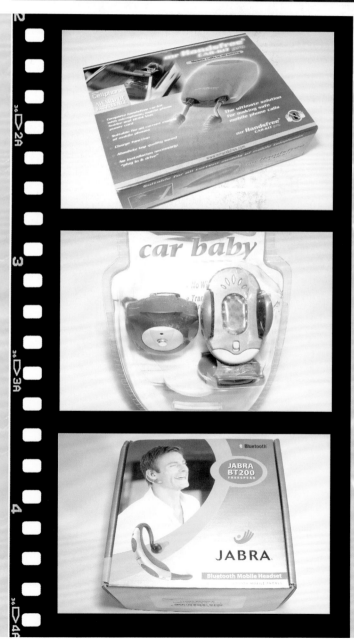

Kit fitting

Fitting details are obviously going to vary, depending on what you've bought – the main trick is to get one which doesn't require you to go drilling holes in your dash. Luckily, this is now so unpopular that most modern kits don't even offer hole-drilling as an option.

Mr Handsfree

01 All these kits (apart from the Bluetooth headset) need power, usually conveniently taken from the fag lighter socket.

Insurance & The Law

02 If you're not going to drill holes, you'll be sticking stuff on. If you want things to stay stuck (and you usually only get one shot at this) a little cleaning is in order first.

03 Mostly, it's Velcro pads you get for sticking the various kit bits in place (so they can be easily ripped off and stashed when you leave the car). Leave the two 'halves' of Velcro stuck together while fitting. With the mounting area clean, it's peel . . .

04 . . . and press firmly. This is the main unit, which contains the speaker. We thought the centre console was too good a spot to ignore. You only have to ensure the two curly-cords will reach the lighter socket and the phone.

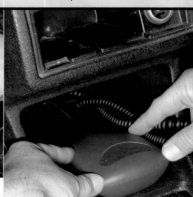

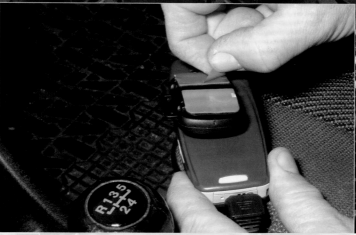

05 Not all fitting is quite this simple, though. With a little clever thinking, you can do a much neater fitting job than one which leaves all the wires hanging out. Take this little mike which comes with the Mr Handsfree kit – by prising out one of the 106's blank switches, we hid the wire inside the dash and stuck the mike to the switch, right where it's needed. Result.

06 For mounting the phone itself, we have a magnetic bracket, again stuck with sticky pads. It's only an old Nokia, but we'd still better make sure it doesn't hit the deck, by making sure it's firmly attached.

07 And there it is – the phone's nice and handy, the mike's discreetly mounted, and the speaker unit's tucked in the console. And this is the first one of these we've fitted!

Pama Plug n Go

This is one neat unit – no dangling wires, a well-designed mounting bracket with a huge sucker for sticking to the windscreen, and a built-in speaker which faces the glass, so sound is 'reflected' back. The unit is self-contained, with a built-in battery (car charger supplied), so it can be used anywhere, not just in-car. Looks sweet, works a treat.

01

Jabra Bluetooth headset

Only any good to you if your phone's got Bluetooth, but like the Pama unit we fitted earlier, there's no mess. The headset needs charging before use, but after that, you just 'pair' your phone and headset together, and start jabbering. If your phone's trendy enough to have voice-activated dialling, this is about as hands-free as you'll get. You don't even need a cradle for your mobile with this one!

01

Security

Lock me or lose me

It's a sad fact, but making your car attractive to the opposite sex also tends to attract attention of a less-welcome kind, from less-than-human pond life.

Avoiding trouble

Now come on - you're modifying your car to look cool and to be seen in. Not a problem - but be careful where you choose to show your car off, and who to. Be especially discreet, the nearer you get to home - *turn your system down* before you turn into your road, for instance, or you'll draw unwelcome attention to where that car with the loud stereo's parked at night.

Without being too paranoid, watch for anyone following you home. At night, if the car behind switches its lights off, be worried. If you suspect this is happening, do not drive home - choose well-lit public places until they give up. Believe us - it happens.

If you're going out, think about where you're parking - well-lit and well-populated is good.

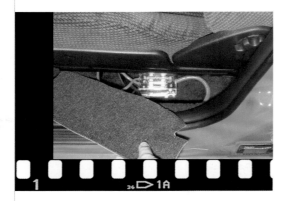

Thieves hate light being on them, so don't make it easy by parking somewhere dark - think about this if you park up in daylight, knowing you won't be back 'til late.

Hands up, who doesn't lock their car when they get petrol? Your insurance company has a term for this, and it's 'contributory negligence'. In English, this means you won't get a penny if your car goes missing when you haven't locked it.

If you're lucky enough to have a garage, use it. On up-and-over garage doors, fit extra security like a padlock and ground anchor.

A clever thief will watch your movements and habits over several days before trying your car. Has it got an alarm, and do you always set it? Do you only fit your steering wheel lock when you feel like it? Do you always park in the same place, and is the car hidden from the house or from the road? Don't make his life easier. Ask yourself how you'd nick your car…

A word about your stereo

From the moment you bolt on those nice alloys, it's taken as read that you've also got stereo gear that's worth nicking - and the thieves know it. All the discreet installation in the world isn't going to deter them from finding out what's inside that nice motor.

Please don't advertise your love of ICE around your car. Your nice stereo gear will fit other cars too, and can be ripped out in nothing flat. You may be very proud of your ICE install, but nothing is more of an 'invite' than a huge ICE sticker or sunstrip. If you've fitted one just to look cool, replace it now with something less provocative - seriously. Your set might not actually be very expensive, but you could still lose a side window for advertising something better.

You'll have got a CD player, obviously, but don't leave discs or empty CD cases lying around inside the car. A nice pair of 6x9s in full view on the back shelf is an invite to having your rear window smashed - stealth shelf, anyone? When you're fitting your system, give some thought to the clues you could accidentally leave in plain view. Oxygen-free speaker cable is great stuff, but it's also a bit bright against dark carpets, and is all the clue necessary that you're serious about your tunes. Hide amps and CD changers under your front seats, or in the boot.

Most modern sets are face-off or MASK, so if they've got security features like this, use them - take your faceplate off when you leave the car, and take it with you rather than leaving it in the door pocket or glovebox (the first places a thief will look).

Things that go beep in the night

Unless your insurance company demands it up front, fitting an alarm is something generally done as an after-thought. We know alarms aren't exactly sexy, but don't skimp - an alarm may never be put to the test, but if it is, you'll be glad you spent wisely…

The simplest first step to car security is to fake it. Tacky *'This car is fitted with an alarm'* stickers won't fool anyone, but if you want cheap, just fit a flashing LED. We know it's not the real thing, but everyone else will think you've got a posh alarm. An LED is cheap to buy and easy to fit, and can be rigged to a discreet switch inside the car.

Don't overlook the value of so-called 'manual' immobilisers, such as steering wheel locking bars and gear-to-handbrake lever locks. These can be a worthwhile deterrent - a thief not specifically after your car may move on to an easier target. Some of the items offered may be 'Sold Secure' or Thatcham Cat 3, accolades well worth checking out, since it means they've withstood a full-on brute force attack for a useful length of time.

The only way to combat the more determined thief is to go for a well-specified and intelligently-installed alarm. Immobilisers alone have their place, but sadly, even a pro-fitted immobiliser on its own won't stop someone pinching your wheels, or having it away with the stereo gear. Neither, incidentally, will a cheap alarm - you have to know how the thieves operate to stand any chance defeating them. Any alarm you fit yourself probably won't gain you any insurance discount, but it will give you peace of mind, and DIY means you can do a real trick installation, to make it very hard work for the crims.

Finally, one other scam which you might fall victim to. If you find your alarm is suddenly going off a lot at night, when previously it had been well-behaved, don't ignore the problem. It's an old trick for a thief to deliberately set off your alarm several times, each time hiding round the corner when you come out to investigate, then to wait until the fifth or sixth time when you don't reset it (in disgust), leaving him a clear run. If your alarm does keep false-alarming

without outside assistance, find out the cause quickly, or your neighbours will quickly become 'deaf' to it.

Thatcham categories and meanings:

1 **Cat 1.** For alarms and electronic immobilisers.
2 **Cat 2.** For electronic immobilisers only.
3 **Cat 2-1.** Electronic immobilisers which can be upgraded to Cat 1 alarms later.
4 **Cat 3.** Mechanical immobilisers, eg snap-off steering wheels, locking wheel bolts, window film, steering wheel locks/covers.
5 **Q-class.** Tracking devices.

Other alarm features

Two-stage anti-shock - means that the alarm shouldn't go off, just because the neighbour's cat jumps on your car roof, or because Little Johnny punts his football into your car. Alarm will only sound after a major shock, or after repeated shocks are detected.

Anti-tilt - detects any attempt to lift or jack up the car, preventing any attempt to pinch alloys. Very unpopular with thieves, as it makes the alarm very sensitive (much more so than anti-shock). Alarm may sound if car is parked outside in stormy conditions (but not if your suspension's rock-hard!).

Anti-hijack - immobiliser with built-in delay. If your motor gets hi-jacked, the neanderthals responsible will only get so far down the road before the engine cuts out.

Rolling code - reduces the chance of your alarm remote control signal from being 'grabbed' by special electronic equipment.

Total closure - module which connects to electric windows/sunroof and central locking, which closes all items when alarm is set. Alarms like this often have other nifty features such as remote boot opening.

Pager control - yes, really - your alarm can be set to send a message to your pager (why not your mobile?) if your car gets tampered with.

Current-sensing disable - very useful feature on some cars which have a cooling fan which can cut in after the ignition is switched off. Without this feature, your alarm will be triggered every time you leave it parked after a long run - very annoying.

Volumetric-sensing disable - allows you to manually disable the interior ultrasonics, leaving the rest of the alarm features active. Useful if you want to leave the sunroof open in hot weather - if a fly gets in the car, the alarm would otherwise be going off constantly.

Talking alarms - no, please, please no. Very annoying, and all that'll happen is you'll attract crowds of kids daring each other to set it off again. Unfortunately, these are becoming more popular, with some offering the facility to record your own message!

The knowledge

What people often fail to realise (at least, until it happens to them) is the level of violence and destruction which thieves will employ to get your stuff - this goes way beyond breaking a window.

It comes as a major shock to most people when they discover the serious kinds of tools (weapons) at many professional thieves' disposal, and how brutally your lovingly-polished car will be attacked. Many people think, for instance, that it's their whole car they're after, whereas it's really only the parts they want, and they don't care how they get them (this means that these parts are still attractive, even when fitted to a basic car which has yet to be fully modded). Obviously, taking the whole car then gives the option of hiding it to strip at leisure, but it won't always be the option chosen, and you could wake up one morning to a well-mangled wreck outside.

Attack 1 The first option to any thief is to smash glass - typically, the toughened-glass side windows, which will shatter, unlike the windscreen. Unfortunately for the thief, this makes a loud noise (not good), but is a quick and easy way in. The reason for taking this approach is that a basic car alarm will only go off if the doors are opened (voltage-drop alarm) - provided the doors aren't opened, the alarm won't go off.

Response 1 A more sophisticated alarm will feature shock sensing (which will be set off by the impact on the glass), and better still, ultrasonic sensing, which will be triggered by the brick coming in through the broken window.

Response 2 This kind of attack can also be stopped by applying security film to the inside of the glass, which holds it all together and prevents easy entry.

Attack 2 An alternative to smashing the glass is to pry open the door using a crowbar - this attack involves literally folding open the door's window frame by prising from the top corner. The glass will still shatter, but as long as the door stays shut, a voltage-drop alarm won't be triggered.

Response This method might not be defeated by a shock-sensing alarm, but an ultrasonic unit would pick it up.

Incidentally, another bonus with ultrasonic alarms is that the sensors are visible from outside - and act as a deterrent.

Attack 3 The next line of attack is to disable the alarm. The commonest way to kill the alarm is either to cut the wiring to the alarm itself, or to disconnect the battery, 'safely' hidden away under the bonnet. And just how strong is a bonnet? Not strong enough to resist being crowbarred open, which is exactly what happens.

Response 1 If your alarm has extra pin-switches, be sure to fit one to the bonnet, and fit it in the bonnet channel next to the battery, so that it'll set off the alarm if the bonnet is prised up. Also make sure that the wire to the pin-switch cannot be cut easily though a partly-open bonnet.

Response 2 Make sure that the alarm module is well-hidden, and cannot be got at from underneath the car.

Response 3 Make the alarm power supply connection somewhere less obvious than directly at the battery terminal - any thief who knows his stuff will immediately cut any 'spare' red wires at the battery. Try taking power from the fusebox, or if you must source it under the bonnet, trace the large red battery lead to the starter motor connections, and tap into the power there.

Response 4 Always disguise the new alarm wiring, by using black insulating tape to wrap it to the existing wiring loom. Tidying up in this way also helps to ensure the wires can't get trapped, cut, melted, or accidentally ripped out - any of which could leave you with an alarm siren which won't switch off, or an immobiliser you can't disable.

Response 4 An alarm which has a 'battery back-up' facility is a real kiss of death to the average thief's chances. Even if he's successfully crow-barred your bonnet and snipped the battery connections, the alarm will still go off, powered by a separate battery of its own. A Cat 1 alarm has to have battery back-up.

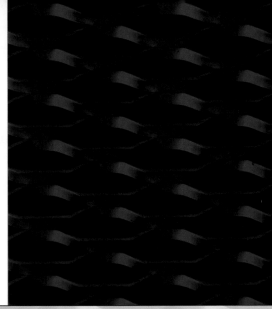

Fitting a basic **LED**

All you need for this is a permanent live feed, an earth, a switch if you want to be able to turn it on/off, and the flashing LED itself (very cheap, from any car accessory shop).

An LED draws very little current, so you'll be quite safe tapping into almost any live feed you fancy. If you've wired in your ICE, take a live feed from the permanent (radio memory supply) wire at the back of your head unit, or have a delve into the back of the fusebox with your test light. An earth can easily be tapped again from your head unit, or you can make one almost anywhere on the metal body of the car, by drilling a small hole, fitting a self-tapping screw, then wrapping the bared end of wire around and tightening it.

The best and easiest place to mount an LED is into one of the many blank switches the makers seem to love fitting. The blank switch is easily pried out, and a hole can then be drilled to take the LED (which usually comes in a separate little holder). Feed the LED wiring down behind the dashboard to where you've tapped your live and earth, taking care not to trap it anywhere, nor to accidentally wrap it around any moving parts.

Connect your live to the LED red wire, then rig your earth to one side of the switch, and connect the LED black wire to the other switch terminal. You should now have a switchable LED! Tidy up the wiring, and mount the switch somewhere discreet, but where you can still get at it. Switch on when you leave the car, and it looks as if you've got some sort of alarm - better than nothing!

Wiring basics

With your wires identified, how to tap into them? Before we even get that far, is that wire you're planning on playing with live?

Switch off the ignition at least - and ideally disconnect the battery before you do anything else. On cars with airbags, don't go tapping into any of the airbag wiring, which is usually bright yellow. With that cleared up, how were you planning on joining the old and new wires together?

Here's our advice:

Soldering - avoids cutting through your chosen wire - strip away a short section of insulation, wrap your new wire around the bared section, then apply solder to secure it. If you're a bit new to soldering, practise on a few offcuts of wire first - it ain't rocket science! Re-insulate the soldered connection afterwards, with tape or heatshrink tube.

Bullet connectors - cut and strip the end of your chosen wire, wrap your new one to it, push both into one half of the bullet. Connect the other end of your victim wire to the other bullet, and connect together. Always use the 'female' half on any live feed - it'll be safer if you disconnect it than a male bullet, which could touch bare metal and send your motor up in smoke.

Block connectors - so easy to use. Just remember that the wires can come adrift if the screws aren't really tight, and don't get too ambitious about how many wires you can stuff in one hole (block connectors, like bullets, are available in several sizes). Steer clear of connectors like the one below - they're convenient, but they can give rise to problems.

With any of these options, always insulate around your connection - especially when soldering, or you'll be leaving bare metal exposed. Remember that you'll probably be shoving all the wires up into the dark recesses of the under-dash area - by the time the wires are nice and kinked/squashed together, that tiny bit of protruding wire might just touch that bit of metal bodywork, and that'll be a fire…

Fitting an
auxiliary
fusebox

Attention!
Disconnect the battery negative (earth) lead before starting work, and only reconnect it when all live leads and terminals have been securely connected.

You'll need plenty of fused live feeds from the battery during the modifying process, for stereo gear, neons, starter buttons - and alarms, and it's always a pain working out where to tap into one. If you make up your own little fusebox, mounted somewhere easy to get at, you'll never have this problem again - and it's easy enough to do.

01 The first part of this process is to mount the fusebox in a suitable location. A good location, is one that's easily accessible in the event of changing a fuse, but sufficiently hidden. The glovebox recess seems as good a place as any – offer it into place to check for size. Remove the glovebox for improved access to this area whilst working (see 'Removing stuff').

02 Trimming of plastic may be required to ensure a snug fit.

03 Some rather fine drilling and bracket work later, and it looks like the fusebox grew there naturally. Nice.

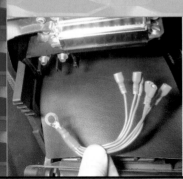

07 At the end of each of the six wires, crimp a female connector into place. The final loom should look a little something like this.

08 Attach the ring connector to a terminal in the junction box, and the female connectors to each pin on the back of the fusebox. It may be necessary to remove the fusebox from its bracket in order to attach the wires more easily.

09 Now go to the engine bay and look at the bulkhead. You're looking for a spot to feed a thick eight-gauge wire from battery into the car. There's a big rubber grommet in the bulkhead for the main wiring loom – by carefully making a slit in the rubber, you can push your new wire through into the car. When you're finished, seal the new hole with some silicone.

10 When the wire finally arrives at the junction box, attach a ring terminal to the end as before, using solder and heat-shrink. Fit it into place on the remaining junction box terminal and close the box.

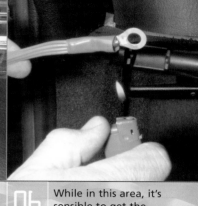

04 Next job is to mount the junction box as close as possible to the fusebox. As luck would have it, there is a space to the left of the fusebox, just waiting to be drilled.

05 A DIY-store L-shaped bracket will keep the junction box in place.

06 While in this area, it's sensible to get the wires from the junction to the fusebox ready. Make sure the wires are long enough to reach all the terminals, then solder a ring connector to one end of the bunch. Cover the join with tape or heat-shrink.

11 Pop back to the engine bay once more, for the final stages of fitment. Tidily route the new thick wire towards the battery by lashing it to the main wiring loom using cable-ties.

12 Before connecting the wire to the battery, you need a fuse in the line (it's a safety thing). You can get in-line fuse assemblies like the one here from any good motor accessory shop.

13 With the fuse in place, all that's left to do is continue routing the wire to the battery, then fit a ring connector to the end - solder, shrink-wrap and attach. Remember to go back and pop a suitable-sized fuse into each of the holders, so you're ready to use the fusebox straight away should you need to.

Alarm fitting

If your 106 already has a decent aftermarket alarm on it, don't mess with it. Otherwise, be prepared for some nasty surprises when you dive behind the dash. How the heck have they wired this in? Will chopping that wire mean the car won't start? If it looks a mess behind there, it's best to leave it - and then hope it never goes wrong, or you'll have to suss it all out anyway.

If your 106 is still a virgin in the aftermarket alarm sense, things are a bit easier. The alarm we've chosen to fit is a MicroScan, which, whilst it isn't a Clifford, still offers a decent level of protection, and a useful array of features for a sensible price. When it goes off, it actually sounds like a Clifford - result!

As with everything else in this book, remember that we're showing you just how this *particular* alarm is fitted. All the same, whatever alarm you fit, it'll still be useful to pick out the fitting principles and tips. Always refer to the instructions which come with your alarm, and don't go joining the red wire to the yellow wire, just because WE say so…

01 Disconnect the battery negative lead, and move the lead away from the battery, or you'll be blowing fuses and your new alarm will go mental the minute it's rigged up.

02 Decide where you're going to mount the alarm/siren. Choose somewhere not easily reached from underneath, for a start, and if you can, pick a location away from where you'll be topping up washers, oil or coolant - fluids and alarm modules don't mix. The only spot on our 106 was on the bulkhead, on the driver's side.

03 To get access for a spot of drilling, first the scuttle panels over the wiper mechanism have to go (check the single wiper fitting section). After that, there's a plastic clip or two holding the sound-deadening in place, and the area has been cleared for drilling.

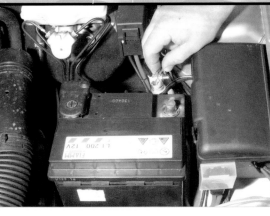

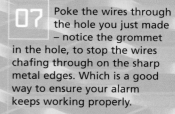

04 Use the module mounting bracket to mark the holes, then get out the drill. Make sure you're not drilling through into anything vital.

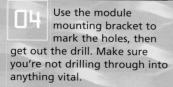

05 Bolt the bracket in place, then fit the module – it doesn't get any easier than this, so if this is any kind of challenge for you, stop now. Next, you need another, bigger, hole in the bulkhead, for feeding all the alarm wires through. Out comes the drill again.

Back to the engine bay, to fit the bonnet pin switch. It should be close to the battery, but this ain't easy on a 106. Use a spot behind the headlight, feeling underneath to make sure there is room. Stick on a few strips of masking tape first – it's something to mark on, and it stops the drill slipping. You need two holes - one large, for the switch body, and a smaller one for the switch screw.

06 Well, that was the easy bit - now there's wires to play with. Most of them need to go through into the car, but not all - check your alarm's instructions. There's a (brown) bonnet pin switch wire which can stay in the engine bay. The rest? Get out the electrical tape (or plastic spiral), and wrap that bunch of wires into a neat loom, to go inside.

07 Poke the wires through the hole you just made – notice the grommet in the hole, to stop the wires chafing through on the sharp metal edges. Which is a good way to ensure your alarm keeps working properly.

When feeding wires through the bulkhead either enlarge a hole in an existing grommet (see 'Fitting an auxiliary fusebox') or drill a new hole. Any wiring holes you drill yourself must be fitted with a grommet if you want the alarm to be reliable.

. . . then mark and drill the screw hole, and tighten the screw securely - this is the switch's earth connection to the car body, so it has to be secure.

08

09

10 With the large hole drilled, slip the switch into its new home . . .

11

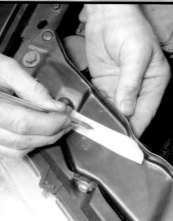

>>

>>

12 Crimp a spade terminal onto the alarm's pin switch wire (brown in this case), and connect to the switch. Sorted.

13 Back inside the car, it's time for some serious wiring-up. Do the immobiliser relay first. This comes with its four wires pre-attached, so all you do is mount it in position, and connect the car's wiring to these wires. Select a spot inside the driver's lower trim panel, which means offering up the relay from outside . . .

14 . . . to mark and then drill a mounting hole. With the relay fixed, you need to make some connections. Gain access to the base of the ignition switch by removing the steering column lower shroud (three screws from below).

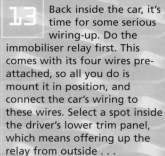

Removing the centre switch panel gives access-all-areas to the hazard warning light switch. Why should you be impressed? Because you have to tap into the indicator wiring, and it's all right here. Using the strip-and-solder method, join the two grey alarm wires to the red and green on the hazard switch plug, and another part of wiring-up is complete.

To give triggering on the interior light, the alarm's red wire has to go straight to the interior light circuit. According to the Haynes wiring diagram, it's wire code B08 (remember, no colour-codes on Pugs) – this is the fused live to the interior light. Remove the glovebox (see 'Removing stuff') and unclip the lower block of fuses . . .

. . . on the back, you should find this large white plug, and a white wire with the right code on it (but go by the code, not the wire colour – yours may be different). Use the strip-and-solder method to join the alrm's red wire to this one, and you're one step nearer having a working alarm.

A good earth is what you need next, for the alarm's black wire. Peugeot thoughtfully provide one, right below the car's fusebox - just remove the bolt, add your ring-terminalled wire, and tighten back up.

19

20

21

22

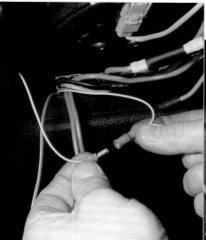

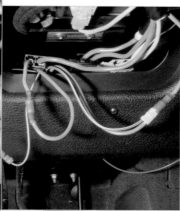

15 The starter wire is a thick blue one (on this car, at least), and this gets cut - leave enough wire either side of the cut to join onto. Following the alarm's instructions, join the relay's yellow wire to the yellow from the alarm. Well, that was easy.

16 Now for the thick blue wire you cut earlier. The wire from the switch gets the red/white and first brown wire joined to it, while the other gets the second brown. Solid, well-insulated connections needed here. Tidy the wiring away, and that's the immobiliser done.

17 Next, you need somewhere to mount the alarm's LED - this needs to be somewhere highly-visible from outside. This XS has a handy blank switch in the centre of the dash, but getting at it means removing the facia centre section (see 'Racing starts' in 'Interiors' for a how-to on this).

18 With the blank switch prised out, all you need do is drill a hole in it (usually 8 mm) – in the centre would be handy. Feed the LED and wire in from behind, and push the holder in from the front. Clip the switch back in place, and the LED's sorted.

Last of all, you're wiring-in the remote central locking function. The Haynes diagram shows the lock/unlock signal wires are code 625 and 623. These wires are on a large brown plug at the back of the fusebox. On go the blue (lock) and green (unlock) alarm wires, and hey presto - remote locking, allowing you **23** to de-lock the doors later on. Sweet.

This alarm has the facility to allow a longer signal or 'pulse' to work the central locking. Some cars need this, some don't. Turns out this Pug does require a bit longer to think about opening its doors, which means this white wire, **24** back at the alarm module, gets the chop.

So come on - does it work? Most alarms require you to 'programme in' the remotes before they'll work. Test all the alarm features in turn, remembering to allow enough time for the alarm to arm itself (usually about 30 seconds). When you test it for the first time, either shut the bonnet completely, or hold the bonnet pin switch down. This way, you can pull out the alarm **25** fuses and shut it up, if something goes wrong!

Set the anti-shock sensitivity with a thought to where you live and park - will it be set off every night by the neighbour's cat, or by kids playing football? Finally, and most important of all - next time you **26** park up, remember to set it!

Body styling

If you're planning a major body job, you've probably already got some good ideas about how you want your 106 to look, from *'Max Power'* or *'Revs'*, or maybe from a friend's car. While it can be good to have a target car to aim for, if you're just starting out on the road towards a fully-loaded car, you probably don't want (or can't quite afford) to go 'all the way' all at once.

If you're new to the world of modifying, it's a good idea to start with smaller jobs, and work up to the full body kit gradually, as your skills increase; spending loads on a body kit is a pretty lame idea if you then make a mess of fitting it! There's plenty of small ways to improve the look of your 106, which don't cost much, and which are simple enough to fit; start with some of these before you go too mad!

One golden rule with any body mods is to plan what you're going to do, and don't rush it. It's better that the car looks a bit stupid for a week (because you couldn't get something finished) than to rush a job and have the car look stupid forever. Do half the job properly instead of messing up all of it. Try and think the jobs through - plan each stage. Have you got all the tools, screws or whatever before you start, or will you have to break off halfway through? If you get stuck, is there someone you can get to help, or have they gone off for the weekend? Above all, if something goes wrong - don't panic - a calm approach will prove to be a huge bonus (that job doesn't have to be done today, does it?).

If a piece of trim won't come off, don't force it. If something feels like it's going to break, it probably will - stop and consider whether to go on and break it, or try another approach. You could even try the Haynes manual… Especially on an older car, things either never come off as easily as you think, or else have already been off so many times that they break or won't fit back on properly. While we'd all like to do a perfect job every time, working on an older car will, sooner or later, teach you the fine art of 'bodging' (finding valid alternative ways of fixing things!). Don't assume you'll have to bodge something back on, every time - if a trim clip breaks when you take something off, it might be easier and cheaper than you think to simply go to your Peugeot dealer, and buy a new clip (remember, even Peugeot mechanics break things from time to time, so they will keep these things in stock!).

Mirror, mirror

Mirrors are another simple to fit, must-have accessory. The DTM or M3-style door mirrors are well established on the modified car circuit, but there are lots of variations of mirror styles and finishes, so finding some you like won't be hard.

If you want to be just a little different, try some 'California' mirrors. The trouble with being different is it's always more work - California mirrors are 'universal fit', meaning you have to make them fit your car. You bought a 106 'cause it's a popular car, so why make life difficult? Buy some 106 mirrors (or at least some 106 mirror bases), and your new mirrors could be fitted in minutes.

There's more to mirrors than just looks, though - some have toys attached. Like side repeater lights (in a Merc stylee) or thumb switches for releasing your de-locked, de-handled doors. We want some of that.

California mirrors

01 Prise away the mirror trim panel from inside edge of the door . . .

02 . . . and you'll see that the adjuster knob is attached to this panel by a screw, so remove this next.

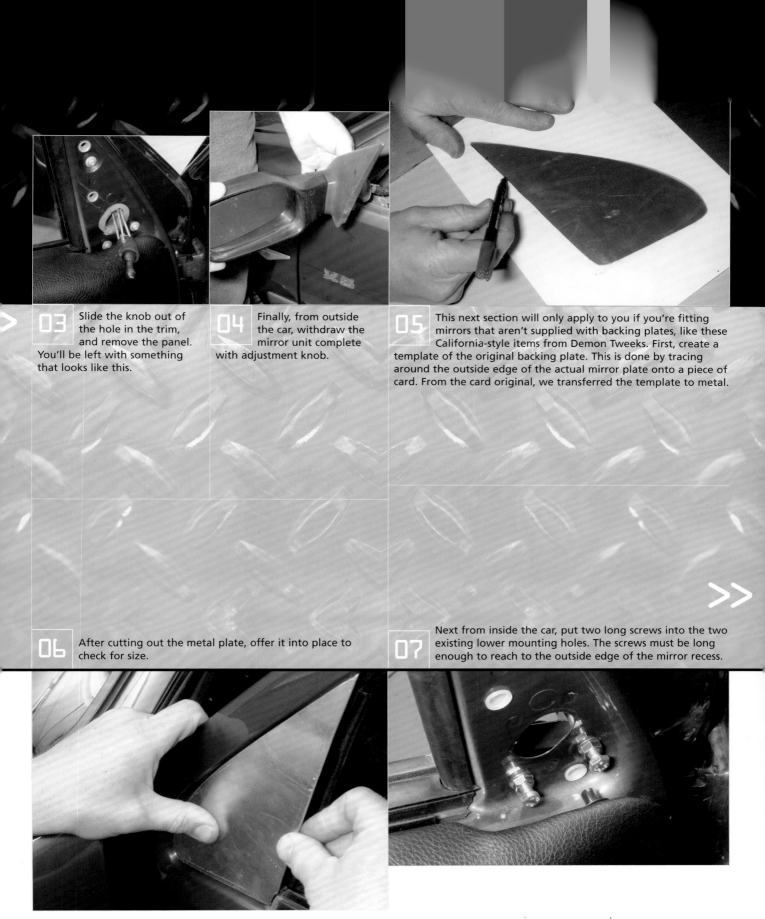

03 Slide the knob out of the hole in the trim, and remove the panel. You'll be left with something that looks like this.

04 Finally, from outside the car, withdraw the mirror unit complete with adjustment knob.

05 This next section will only apply to you if you're fitting mirrors that aren't supplied with backing plates, like these California-style items from Demon Tweeks. First, create a template of the original backing plate. This is done by tracing around the outside edge of the actual mirror plate onto a piece of card. From the card original, we transferred the template to metal.

06 After cutting out the metal plate, offer it into place to check for size.

07 Next from inside the car, put two long screws into the two existing lower mounting holes. The screws must be long enough to reach to the outside edge of the mirror recess.

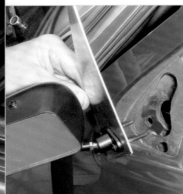

>>

08 Spread some copper grease on the ends of these two screws, and put the newly-created backing plate into place. As if by magic, the grease marks exactly where you need to drill your mounting holes for your new mirrors. We like it this way because you don't need to go drilling extra holes in your doors!

09 Fix the mirror to the plate, remove the positioning screws, and offer the whole unit into place, just to check that everything's gone according to plan.

10 To create a more-sporty look to our 106, we've decided to cover our backing plate in carbon fibre film. Unbolt the mirror and, using the backing plate as a template, cut out the film, leaving a 1 cm border around each edge.

11 Check out the instructions on your film, as product fitment details vary between manufacturers. In our case, just remove the backing paper and stick the film onto the metal.

12 The sticky film is then pressed into place, with any excess film at the corners cut off to create a nicer finish. Remember to punch through the film to uncover the mirror mounting holes!

13 Nearly there - all that's left now is to pop some adhesive pads onto the top of the plate to keep everything in place. This is important because we only have mounting holes for retaining screws at the bottom edge of the plate. We don't want any sagging, do we?

14 The final part requires two people. One to sit in the driver's seat, the other adjusting the mirror angle until the driver's happy. Once this has been done, tighten the screw that will keep the mirror stationary at that angle. This is the only form of adjustment possible with these mirrors. Call it the price of fashion.

15 That's it - just a case of fixing the mirror plate in place by tightening the retaining nuts on the inside of the door and clipping the trim panel into position.

Fill 'er up!

Ah, the humble fuel filler cap - what you decide to do here really is a matter of taste. The 106 item's not offensive – at least it's colour-coded, which is more than some cars. Which means it doesn't stand out. Which, for some people, is a problem.

For those who really want to impress, it's got to be a complete racing conversion, which does away with the dull standard filler cap, in favour of a fully-functional alloy item to grace the 106 flanks. Trouble is, 'proper' aero-style filler caps need bodyshop work to fit – so what's the answer? Our Sparco race cap looks good, and should fit straight on – let's find out.

Fitting a racing **filler cap**

The most strenuous thing about fitting this replacement fuel filler cap is peeling off the backing paper from the sticker that sits around the middle of the cap. Yeah, but then there's the stress of getting it **01** on straight, with no air bubbles…

Fitting involves the very difficult task of holding the cap with the key, and twisting it into place. Pretty damn tricky, we think you'll agree. Anyone who can't fit one of these very fine caps should **02** probably sell their Pug now, and forget all about modifying.

Smoothly does it

If you've bought a basic 106, it's understandable that you might not want to declare this fact loudly from the rear end of your car. Badges also clutter up the otherwise clean lines, and besides, you're trying to make your 106 look different, so why give them obvious clues like a badge? Most 106s also come with admittedly-useful but actually quite ugly side rubbing strips of some sort - lose these, or at least colour-code, if you're at all serious about raising your game.

De-badging

01 To remove the badges from the rear of your car, simply use a flat-bladed prising tool. To save scratching the bodywork, why not wrap some masking tape around the end of the tool. Badges are often easier to remove if you warm them up first – this softens the glue, making it easier to peel.

02 Most of the foam part of the badge has actually stayed on the car, but fear not – this can easily be removed by hand.

03 Finally, give the area a good clean-up with some polish, preferably something with at least a light 'cut', to blend the paint behind the badge with the rest of the car. Don't go mad with regular T-Cut, though – most 106s are lacquer-finished (even the non-metallic ones), and if you go through the lacquer, it'll look very poor.

De-stripping

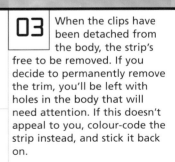

01 Side rubbing strips. Good - they save your paint if Mr Numpty opens his rusty Metro door into your car. Bad - they look hideous. If looks are important, removal is an option (as is colour-coding, if you want to keep them). Use a flat prising tool to lever the side rubbing strips away from the body – protect the bodywork by putting something like a rag or cardboard between the tool and the metal.

02 There is a chance that some of the body clips may get stuck on the car whilst removing the strip, so some individual clips may require extra levering.

03 When the clips have been detached from the body, the strip's free to be removed. If you decide to permanently remove the trim, you'll be left with holes in the body that will need attention. If this doesn't appeal to you, colour-code the strip instead, and stick it back on.

When it comes to car bodywork, every hole is not a goal. At least small holes can be filled without stretching your talent envelope too far. First, cover the area around your chosen hole (two holes, in this case) with masking tape - make sure you get a decent working area around the hole.

01

Filling holes - a cunning plan

02 Now neatly cut out your holes in the tape.

Here's where we start to see the true cunning of this plan - mix up some Araldite (or similar glue for bonding metals), and apply a blob of it to a washer large enough to cover the hole, on the inside. Rich types among you may prefer to use a coin.

03

Stick the washer or coin on from inside, then stand around looking stupid, holding it in place while the glue dries.

04

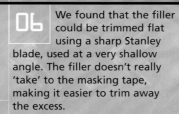

05 Mix up some filler, and apply to your hole - the masking tape prevents any getting on the paintwork. Apply more than one layer, and build the filler up evenly.

06 We found that the filler could be trimmed flat using a sharp Stanley blade, used at a very shallow angle. The filler doesn't really 'take' to the masking tape, making it easier to trim away the excess.

07 Peel away the masking tape, and your hole is filled - all it needs is paint.

08 If you haven't done such a great job, remember that you can improve things by applying layer after layer of paint (wait for each one to dry). When you've built the paint up proud of the hole, T-Cut it back smooth.

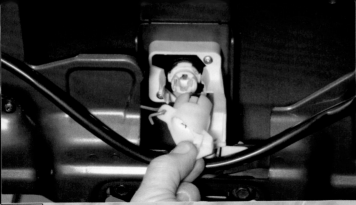

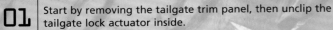

01 Start by removing the tailgate trim panel, then unclip the tailgate lock actuator inside.

02 Next, remove the locking motor left-hand screw, and loosen the slotted right-hand screw.

03 The motor, actuator and link rod assembly can now be removed in one piece, disconnecting the wiring to the motor as you lift it out from the tailgate.

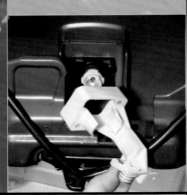

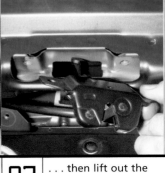

04 Remove the two screws and take out the lock lever. Big, innit?

05 Lower the tailgate to recover the outer lock trim and cylinder assembly from the car. Leaves just a bit of a hole, doesn't it? Don't think we're talking bodyfiller for that one.

06 Next remove the tailgate catch, held on by two bolts . . .

07 . . . then lift out the catch from its recess. This bit holds the tailgate shut, so with it gone… it won't stay shut. Which is another way of saying – don't lose it, as it's going back on.

Tailgate smoothing

01 Once you've de-wipered and de-locked the cluttered 106 rear end, what's next? A full flush, that's what. You won't get rid of the tailgate lock hole using filler, so a more permanent solution's needed. Make a cardboard template of the tailgate's lock handle recess (which is just a smaller version of the number plate recess we're doing on this car) . . .

02 . . . use the template to cut out the same shape from metal plate . . .

03 . . . and try it for size. After a little fine-tuning, the new plate's ready to be welded-in.

04 Every edge must be welded up, and this is best done using short, measured blasts of the welder, so that excessive heat is not applied to the tailgate. The new plate must be well-welded all round, or it could flex, cracking any filler that sits on top of it and taking your paint with it.

05 Once the welding has been completed and the metal cooled (so that it is cold to touch), run an angle grinder over the weld to smooth down any large blobs. Once this has been done, a skim of filler can be applied to the area and left at least 24 hours to dry. The longer you can leave the filler to dry, the better.

Tailgate **solenoid**

01 Place the tailgate catch on a clean flat surface. You need to trim away the plastic strengthening webbing from the operating arm, to get a flat surface to drill into. Not a problem if your knife's sharp enough – just don't chop the operating arm off completely.

02 If the trimming went as planned, you can now drill a small hole in the operating arm (about 3 mm should do it).

03 Next, using some suitable 2.5mm diameter rod (we used welding wire), make up a new link rod at least 150mm in length. Hook it through the hole you've just created on the tailgate catch, and bend the end around using pliers to keep it from unhooking.

04 In exactly the same way as above, create a second 150 mm link rod that will be attached to the lock motor arm. There's a hole in this arm already – no drilling needed.

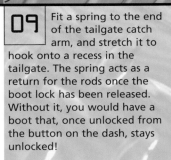

09 Fit a spring to the end of the tailgate catch arm, and stretch it to hook onto a recess in the tailgate. The spring acts as a return for the rods once the boot lock has been released. Without it, you would have a boot that, once unlocked from the button on the dash, stays unlocked!

10 Inside the car now, for the final stages of fitment to begin. Start by removing the rear shelf support panel. Located under this trim is the main wiring loom that feeds the light clusters (and more importantly, the tailgate central locking).

11 Check out the wiring diagram found in your Haynes 106 manual, to find the two wires that control the feed to the central locking. In our case, it was wire codes 6206 and 6216 (if it helps, these were a yellow and a white – just don't expect yours to be the same).

12 Connect two lengths of wire that are long enough reach to the dash (and then some), to the existing yellow and white wires, using bullet connectors. Tape up the ends of the yellow and white wires that are now redundant. Route the two wires down the car, under the carpets to the passenger footwell. Use cable-ties to attach the wire to existing loom.

05 Join the two rods together using a suitable clamp. If you buy a central locking kit from Microscan, you'll get everything you need for this job, including, rods, clamps, and even a motor (if your 106 doesn't have central locking on the tailgate).

06 Dismantle the clamp temporarily, and refit the modified tailgate catch assembly . . .

07 . . . followed swiftly by the motor and newly-created link rod.

08 With the rods clamped back together, you should at this point have something that looks like this.

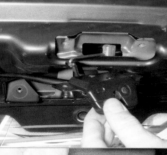

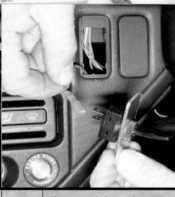

13 On arrival at the passenger footwell the two wires branch off. One must be connected to a suitable fused live feed – for us that's easy, as we've fitted an auxiliary fusebox, but for those of you who aren't so fortunate, you'll have to find yourself a live feed – possibly directly off the battery. Fit an in-line fuse to any battery feeds.

14 The remaining wire must be routed up under the dash to the switch pins. It's preferable to fit a spring-return 'flick' switch for a boot solenoid – it's just way cooler, that's all. We made up this retro-look switch from a basic switch bought in a car accessory shop, and a home-made ally plate.

15 Take one final piece of wire that is long enough to reach the nearest earth point. Attach one end of the wire to the remaining pin on the back of the switch, and the other to the earth point, using a ring terminal.

Single wiper
conversion

Another saloon-car racing-inspired item, the single wiper conversion is a really smart way to make your 106 stand out from the crowd. Presumably, the saloon racers fit single wipers to enhance the view forward (one less wiper arm obscuring the view could make all the difference), improve the aerodynamics, and maybe even to save weight! Many 106 owners want the single wiper because it helps to remove clutter - park two 106s side by side, and the one with one less wiper looks way better.

01 First things to go are your old wipers (well, no surprise there, then). Make sure the wipers are 'parked' by switching them on, then quickly off, then let the wipers come to rest before switching off the ignition. With the bonnet open, remove the retaining nuts at the base of each arm. Then lower the bonnet down and prise off each wiper arm from its splines.

02 Next, remove the scuttle panel. This clips under the screen, and is also held in place by a nut at each end and a Torx screw in the middle of the panel. Once the nuts and screw are removed, lift the panel over the end studs and pull the panel towards the engine to detach the clips.

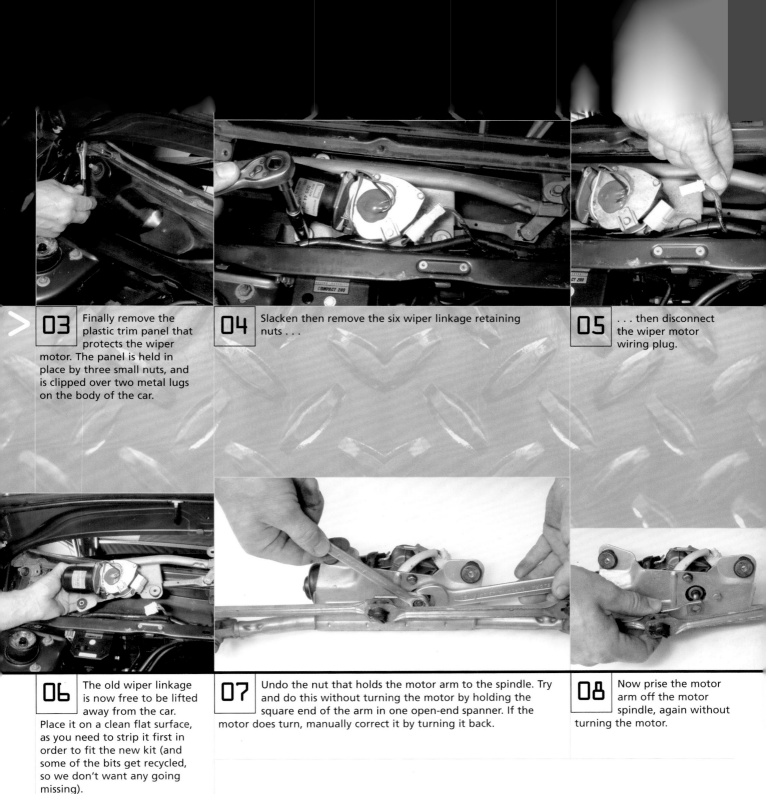

03 Finally remove the plastic trim panel that protects the wiper motor. The panel is held in place by three small nuts, and is clipped over two metal lugs on the body of the car.

04 Slacken then remove the six wiper linkage retaining nuts . . .

05 . . . then disconnect the wiper motor wiring plug.

06 The old wiper linkage is now free to be lifted away from the car. Place it on a clean flat surface, as you need to strip it first in order to fit the new kit (and some of the bits get recycled, so we don't want any going missing).

07 Undo the nut that holds the motor arm to the spindle. Try and do this without turning the motor by holding the square end of the arm in one open-end spanner. If the motor does turn, manually correct it by turning it back.

08 Now prise the motor arm off the motor spindle, again without turning the motor.

>>

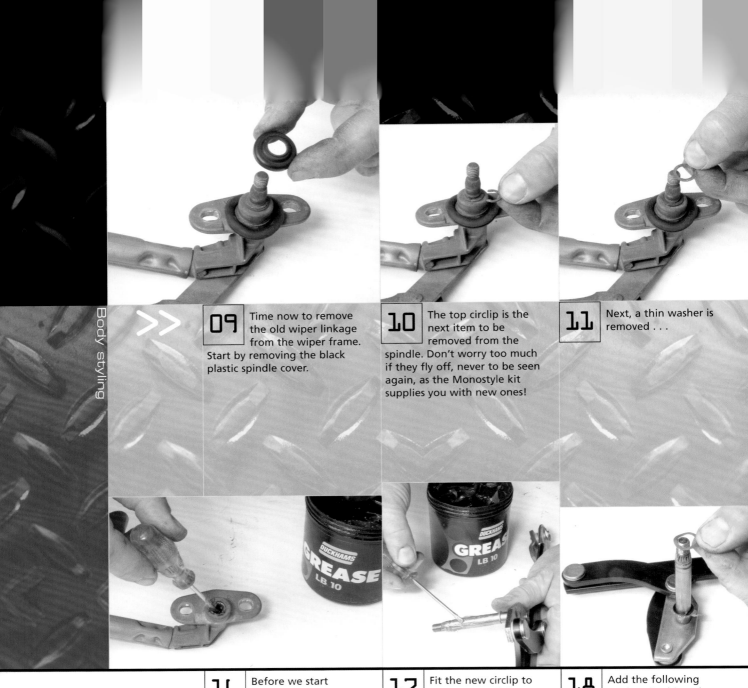

>>

09 Time now to remove the old wiper linkage from the wiper frame. Start by removing the black plastic spindle cover.

10 The top circlip is the next item to be removed from the spindle. Don't worry too much if they fly off, never to be seen again, as the Monostyle kit supplies you with new ones!

11 Next, a thin washer is removed . . .

16 Before we start rebuilding the frame with new parts, make sure you give the spindle sleeve a dose of grease for the big-boy spindle.

17 Fit the new circlip to the bottom of the spindle on the new motor arm, then grease that spindle!

18 Add the following washers in this order – the original flat washer goes on first, and then the spring washer.

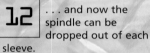

12 . . . and now the spindle can be dropped out of each sleeve.

13 Where applicable, recover the tiny rubber O-ring from inside the spindle sleeves.

14 Lastly, the spring washer and then the flat washer can be removed from the base of the spindle on the linkage.

15 Finally, to leave you with the required bare frame, remove the rubber washer. The old linkage is now redundant, but best kept if you ever decide to refit the original wipers.

19 Insert the spindle into the spindle sleeve, and pop the thin washer into place.

20 Last job now is to fit the new circlip to the top of the spindle, to keep everything in its rightful place.

21 We now have to secure the new linkage's motor arm to the motor. Turn the assembly over so the motor itself is on the back. You'll now see the splined shaft that the motor arm locates onto. Line up the new linkage so the stepped brass-coloured motor arm sits parallel with the black metal link arm, as shown.

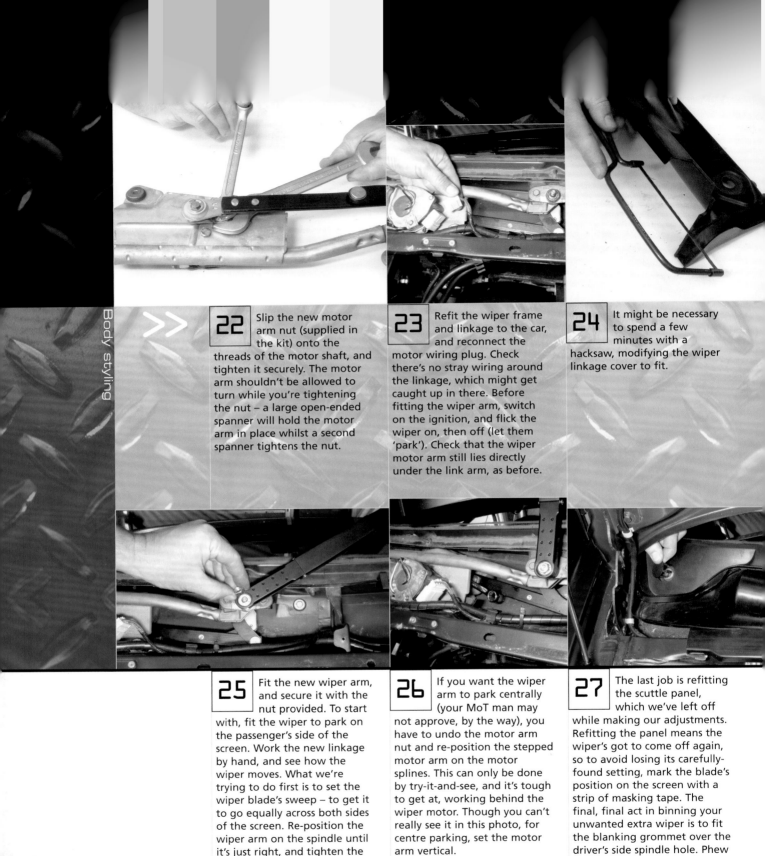

>>

22 Slip the new motor arm nut (supplied in the kit) onto the threads of the motor shaft, and tighten it securely. The motor arm shouldn't be allowed to turn while you're tightening the nut – a large open-ended spanner will hold the motor arm in place whilst a second spanner tightens the nut.

23 Refit the wiper frame and linkage to the car, and reconnect the motor wiring plug. Check there's no stray wiring around the linkage, which might get caught up in there. Before fitting the wiper arm, switch on the ignition, and flick the wiper on, then off (let them 'park'). Check that the wiper motor arm still lies directly under the link arm, as before.

24 It might be necessary to spend a few minutes with a hacksaw, modifying the wiper linkage cover to fit.

25 Fit the new wiper arm, and secure it with the nut provided. To start with, fit the wiper to park on the passenger's side of the screen. Work the new linkage by hand, and see how the wiper moves. What we're trying to do first is to set the wiper blade's sweep – to get it to go equally across both sides of the screen. Re-position the wiper arm on the spindle until it's just right, and tighten the arm nut securely.

26 If you want the wiper arm to park centrally (your MoT man may not approve, by the way), you have to undo the motor arm nut and re-position the stepped motor arm on the motor splines. This can only be done by try-it-and-see, and it's tough to get at, working behind the wiper motor. Though you can't really see it in this photo, for centre parking, set the motor arm vertical.

27 The last job is refitting the scuttle panel, which we've left off while making our adjustments. Refitting the panel means the wiper's got to come off again, so to avoid losing its carefully-found setting, mark the blade's position on the screen with a strip of masking tape. The final, final act in binning your unwanted extra wiper is to fit the blanking grommet over the driver's side spindle hole. Phew - that's it. Time for a well-earned pint.

Travelling incognito

If you is a gangsta wiv da Staines massive, blacking those windows is a must. Window tinting is also one of the best ways to disguise a naff standard interior, or a good way to hide a sorted interior (or ICE install) from the pikeys…

Tints look right with almost any car colour (limo-tint on a black 106 is virtually essential, while mirror film looks trick on a silver car), and with 'reflex film' available in various rainbow colours, there's something for everyone. Only downside is - not all tints are legal to be run on the road, and you'll be chancing it buying any advertised as 'for show cars only'. The boys in blue don't like to see tinted front windows (at cruises, it can be an instant pull), but just doing the rear windows looks a bit stupid. Tints don't suit everybody - if you're doing your car to pose around in (and why not?) it's hard enough to see you in there anyway, without blacking-out the windows!

Because window tinting involves sticking a layer of film to the inside of the glass, fitting tints might help to prevent a break-in, since your side windows won't shatter when hit. Car security firm Toad market an adhesive film specifically designed to prevent break-ins in this way, and even humble window-tinting kits are claimed to offer the same effect.

Generally, window tint comes on a roll, but you can sometimes buy pre-cut kits for popular cars. Buying a kit (if you can) sounds a better deal, but if you muck up fitting one section, you'll be buying another complete kit. With a roll of film, check how many windows you'll be able to do with it - one roll usually isn't enough for the whole car.

At this point, we'd better 'fess up and tell you that tinting will severely try your patience. If you're not a patient sort of person, this is one job which may well wind you up - you have been warned. Saying that, if you're calm and careful, and you follow the instructions to the letter, you could surprise yourself - our mechanic did, when we tried it for the first time and got a near-perfect result!

In brief, the process for tinting is to lay the film on the outside of the glass first, and cut it exactly to size. The protective layer is peeled off to expose the adhesive side, the film is transferred to the inside of the car (tricky) and then squeegeed into place (also tricky). All this must be done with scrupulous cleanliness, as any muck or stray bits of trimmed-off film will ruin the effect (almost impossible, if you're working outside). The other problem which won't surprise you is that getting rid of air bubbles and creases can take time. A long time. This is another test of patience, because if, as the instructions say, you've used plenty of spray, it will take a while to dry out and stick… just don't panic!

Legal eagle

The law on window tinting currently is that there must be no more than a 25% reduction in light transmission through windscreens, and a limit of 30% reduction on all other glass. How the heck do you measure light reduction? Also, many cars come with tinted glass as standard - so can you fit a tinting kit on top and still be legal? Hard to know what line to take, if you're stopped by Plod - try and choose a tinting kit which is EC-approved (ask before you buy, and if you think it could be a serious issue, get a letter from the company to support the legality of the kit, to use in your defence). Some forces now take this seriously enough to have portable test equipment they can use at the roadside - if your car fails, it's an on-the-spot fine.

Tinting windows

It's worth picking your day, and your working area, pretty carefully - on a windy day, there'll be more dust in the air, and it'll be a nightmare trying to stop the film flapping and folding onto itself while you're working.

Applying window tint is best done on a warm day (or in a warm garage - if there is such a thing), because the adhesive will begin to dry sooner. For fairly obvious reasons, don't try tinting when it's starting to get dark! It's a good idea to have a mate to help out with this job, but you might get fed up hearing 'you've missed another bubble' or 'you can still see that crease, y'know'.

01 Get the window being tinted clean - really clean - inside and out. Don't use glass cleaners (or any other product) containing ammonia or vinegar, since both will react with the film or its adhesive, and muck it up. Also clean the area around the window - it's too easy for stray dirt to attach itself to the film - and by the time you've noticed it, it could be too late. On door windows, wind them down slightly, to clean all of the top edge, then close them tight to fit the film.

02 Before you even unroll the film, take note - handle it carefully. If you crease it, you won't get the creases out - ever. First work out which way up the film is, by applying a small bit of really sticky tape to the front and back side - use the tape to pull the films apart, just at one corner.

03 Lay the film onto the glass, with the clear side facing you. Unroll the film, and cut it roughly to the size of the window (on a door window, leave plenty at the bottom edge for now). Some kits have a logo on the film, which seems daft - tinting's difficult enough, without having to get a logo straight! The only benefit of a logo is to establish which layer is the tint. Make life easier - lose the logo.

04 Spray the outside of the window with a weak soapy water solution (Folia Tec supply a small bottle of Joy fluid in their kit, but you could use a few drops of ordinary washing-up liquid). Get one of those plant sprayers you can buy cheap in any DIY store, if your kit doesn't contain a sprayer.

05 Lay the roughly-cut sheet of tint back onto the glass, and spray the outside of the film with soapy water . . .

06 . . . then use a squeegee to get out the air bubbles, sticking the film to the outside of the glass.

07 On a door window, trim the bottom edge to leave some excess to tuck down inside the door - this stops the film peeling off on the bottom rubber when you roll the window down!

08 Using a sharp knife (and taking care not to damage your paint or the window rubber), trim round the outside of the window. An unimportant piece of plastic (like an expired video club card) is brilliant for tucking the film into the edges to get the shape right, but don't trim the film right to the absolute edge - leave a small, even gap of just a few mill all round (this helps to get rid of excess water when you squeegee it on the inside - you'll see).

09 Now go inside, and prepare for receiving the tint. On fixed glass, waterproof the side trim panels in anticipation of the soapy water which will be used, by taping on some plastic sheet (otherwise, you'll have some very soggy panels. And seats. And carpets). Spray the inside of the glass with the soapy solution.

10 Back outside, it's time to separate the films. Use two pieces of sticky tape to pull the films slightly apart at one corner. As the films come apart, spray more solution onto the tinted piece underneath, to help it separate cleanly. Try not to lift the tint film too much off the glass when separating, as this increases the risk of creasing.

11 Have your willing helper on standby, to assist with transferring the film to the inside (a prime time for messing it all up). Peel the tint film off the glass, keeping it as flat as you can. Without letting it fold onto itself, move it inside the car and place it fairly accurately on the inside of the glass. The surface which was outside should now be on the inside of the glass (now that you've cut it, it will only fit one way!). Carefully slide the film into the corners, keeping it flat.

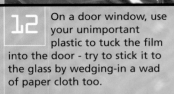

12 On a door window, use your unimportant plastic to tuck the film into the door - try to stick it to the glass by wedging-in a wad of paper cloth too.

13 Spray the film with the soapy water . . .

14 . . . then carefully start to squeegee it into place, working from top to bottom. We found that, to get into the corners, it was easier to unscrew the blade from the squeegee, and use that on its own for some of it.

15 You'll end up with a few strips at the bottom, which seemingly will not stick to the glass. Don't panic. First, soak up any excess water at the base of the film, with paper towels. Now using a hot-air gun to very gently warm the film should help to finish drying, and encourage the film to stick. Be careful squeegee-ing the film when it's dry - risk of damage. Don't lift the film off the glass - the adhesive will stick, given time. Persistence pays off.

Fitting a sunstrip

The modern sunstrip, first seen as a lovely green shadeband on Cortinas and Capris back in the 70s, usually bearing imaginative slogans such as 'DAVE AND SHARON'. Just goes to show that some things improve with age.

There are two options to make your car look (and maybe even feel) cooler:

a The sunvisor, a screen tint band inside the screen, which is usually a graduated-tint strip. As this fits inside, there's a problem straight away - the interior mirror. Your 106 mirror may be bonded to the screen, and it seriously gets in the way when trying to fit a wet and sticky (nice!) strip of plastic around it. Go for a sunstrip instead.

b The sunstrip, which is opaque vinyl, colour-matched to the car, fits to the outside of the screen. Much more Sir.

A really wide sunstrip imitates the 'roof chop' look seen on American hot rods, and colour-coded, they can look very effective from the front - plus, of course, you can use the space to advertise your preferred brand of !CE (no, no, NO! Not a good idea!). As it's fitted to the outside of the screen, the sunstrip has a good chance of seriously interfering with your wipers (or wiper, if you've been converted). If this happens to the point where the wipers can't clean the screen, Mr MOT might have a point if he fails your car… The wiper blades may need replacing more often, and the sunstrip itself might start peeling off - still want one? Well, you've got to, really.

01 This is only stuck to the outside, so only the outside of the screen needs cleaning - excellent! Do a good job of cleaning, though - any dirt stuck under the strip will ruin the effect.

02 With the help of an assistant (if you have one handy), lay the strip onto the car, and decide how far down the screen you're going to go. Legally-speaking, you shouldn't be lower than the wiper swept area - so how much of a 'badboy' are you? If you measure and mark the bottom of the strip with tape, you'll be sure to get it level, even if it's not legal.

Legal eagle
The rule for tinting or otherwise modifying the windscreen is that there must be no more than a 25% light reduction from standard. In theory, this means you can have a sunstrip which covers up to 25% of the screen area, but some MOT testers may see it differently. A sunstrip's got to come down the screen a fair way, to look any sense (otherwise, why bother?). You could argue that accurately measuring and calculating the windscreen area isn't actually that easy, if you get stopped, and anyway, a sunstrip also cuts out harmful glare! If you go so far down the screen that you can't see out, though - well, that's just stupid.

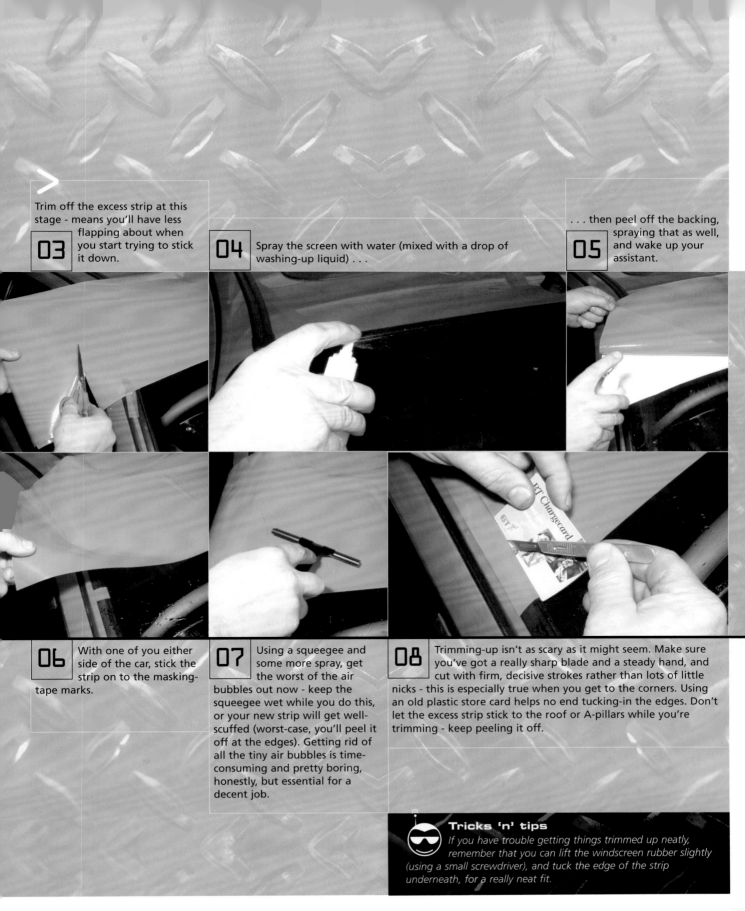

03 Trim off the excess strip at this stage - means you'll have less flapping about when you start trying to stick it down.

04 Spray the screen with water (mixed with a drop of washing-up liquid) . . .

05 . . . then peel off the backing, spraying that as well, and wake up your assistant.

06 With one of you either side of the car, stick the strip on to the masking-tape marks.

07 Using a squeegee and some more spray, get the worst of the air bubbles out now - keep the squeegee wet while you do this, or your new strip will get well-scuffed (worst-case, you'll peel it off at the edges). Getting rid of all the tiny air bubbles is time-consuming and pretty boring, honestly, but essential for a decent job.

08 Trimming-up isn't as scary as it might seem. Make sure you've got a really sharp blade and a steady hand, and cut with firm, decisive strokes rather than lots of little nicks - this is especially true when you get to the corners. Using an old plastic store card helps no end tucking-in the edges. Don't let the excess strip stick to the roof or A-pillars while you're trimming - keep peeling it off.

Tricks 'n' tips
If you have trouble getting things trimmed up neatly, remember that you can lift the windscreen rubber slightly (using a small screwdriver), and tuck the edge of the strip underneath, for a really neat fit.

Painting by numbers

This is not the section where we tell you how to respray your entire 106 in a weekend, using only spray cans, okay? Mission Impossible, we ain't. This bit's all about how to spray up your various plasticky bits before final fitting - bits such as door mirrors, light brows, spoilers, splitters - hell, even bumpers if you like. As we've no doubt said before, with anything new, fit your unpainted bits first. Make sure everything fits properly (shape and tidy up all parts as necessary), that all holes have been drilled, and all screws etc are doing their job. Then, and only when you're totally, completely happy with the fit - take them off, and get busy with the spray cans.

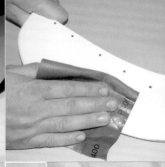

01 The first job is to mask off any areas you don't want painted. Do this right at the start, or you could be sorry; on these door mirrors, we decided to mask off just at the lip before the glass, to leave a black unpainted edge - if we hadn't masked it as the very first job, we would've roughed up all the shiny black plastic next, and wrecked the edge finish.

02 Remove any unwanted 'seams' in the plastic, using fine sandpaper or wet-and-dry. Some of these seams look pretty cool, others don't - you decide. Also worth tidying up any other areas you're not happy with, fit-wise, while you're at it.

03 Especially with 'shiny' plastic, you must rough-up the surface before spray will 'bite' to it, or - it'll flippin' flake off. Just take off the shine, no more. You can use fine wet-and-dry for this (used dry), but we prefer Scotchbrite. This stuff, which looks much like a scouring pad, is available from motor factors and bodyshops, in several grades - we used ultra-fine, which is grey. One advantage of Scotchbrite is that it's a bit easier to work into awkward corners than paper.

04 Once the surface has been nicely 'roughened', clean up the surface using a suitable degreaser ('suitable' means a type which won't dissolve plastic!). Generally, it's ok to use methylated spirit or cellulose thinners (just don't inhale!), but test it on a not-so-visible bit first, so you don't have a disaster.

05 Before you start spraying (if it's something smaller than a bumper) it's a good idea to try a work a screw into one of the mounting holes, to use as a 'handle', so you can turn the item to spray all sides.

06 Another good trick is to use the screw to hang the item up on a piece of string or wire - then you can spin the item round to get the spray into awkward areas.

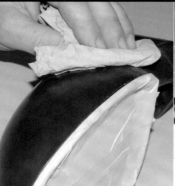

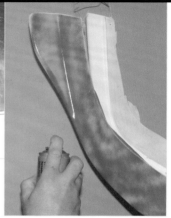

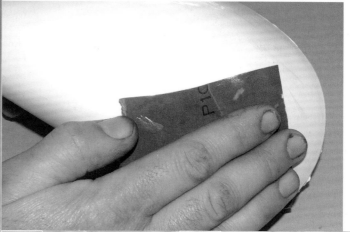

07 If you like a bit of wildlife in your paint, you can't beat the great outdoors. If it's at all windy, you'll end up with a really awful finish and overspray on everything (which can be a real pain to get off). Even indoors, if it's damp weather, you'll have real problems trying to get a shine - some kind of heater is essential if it's cold and wet (but not one with a fan - stirring up the dust is the last thing you want).

08 If you're a bit new at spraying, or if you simply don't want to balls it up, practise your technique first (steady!). Working left-right, then right-left, press the nozzle so you start spraying just before you pass the item, and follow through just past it the other side. Keep the nozzle a constant distance from the item - not in a curved arc. Don't blast the paint on too thick, or you'll have a nasty case of the runs - hold the can about 6 inches away - you're not trying to paint the whole thing in one sweep.

09 Once you've got a patchy 'mist coat' on (which might not even cover the whole thing) - stop, and let it dry (primer dries pretty quickly). Continue building up thin coats until you've got full coverage, then let it dry for half an hour or more.

10 Using 1000- or 1200-grade wet-and-dry paper (used wet), very lightly sand the whole primered surface, to take out any minor imperfections (blobs, where the nozzle was spitting) in the primer. Try not to go through the primer to the plastic, but this doesn't matter too much in small areas.

11 Rinse off thoroughly, then dry the surfaces - let it stand for a while to make sure it's *completely* dry, before starting on the top coat.

12 Make sure once again that the surfaces are clean, with no bits left behind from the drying operations. As with the primer, work up from an initial thin mist coat, allowing time for each pass to dry. As you spray, you'll soon learn how to build a nice shine without runs - any 'dry' (dull) patches are usually due to overspray landing on still-wet shiny paint. Don't worry if you can't eliminate all of these - a light cutting polish will sort it out once the paint's hardened (after several hours).

13 Especially with a colour like red (which is notorious for fading easily), it's a good idea to blow on a coat or two of clear lacquer over the top - this will also give you your shine, if you're stuck with a very 'dry' finish. It's best to apply lacquer before the final top coat is fully hardened. The spraying technique is identical, although pro sprayers say that lacquer should be applied pretty thick - just watch those runs! Lacquer also takes a good long while to dry - pick up your item too soon, for that unique fingerprint effect!

There's no way in

One way to tidy up the 106 lines is to do away with the door locks, and even the door handles - but be careful. Flushing the rear door handles (on 5-door models) is okay, legally/MOT-speaking, but removing the front door handles will land you in trouble, come MOT time.

Construction & Use regs require your car to have an independent mechanical means of door opening from outside (so fire-fighters can get you out, if you stick your all-action 106 on its roof, or in a ditch…) If you must lose the front handles, find some trick mirrors which have door catches built-in, underneath.

At least most 106s (apart from the billy-basic models) have central locking as standard, meaning all you need is a remote alarm with a central locking interface (like the one we fitted in the Security section) and you're sorted.

01 De-locking your 106 doors means removing the lock barrels and plating over the holes. First, remove the door card (see 'Interiors'). When the plastic membrane is pulled back, you'll see a metal retaining clip, which you slide sideways from the lock barrel . . .

02 . . . unclip the lock rod from the back of the lock, and . . .

03 . . . the lock is then free to be removed from the car by hooking it out through the hole. The hole that's left behind is now ready to be filled in. The most DIY-friendly way of plugging this hole is by gluing a metal plate into place behind the hole (no, really – it can work).

04 Otherwise, make up a card template of the hole where the lock used to be, then create a metal plate that shape. Weld the plate to the door, smooth the weld with a grinder, and add a touch of filler. Your de-locked door is now ready to be sprayed. Course, now you've come this far, colour-coding the door handles would be nice…

Body styling

Remote **locking**

So you can lock and unlock your freshly de-locked doors, you'll need to buy and fit a remote central locking kit, which you can get from several Max Power-advertised suppliers (our Microscan kit is an extra for our chosen alarm, but is pretty typical of what you'll get). If your 106 already has central locking, you're in luck - buy yourself a cheap car alarm, and a central locking interface.

Tricks 'n' tips
If your battery goes flat, you'll be locked out. We ran two thin wires from the battery terminals (with a 10-amp fuse in the live, and the ends insulated), and tucked them away for access from below in an emergency. By connecting a slave battery to these wires (do not try jump-starting), you'll put enough juice into the system to operate the locks, saving you a red face. Think it over.

Central locking **kit**

If your 106 doesn't have central locking as standard, don't despair - there's several kits out there to help you towards your goal. Our project 106 already had central locking, so regrettably there are no 106-specific photos to show you, but hopefully, the details below, together with your kit's instructions, will help you out.

Before you start fitting your new lock solenoids, it makes sense to test them. Connect them all together as described in your kit's instructions - with power connected to all the solenoids, pull up on the operating plunger of one, and all the rest should pop up too - clever, eh?

Decide where you're going to mount the lock control unit, then identify the various looms, and feed them out to the doors.

The new lock solenoids must be mounted so they work in the same *plane* as the door lock buttons. What this means is it's no good having the lock solenoid plungers moving horizontally, to work a button and rod which operates vertically! Make up the mounting brackets from the metal bits provided in the kit, and fit the solenoids loosely to the brackets, and to the doors.

The kit contains several items which look uncannily like bike spokes - these are your new lock operating rods, which have to be cut to length, then joined onto the old rods using screw clamps. It's best to join the old and new rods at a straight piece of the old rod, so feed the new rod in, and mark it for cutting.

Cut the new rod to the marked length, fit the cut rod to the solenoid, then slip the clamp onto it. Fit the solenoid onto its bracket, and offer the rod into place, to connect to the old rod. Join the new rod and old rod together, and fasten the clamp screws tight. If the clamp screws come loose, you're basically going to be locked out.

Now you can connect up the wires - the easy bit is joining up inside the door. Hopefully, your kit's instructions should be sufficient, but if not, you'll have to resort to the Haynes manual wiring diagrams.

PEUGEOT
106

Haynes Service and Repair Manual

Don't mesh with me, boy

A meshed grille or bumper is just one way to demonstrate who's the daddy of the cruise, and it does a great job of dicing any small insects or rodents foolish enough to wander into the path of your motor. So if you're sick of scrubbing off insect entrails from your paint, and fancy getting even, read on...

Which style of mesh to choose? Classic diamond-shape, or round-hole? In our humble opinion, the round-hole mesh works best on modern roundy-shaped cars (like say, a Corsa) - for everything else, we'll settle for the original and best. But wait - the choice doesn't end with what shape you want. Mesh can now be had in various anodised colours too, to match or contrast with the rest of your chosen paint scheme.

01 Anyone can mesh a hole. Ab-so-lutely anyone - it's dead easy. First, measure your hole, then cut out a roughly-sized piece of mesh, leaving some over the sides to bend around the edges of your hole.

02 Of course, holes usually have corners - and some of the sides you'll encounter aren't exactly straight. Make small cuts in the edge of the mesh at strategic points . . .

03 . . . and bending over the edges will be much easier. The main mesh panel will also stay flatter, and you'll be less stressed, too.

04 There's loads of ways to secure your mesh. One of the most permanent is to use small self-tapping screws, but this won't always be possible. Our hot-glue gun method worked a treat, as the glue flows into place. You can use mastic (quick-setting, exterior-use type) or even builder's 'no-nails' adhesive, but you squirt on a bead of the stuff, and then have to smooth it on by hand, to 'squidge' it over the mesh. Very meshy - sorry, messy.

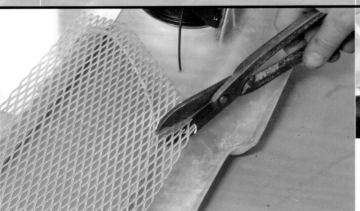

Bumpers 'n' bodykits

If you can't find a kit you like for a 106, you're not trying - check the various 106 modding websites and chat forums for ideas if you're stuck. Some people like to mix it up with stuff for the 106, if they find one kit too limiting. Kit suppliers worth checking out include Carcept, Carzone, CCM, Dimma, Ibherdesign, and that's just for starters. But we've forgotten the most famous of all Peugeot kit makers – Ecosse, who kindly supplied us with a full kit for our 106.

One thing you should be concerned about is how well it's all going to fit. Even if you're giving the joy of fitting to a bodyshop, they'll still charge you more if your cheap duff kit takes a week longer to fit than expected. Ask around (or check the 106 web forums) before splashing the cash.

Front bumper

It's not absolutely necessary for you to have the car up on axle stands, but if you do, it gives you much better access to those hard-to-reach areas (see 'Wheels & tyres' for info on jacking-up). Start removing the bumper by prising off the body clip that secures the wheel arch liner to the bumper.

01

02 Pull down the access panel in the wheel arch . . .

>>

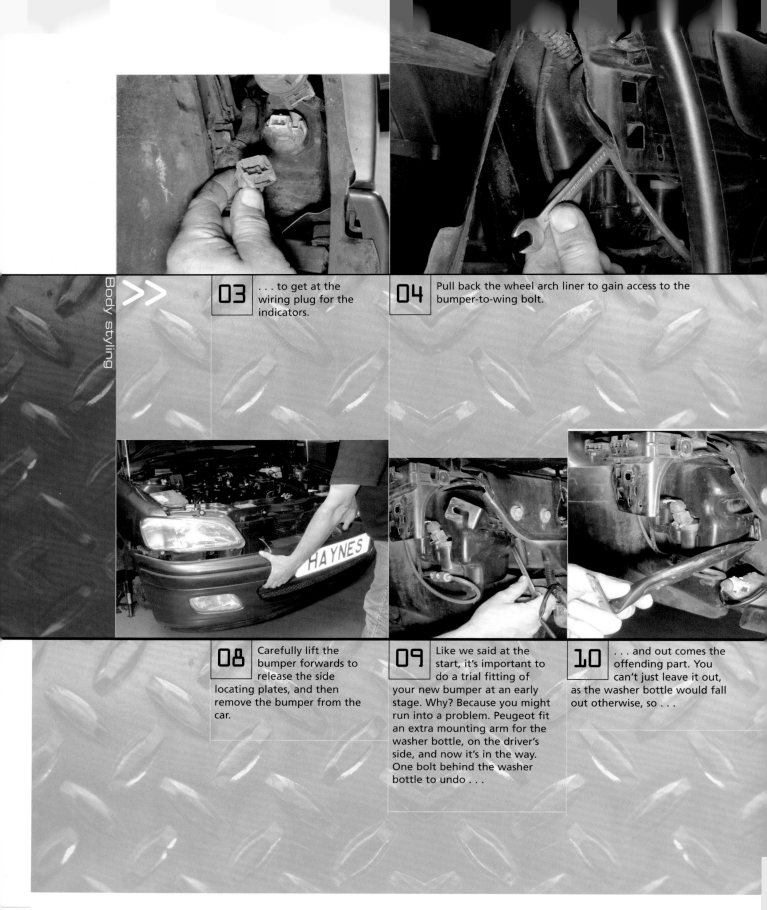

03 . . . to get at the wiring plug for the indicators.

04 Pull back the wheel arch liner to gain access to the bumper-to-wing bolt.

08 Carefully lift the bumper forwards to release the side locating plates, and then remove the bumper from the car.

09 Like we said at the start, it's important to do a trial fitting of your new bumper at an early stage. Why? Because you might run into a problem. Peugeot fit an extra mounting arm for the washer bottle, on the driver's side, and now it's in the way. One bolt behind the washer bottle to undo . . .

10 . . . and out comes the offending part. You can't just leave it out, as the washer bottle would fall out otherwise, so . . .

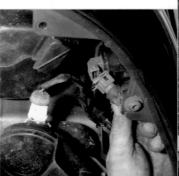

05 Unlike the rest of the operations in removing the bumper, the next bolt you have to remove is only found on the driver's side – it's the bolt that attaches the bumper to the washer fluid reservoir support strap.

06 On models with front foglights, disconnect the foglight wiring.

07 Finally, working under the bumper, remove the bumper lower mounting bolts. There's one bolt either side of the bumper, securing the bumper to the front panel (they're a bit hard to see, and you'll need a socket and long extension, but they're in there somewhere).

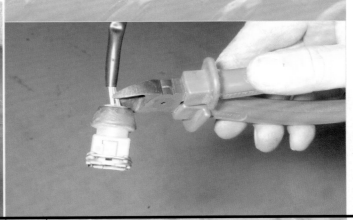

11 . . . it's over to the workbench, where the bar gets a little 'modification' with the hacksaw, before being refitted.

12 Other than figuring out ways round obstacles like the washer bottle mounting bar, the only other 'problem' to deal with is wiring-up the extra fog and spotlights in the new Ecosse bumper. Our 106 XS came with front fogs as standard, but even the stock wiring needed a mod – carefully trim off the old wiring plug . . .

>>

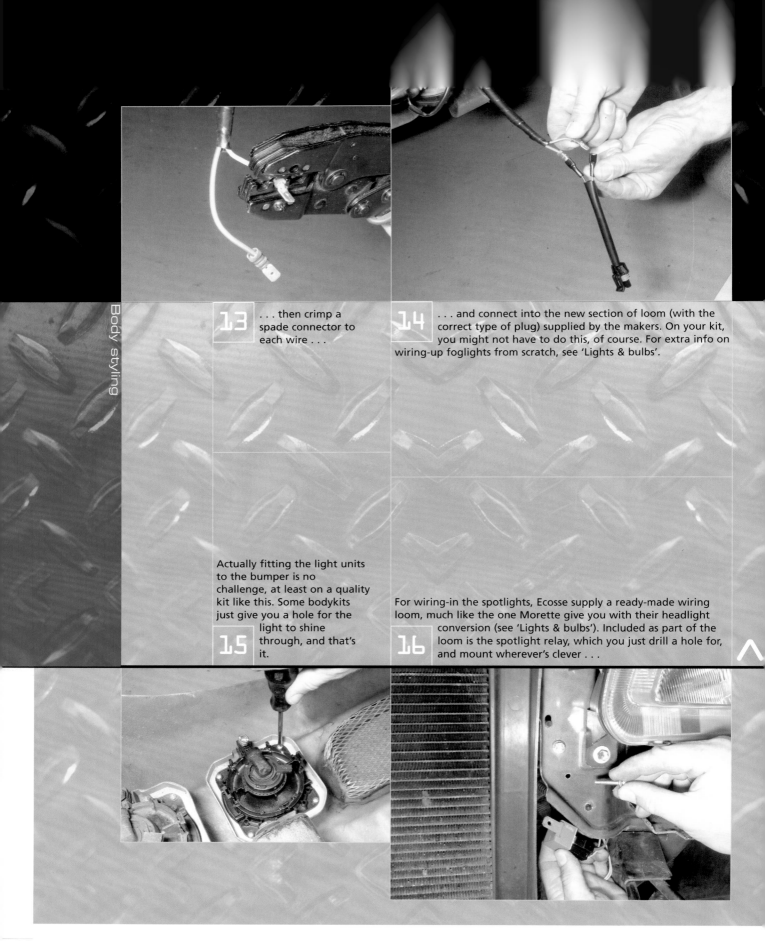

13 . . . then crimp a spade connector to each wire . . .

14 . . . and connect into the new section of loom (with the correct type of plug) supplied by the makers. On your kit, you might not have to do this, of course. For extra info on wiring-up foglights from scratch, see 'Lights & bulbs'.

15 Actually fitting the light units to the bumper is no challenge, at least on a quality kit like this. Some bodykits just give you a hole for the light to shine through, and that's it.

16 For wiring-in the spotlights, Ecosse supply a ready-made wiring loom, much like the one Morette give you with their headlight conversion (see 'Lights & bulbs'). Included as part of the loom is the spotlight relay, which you just drill a hole for, and mount wherever's clever . . .

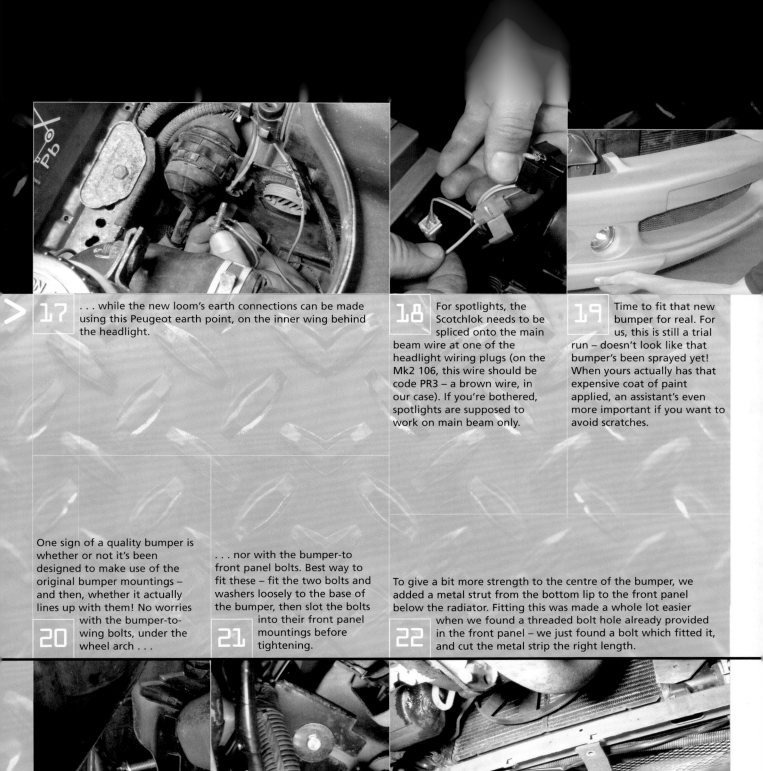

17 . . . while the new loom's earth connections can be made using this Peugeot earth point, on the inner wing behind the headlight.

18 For spotlights, the Scotchlok needs to be spliced onto the main beam wire at one of the headlight wiring plugs (on the Mk2 106, this wire should be code PR3 – a brown wire, in our case). If you're bothered, spotlights are supposed to work on main beam only.

19 Time to fit that new bumper for real. For us, this is still a trial run – doesn't look like that bumper's been sprayed yet! When yours actually has that expensive coat of paint applied, an assistant's even more important if you want to avoid scratches.

20 One sign of a quality bumper is whether or not it's been designed to make use of the original bumper mountings – and then, whether it actually lines up with them! No worries with the bumper-to-wing bolts, under the wheel arch . . .

21 . . . nor with the bumper-to-front panel bolts. Best way to fit these – fit the two bolts and washers loosely to the base of the bumper, then slot the bolts into their front panel mountings before tightening.

22 To give a bit more strength to the centre of the bumper, we added a metal strut from the bottom lip to the front panel below the radiator. Fitting this was made a whole lot easier when we found a threaded bolt hole already provided in the front panel – we just found a bolt which fitted it, and cut the metal strip the right length.

Rear bumper

01 To make life a little easier for you, put the car up on axle stands, and get the wheels off (see 'Wheels & tyres' for info on jacking the car up). Then open the tailgate and prise the plastic cover from the rear of each light cluster.

02 Remove the securing screw and unclip the air extraction grille from the side of the luggage compartment. Oh look – the wheelbrace just came off in our hand as well.

03 Pull the carpet out from behind the grille, and reach in to disconnect the number plate wiring connector.

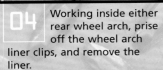

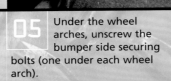

04 Working inside either rear wheel arch, prise off the wheel arch liner clips, and remove the liner.

05 Under the wheel arches, unscrew the bumper side securing bolts (one under each wheel arch).

06 Prise off the rubber grommets at the back of the luggage compartment to reveal the bumper securing bolts and the central nut – remove these now.

07 Lift the bumper off the car, unclipping it from the side plates as you lift. Carefully feed the number plate wiring through the aperture in the bodywork before you lift the bumper away from the car. You still need bits from this bumper for later, so keep it close to hand.

08 When fitting any aftermarket bumper, it's always a good idea to offer it into place on the car to check for fitment – at least that way you know how much work's involved in fitting it. The only obstacle encountered was that the towing eye was fouling the bumper, so unfortunately it's gotta go.

09 To keep MOT-dude happy, your new bumper still needs a number plate light. If your new bumper comes with one, you're laughing (we suspect you're lying, actually) – if not, you'll have to recover the original. Go back to the old bumper now, and remove the bumper bar from the bumper plastic cover – it's held in place by a series of bolts.

10 Now you can see the wiring plug that feeds the number plate light – disconnect this, then release the light's retaining clip and remove the light from the bumper. And would you believe it – the light clips straight into the new bumper, and can be connected back up as the new bumper's fitted. Being legal has never been easier.

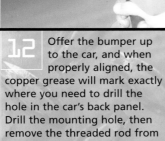

11 The new bumper used all the existing mounting holes, except one – how very annoying. The central mounting is a plastic platform with a threaded hole in the centre of it. Buy a section of threaded rod (from a DIY store), screw into this hole, leaving some sticking out, then apply a little copper grease to the end.

12 Offer the bumper up to the car, and when properly aligned, the copper grease will mark exactly where you need to drill the hole in the car's back panel. Drill the mounting hole, then remove the threaded rod from the mounting platform.

13 From inside the boot, put a bolt through the newly-created hole. When fitting the new bumper, this bolt will screw into the threaded hole and hold the bumper in place. The bumper can now be secured in place using the remaining mounting points. Route the number plate wiring back through properly so that it can reconnected inside the boot.

Tricks 'n' tips
If your bumper doesn't have a central mounting platform like ours, you can always create your own by securing a long bolt to the bumper cover using fibreglass, drilling a mounting hole in the car's back panel, and attaching a washer and nut to the bolt inside the boot.

Side skirts

together' the front and rear sections of a bodykit. This much we know from our magazines. But where did skirts really come from?

As with so much else in modifying, it's a racing-inspired thing. In the late 70s, the Lotus 'ground-effect' F1 cars ran very, very low (for the time) and had side skirts made of rubber (or bristles), to give a flexible seal against the track. With a clear downforce advantage, Lotus blew the opposition away.

So will fitting skirts to your 106 give you race-car levels of downforce, greatly increasing your overtaking chances at the next roundabout? You already know the answer, I'm afraid…

Tricks 'n' tips

Only attempt to carry out procedures such as this one on a dry day. The car will be out of action for a maximum of 24 hours, so make prior arrangements, and try not to drive the car during this time.

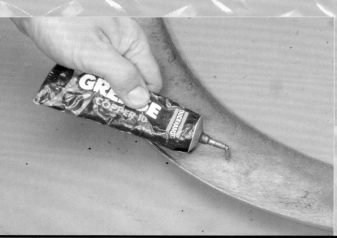

01 To fit the new Ecosse side skirts, the front section of the side rubbing strips has to go (your kit may be different). Start by prising the plastic clip from the wheel arch liner, and pull it back so you can reach in behind the arch. Locate the body clip that secures the strip to the body, and squeeze the bottom of the clip to release it. Oh whoops – more holes in the bodywork.

02 The skirts are an all-in-one arch extension and skirt kit. Slightly more work to fit than conventional skirts – but they look great, so who cares? You can fit this by drilling holes in the arches, or by bonding the extension on with panel bond or equivalent adhesive. Apply copper grease to the kit's pre-fitted studs . . .

03 . . . then offer it up to the car. The copper grease acts as a marker to show where to drill the mounting holes. Some masking tape stuck to the car protects the paint, and makes the marks easier to see, too. If the kit doesn't have studs, either stick on your own bolts/screws with fibreglass, etc – or re-consider the panel bond method of fixing.

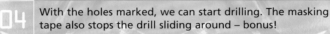

04 With the holes marked, we can start drilling. The masking tape also stops the drill sliding around – bonus!

05 Once the holes are drilled in both the front and rear arches, and the masking tape removed, the kit can be put into place and primarily secured with a washer and nut on the end of each stud. A few self-tapping screws into the sills will stop any flexing of the skirt, so drill a couple more holes in the sill, why don'tcha?

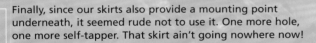

06 Finally, since our skirts also provide a mounting point underneath, it seemed rude not to use it. One more hole, one more self-tapper. That skirt ain't going nowhere now!

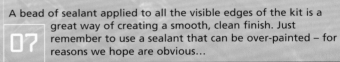

07 A bead of sealant applied to all the visible edges of the kit is a great way of creating a smooth, clean finish. Just remember to use a sealant that can be over-painted – for reasons we hope are obvious…

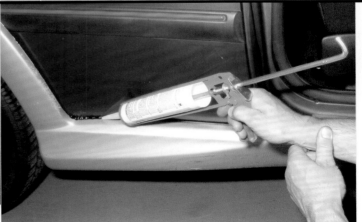

Spoil your 106 rotten

A must for any 106, a rear spoiler makes a very clear statement to the car you just passed - do not mess. Our very fine Ecosse spoiler (with side repeater lights) should do the trick.

Tricks 'n' tips

Fitting a spoiler is actually one of the easier jobs in modifying - just make sure you've got it straight, which means lots of eyeing-up, measuring, and getting a second opinion from a mate. Before you drill any holes, make sure you can actually use those holes to fit bolts through, and nuts to. Get some sealant, too, to keep water out of your boot.

01 Some models come fitted with what can only be described as a very lame standard spoiler. Bigger is so much better – but first you gotta get that old one off. Start by removing the grommet either side of the high-level brake light, and then remove the retaining nuts.

02 At either end of the spoiler, remove the Torx bolt . . .

03 . . . and the old spoiler's free to be lifted away from the car.

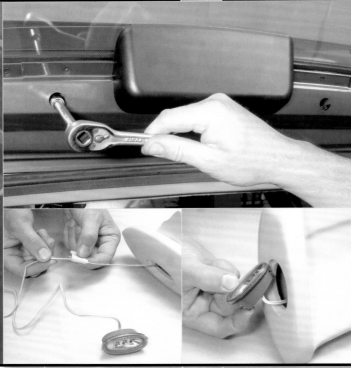

04 The Ecosse spoiler has the trademark side repeaters mounted at either end. This creates slightly more work, but it's worth it. Start by feeding the side repeater wire through the inside of the spoiler and out the hole in the middle. Tape the wiring to a piece of welding wire to help you route it through the spoiler, then repeat the process for the other side.

05 Fit the rubber seal, then the spring steel retaining clip to the repeater, then it can be slotted into place at either end – they'll only fit one way, so if they don't easily push into place, don't force them.

06 Offer the spoiler into place on the roof. Your next job will be to separate the two wires so that the left hand repeater wiring can be routed down the left hand side of the car. So start with the left hand wire first, attach it to a piece of welding wire or equivalent, and route it through the corresponding hole in the middle of the tailgate . . .

07 . . . out to the nearside edge of the tailgate . . .

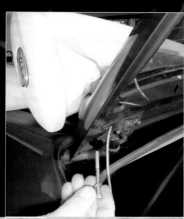

08 . . . then bolt the spoiler in place. Repeat this process for the opposite side, and in the centre of the tailgate, and refit the rubber grommets.

09 Before you go much further, you'll have to start removing some trim in order to feed the wire down to the rear light cluster. Start by removing the knob from the seat backrest release catch.

10 The rear parcel support shelf is held in place with two screws – one located under the rear seat catch, so you'll need to release the catch and push the seat forwards to get on it.

11 The rear seat belt is the last thing you have to remove, so prise off the plastic cover and remove the seat belt top mounting bolt.

12 Unclip the side trim panel, then pull off the tailgate rubber seal around the top edge of the boot.

13 Route the wire from the spoiler through the protective rubber piping and into the car. The faithful old welding wire will help you achieve this – once it's in, routing the wire down to the rear lights is easy.

14 Use a test light to check each wire in turn on the rear cluster wiring plug, to locate the indicator feed. The indicators will need to be on for this, obviously (duh). Wire colours won't be much help to you – you're looking for number codes printed on the wires (and it's 2333 or 2343 you want). Or check your Haynes manual, of course.

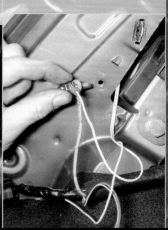

15 Join the spoiler left indicator wire to the live feed on the left-hand light cluster (we think you can figure the rest out yourself). The spoiler earth wires get joined to an earth point on the metalwork – and oh look, there's one they made earlier, next to the rear seat belt reel. Sorted.

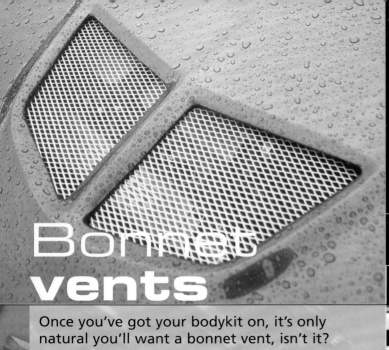

Bonnet vents

01 Start by creating a full-size card template of the bonnet vent.

02 Next mark the areas of the vent that are going to be recessed down through the bonnet.

Once you've got your bodykit on, it's only natural you'll want a bonnet vent, isn't it? Respect.

But this is one scary job to tackle yourself, unless you're really that good, or that brave. Plenty of options - you can get little louvres stamped in as well, to complement your Evo, Impreza, Integrale or F50 main vent. And, like Focus side repeaters, Focus WRC bonnet vents have now been fitted to everything from Novas upwards (so you may want to scope around for something more original). Speaking of which, there's even been a feature car with a bonnet scoop from a (sensible) Kia Sedona people carrier! Truly, anything goes.

A less-scary option is to buy a ready-made, pre-vented bonnet - fitting one of these is about as easy as it gets. But we like a challenge. With this car (ok, so it's a Punto, but a bonnet's a bonnet, innit?), not only are we fitting a vent ourselves, it's an F50 vent. One of the biggest you can get. Game on.

There are two main ways of fitting a bonnet vent, and both include chopping your bonnet about. The first option is to cut a complete-vent-size hole in the bonnet, and fit it up from below - this way, the vent is sunk into the bonnet and doesn't stand proud. The second is to place the vent on top of the bonnet, cut out the shapes of any recessed parts, so that the vent actually sits on the bonnet. The process you choose will to a certain extent depend on the size and thickness of the vent you're fitting. Option 1 for fitting a vent is the preferred way, but not always easy at home in the garage. We're going to show you Option 2.

03 The template must now be put into place on the bonnet. Take your time to measure the bonnet, and place the vent centrally (and straight!).

04 Hold the template in place with masking tape, and mark the holes for cutting . . .

05 . . . you should now be left with something that looks like this. So far, all you've done is create a piece of card with holes in, and drawn on your bonnet - both processes which are reversible. The next bit isn't, really - are you up for the challenge of cutting large holes in your bonnet?

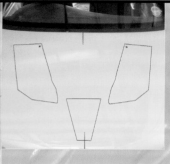

06 Taking a jigsaw with the right blade, begin cutting out the holes. This is harder than it looks - at times you'll be cutting through the bonnet braces inside. Prop the bonnet open slightly using some wood (so your blade doesn't hit any engine bits), and put something over the engine to protect it from the shower of swarf it's about to receive.

07 When the holes have been cut, try the vent in place and it should sit nicely on the bonnet. If you've been holding your breath until now, allow yourself one sigh of relief.

08 Next job is to find a way of securing the vent in place whilst the adhesive, which you'll be adding later on, gets to work. Screws are the easiest option, so start by drilling a series of holes along the edges of the vent.

09 Now drill the corresponding holes in the bonnet. The easiest way of doing this is to put the vent on centrally, hold it still (or tape it in place) and drill down through the holes in the vent and into the bonnet.

10 Add some self-tapping screws and washers, and that vent's going nowhere . . .

11 . . . or is it? Once you've gone to all that bother of fixing the vent in place, now you have to remove it. It's time to apply a nice thick bead of heavy-duty adhesive (proper bodyshop mastic, please). At the end of the day, this bond is what's going to be holding the vent in place, so don't be stingy - give the whole area a hefty squirt.

12 Once the bond has been applied, the vent can be put back into place and screwed in securely until the glue has dried. Any excess that squeezes out can be smoothed around the edge of the vent with a finger.

13 Once the adhesive has dried, we're able to remove the screws - as if by magic, the vent stays where it is. The really time-consuming bit is smoothing the vent into the bonnet - lots of filing-down the edges, lots of filler. Once this stage is complete, the bonnet's ready to be primed and painted.

Wheelarch mods

The law states that your wide rubber shouldn't be so wide that it sticks out from your arches, and the MOT crew will not be impressed if your new rubber's rubbing, either. This presents something of a problem, if you're determined to get 17s on, especially if the car's also having a radical drop job. If you've got rubbing problems on 15s (or even 16s), something's very wrong. Check that your wheels are the right offset (see 'Wheels & tyres'), or chat to your wheel supplier about spacers.

Sometimes, all you need to stop those nasty grinding noises is a small amount of violence. Any non-vital protrusions into the under-arch area can be trimmed off or flattened with a hammer. Also, try removing those (oh-so-practical) wheelarch liners.

Serious wheelarch mods are best done at a bodyshop. Having the arches professionally rolled, using the proper tool, should only cost about £50 per arch (assuming they haven't also got rust or filler to deal with as well). Less satisfactory would be having the arch edges cut or ground off - this leaves a bare-metal edge, and encourages rust (as well as weakening the wings).

The best answer to arches which just aren't roomy enough is, of course, a wide-arch bodykit. And bank loans are so cheap these days.

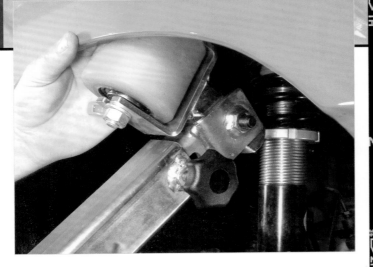

Not happy with your 106's 'pensioner blue' paint? Time to call in the pros. There's no such thing as a simple DIY respray (not one that'll look good afterwards, at any rate). We just thought you'd like to see some of the stages involved.

01 A respray involves massive amounts of rubbing-down - and not just between the various coats, either. Even perfectly-sound original paint has to have a touch of the rough stuff, to take the shine off, and give the new primer something to "bite" to. Edges are favourite areas for paint to start lifting and peeling, so nothing can be missed.

02 Doing a full respray means getting all those door shuts and other areas of painted metal inside, but not the dash, seats, and carpets (unless you're going to completely gut the entire dash and interior afterwards). You can never do too much masking.

03 Hang on, are you sure that's still our car under there? For a full respray, it's often better to remove fixed glass completely, rather than spend time masking it all up. That means windscreen, tailgate, and all the side glass. Still fancy having a go yourself?

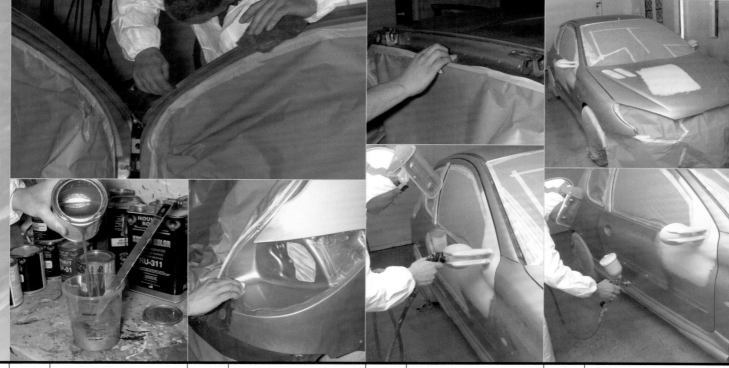

04 Mixing the paint is an important, but often overlooked, stage in any spraying process - even ambient temperatures have a bearing on the final paint mix. Topcoats and lacquer especially have complex mixing ratios for the thinners, hardener, activator, and any 'flex' additives for bumpers and such - get it wrong, and even top-notch paint like this won't work.

05 Making sure the paint surface is clean between steps is another often-overlooked essential item. Our bodywork experts use a water-based wash, as solvent-based products can lift the paint (or react with the next coat). The final stage is cleaning using tack-rags (net-like material, impregnated with resin - very sticky, picks up any bits).

06 What's this? Spraying primer - that's pretty boring, isn't it? Well, no - this green stuff's an epoxy primer, used to ensure good paint adhesion on any bodywork that's had "extreme" work done. The main primer for this colour is actually metallic itself, which enhances the finished shine. Metallic primers (base coats) are unique to House of Kolor, apparently. Still think it's boring?

07 Now we're ready for some real paint. Got your shades handy? Of course, in proper custom paint like this, there's flakes and pearls as well - the choice is bewildering - ask your bodyshop for some test cards before you decide! Several coats of lacquer later, and we'll have an amazing shine.

Lights
& bulbs

Being scene

Lights - one of the easiest and coolest ways to trick up your 106. Several options here, so we'll start at the front, and work back.

Headlights

Almost nothing influences the look of your 106 more than the front end, so the headlights play a crucial role.

What's available?

The popular cheap option is stick-on headlight 'brows', which do admittedly give the rather bland 106 front end a tougher look. The brows are best sprayed to match the car, before fitting - most are fitted using stick-on Velcro pads. Street-cred on the cheap, and (if you choose the Fox-style brows) a cheap alternative to a proper 'badboy' bonnet.

Another cheap option is again stick-on - this time, it's stick-on covers which give the twin-headlight look. This is basically a sheet of vinyl/plastic (shaped to the headlights, and colour-matched to your car) with two holes cut in it. Dead easy to fit, but dare we say, a bit tacky? Just our opinion. A cheap and simple way to get close to the twin-light look.

If you want tinted headlights, you could try spray-tinting them, but go easy on the spray. Turning your headlights from clear glass to non-see-through is plain daft, even if it's done in the name of style. A light tint is quite effective, and gives you the chance to colour-match to your 106. With tinted headlights, you'd be wise to tint those (Mk 1) clear front indicators too, of course.

> ### Pub trivia
> *The popular twin-headlight look was derived from a cunning tweak first employed in the Touring Cars, years ago. Some teams homologated a twin-headlight unit, but for racing, turned one pair of the 'headlights' into air inlets, to direct air from the front of the car to brake ducts or into the engine air intakes, as required. Think about it - why else would the touring cars bother with headlight mods? Until recently, there were no night races!*

Another 'headlight' option sometimes featured on 106s actually belongs in the bodywork section - it's the 'badboy' bonnet. By cunningly welding-in a couple of triangular plates to your standard 106 bonnet, a bodyshop (or handy DIY-er) can create a really mean look, using just the standard lights. Excellent. Still on the subject of bodywork, you'll need a few minor body mods if you fancy fitting some 106 Mk 2 headlights to a Mk 1, but it's far from impossible, and really improves the look.

Getting more expensive, we're looking at complete replacement lights - 'proper' twin-headlights, available as a kit from the French company Morette. Typically around £300 a set at time of writing, these are for lads who're seriously into their cars - maximum cred, and no-one's gonna accuse you of owning a 'boring' Peugeot ever again! The light surrounds have to be sprayed to match your car, and fitting is not without some difficulties, but the finished result is SO worth it.

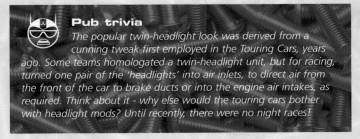

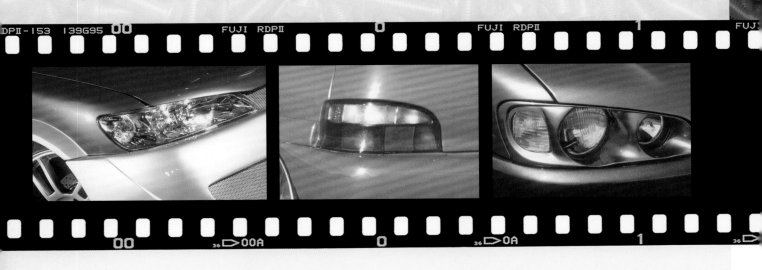

Headlight
brows

This is the cheap 'n' cheerful approach, and it really doesn't get much simpler than this. This is even a mod you can 'undo' easily, if your MOT geezer objects. So what do you get? Two bits of triangular plastic, and two strips of Velcro - how hard can this be?

01 For a cheaper simpler way of updating the look of your car, these brows are ideal. Before attempting to fit them, offer one into place first, just to check that they fit. No major trimming should be needed – have they sent you the right ones? There are two 'generations' of 106, remember. Our 106 is looking better already!

02 You'll have to paint the brows, obviously. In order for the paint to stick, you'll have to roughen it up a little using some Scotchbrite – available from bodyshops or motor factors (or get cheaper pan-scrubbing alternatives from your local supermarket?).

07 Lastly, the lacquer goes on. Though several coats will again be needed, to get a shine, you might have to blast the lacquer on a little heavier than before – too little, and you'll get an un-shiny 'dusty' finish. Leave plenty of time for it to dry – don't rush on at this stage, or there's a fair chance you could wreck all your efforts so far, and you'll be gutted.

08 Whilst the brow finishes drying, you can get on with cleaning the headlight. Our kit came with a 3M cleaning cloth impregnated with suitable cleaning agents, so it made sense to use this.

09 Then when the brow is ready to be fitted to the car, raise the surface temperature of the headlight using a heat gun or hairdryer on a low heat.

10 Then apply the same low heat to the back of the brow. Preferably without warping or melting it.

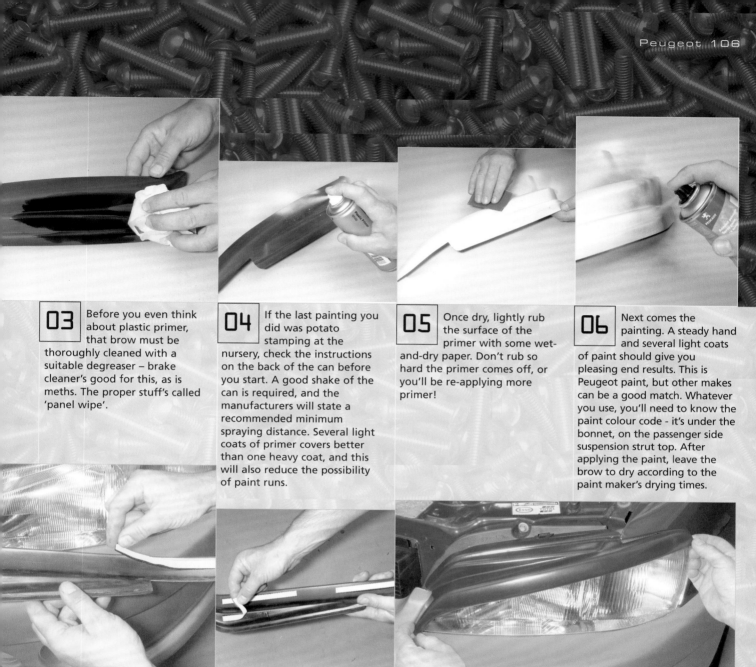

03 Before you even think about plastic primer, that brow must be thoroughly cleaned with a suitable degreaser – brake cleaner's good for this, as is meths. The proper stuff's called 'panel wipe'.

04 If the last painting you did was potato stamping at the nursery, check the instructions on the back of the can before you start. A good shake of the can is required, and the manufacturers will state a recommended minimum spraying distance. Several light coats of primer covers better than one heavy coat, and this will also reduce the possibility of paint runs.

05 Once dry, lightly rub the surface of the primer with some wet-and-dry paper. Don't rub so hard the primer comes off, or you'll be re-applying more primer!

06 Next comes the painting. A steady hand and several light coats of paint should give you pleasing end results. This is Peugeot paint, but other makes can be a good match. Whatever you use, you'll need to know the paint colour code - it's under the bonnet, on the passenger side suspension strut top. After applying the paint, leave the brow to dry according to the paint maker's drying times.

11 Quickly now before the brow cools, remove the backing paper and stick the Velcro pads onto the rear of the brow. Don't separate the two 'halves' of Velcro - just peel off one of the backing papers, and stick firmly. You'll need to trim the Velcro into shorter strips, to get the top and bottom edges of the brow covered.

12 Remove the backing paper on the top of the sticky pads . . .

13 . . . then finally position the brow onto the headlight, and press firmly down when you're happy. Take your time lining it up – that adhesive's well-sticky, and you really want to get it on there right, first-time.

Morette lights

01 Right - let's start by ripping out the old lights. Not a bad idea to disconnect the battery at this point. Next, the front bumper has to come off (see 'Body styling'). Once you're bumper-less, you can clearly see the three headlight retaining bolts. Remember to support the weight of the unit with one hand while you do this, or the Morette conversion won't be optional.

02 Slide the headlight forwards, then twist the headlight rear cover anti-clockwise to remove it from the headlight.

03 Disconnect the headlight and sidelight wiring plugs from the rear of the headlight . . .

 Tricks 'n' tips
Our Morette light-fitting procedure's really for Mk2 106s – not surprising, since we had a Mk2 project car. But if you've got a Mk1, don't feel too bad – this is a good excuse to buy the 106 Haynes manual, which tells you all you need for removing the old lights. Wiring-up the Mk1 Morettes will be very similar to our Mk2s, so you're sorted.

08 With the harness nailed in place and both new lights fitted, the bumper can go back on. Take care as you offer the bumper in place – the new lights are supposed to be a precision fit with the bumper moulding, and some 'adjustment' of the new lights may be needed. When you're happy, the light mountings can be tightened fully.

09 Over to the driver's-side headlight now, for the easiest part of the wiring process. First, plug the new loom straight into the socket behind the new unit's inner light (this is the main beam unit, if you're interested).

10 Now the Peugeot's original headlight wiring plug can be pushed onto the rear of the outer light . . .

11 . . . and there's just the sidelight and indicator to go. The original Peugeot sidelight plug is a two-pin square-ish effort in white – all you do is push the two grey wires with spade terminals (on the back of the new light) into the original plug, and your sidelights are connected. Doesn't matter which grey wire goes where – honest.

04 . . . then unhook the wiring loom from the light, and lift the assembly from the car. No more gakky standard headlights for you! So do you keep them, to put the car back to stock for selling-on, or get them down to the next car boot?

05 We know you'll be just itching to get your new lights bolted in. This is one time you can safely give in to those natural urges – let's get 'em on. There's one bolt at the top (same as the old light) . . .

06 . . . while at the back, there's two funny clamp bolts, which are a wee bit fiddly to work with. Don't do anything up fully tight just yet, until the bumper's back on. There's also the question of when you'll be painting the headlight shells – if you do it now, the lights can be fitted permanently. We're doing a trial fitting, to make sure everything works first.

07 In the box with your new lights, you'll find the (scary) wiring loom. You'll find that one end of this loom looks way more complex than the other – this is the passenger side, where most of the wiring-up gets done. Feed the simpler driver's-side end of the loom across the car, avoiding the radiator, pinning it in place as you go with the cable-ties provided in the kit.

12 The indicator wiring's the same as the sidelight wiring, only simpler still. Morette give you an indicator wiring plug straight off the back of the light, and all you do is run this down to the plug socket inside the wheel arch, and plug it in. Twist out the indicator bulbholder if you need a bit more slack. Told you it was simple.

13 The passenger-side headlight gets wired-up as per the driver's-side, but with a few extras. First, the loom's black plug goes to the green relay on the back of the light. Next, take the new yellow wire (with the Scotchlok connector), and crimp it onto the original headlight wiring plug's main beam wire. This wire should be code PR3 (it was brown on our Mk2, if that helps).

14 The new loom also has two brown earth wires, with ring terminals attached – these should be pinned to a good earth point on the car's metal bodywork. You could drill your own hole, and attach these wires with a self-tapping screw, but there's a ready-made Peugeot earth point on the inner wing behind the headlight – remove the bolt, add your wires, re-tighten the bolt. Easy.

15 The last wire of all is black, and has an in-line fuse fitted – all the clue necessary that this is a live feed. Peugeot even provide a handy little wiring post (with nut) next to the battery's main positive terminal, so connect your new wire right there. These things look so cool, it almost doesn't matter if they don't work, does it? Just kidding - you'll be smiling, same as us.

Headlight
bulbs

Make your 106 look like an Audi or a Beemer, the easy way. Bad-weather and 'blue' headlight bulbs are an excellent way to boost headlight performance, and are perfect with other blue LED accessories like washer jets and number plate screws. The blue bulbs you buy in most accessory shops will be legal, 60W/55 bulbs, and are no problem. Don't be tempted to buy the mega-powerful bulbs you can get from rallying suppliers (any over 60W/55 are in fact illegal for use in this country) - as with all other non-standard lights, the boys in blue will love pulling you over for a word about this, so ask before you buy.

Even if you're not bothered about the legality of over-powerful bulbs (and you might well argue that being more powerful is the whole point of fitting), there's other problems with monster bulbs.

First, they give off masses of heat, and loads of people have melted their headlights before they found this out. Don't believe us? Try fitting some 100W/90s and put your hand in front of the light, close to the glass. Hot, isn't it? The excess heat these bulbs generate will damage the headlights eventually, either by warping the lens, burning off the reflective coating, or melting the bulbholders. Maybe all three.

The increased current required to work big bulbs has also been known to melt wiring (this could lead to a fire) and will almost certainly burn out your light switch. There's no headlight relay fitted as standard, so the wiring and switch were designed to cope only with the current drawn by standard-wattage bulbs; if you're going for high power, a relay must be fitted (much as you'd have to, to fit foglights or spots).

Tricks 'n' tips
Put the old bulbs in the glovebox - carrying spare bulbs is a good way to get a let-off from Plod, if they stop you for having a bulb gone. Be smart. Carry spares.

Front fog/spotlights

Extra lights are useful for adding features to the 106's rather bland front end, even if they are a bit harder to fit than mesh. Most front bumpers have the facility for one or more pairs of lights, so it's gotta be done, really.

If you're fitting fogs, they must be wired in to work on dipped-beam only, so they must go off on main beam. The opposite is true for spotlights. Pop out the main light switch (or pull down the fusebox) and check for a wire which is live only when the dipped beams are on. The Haynes wiring diagrams will help here - on our 106, it was wire number PC3 or PC4 we needed (Peugeot wiring has numbers, not colour-codes, to identify it). Start your search at the wiring plugs on the back of the headlights.

Once you've traced a suitable wire, this is used as the live (+ve) feed for your foglight relay. Did we mention you'll need a relay? You'll need a relay. A four-pin one will do nicely. Splice a new wire onto the feed you've found, and feed it through to the engine (use one of the bulkhead grommets). Decide where you'll mount the relay (next to the battery seems obvious) and connect the new wire onto terminal 86.

For your other relay connections, you'll need an earth to terminal 85 (plenty of good earth spots around the battery). You also need

a fused live supply (buy a single fuseholder, and a 15 or 20-amp fuse should be enough) and take a new feed straight off the battery positive connection - this goes to terminal 30 on your relay.

Terminal 87 on your relay is the live output to the fogs - split this into two wires, and feed it out to where the lights will go. Each foglight will also need an earth - either pick a point on the body next to each light, or run a pair of wires back to the earth point you used earlier for your relay. Simple, innit?

With the wiring sorted, now you'd best fit the lights. Over to you. Most decent foglights come with some form of mounting brackets - you must be able to adjust the aim, even if only slightly. To look their best, hopefully your new lights can slot into pre-cut holes in your new front bumper/bodykit.

To connect the wiring to the lights, you'll probably need to splice on your wires from terminal 87 to the new wiring plugs which came with the lights - not too difficult. Plug it all together, and test - you should now have some rather funky fogs!

There's a range of 'standard' colours that side reps come in, but most people go for clear or smoked, to colour-code with their rear clusters. Clear lenses can be coloured using special paint, but the paint must be applied lightly and evenly to the lens, or this will invite an easily-avoided MOT failure. Bodyshops can colour clear lenses to the exact shade of your car, by mixing a little paint with loads of lacquer - very trick.

Side repeaters must still show an orange light, and must be sufficiently bright (not easy to judge, and no two coppers have the same eyesight!). The stock bulbs are clear, so make sure you get orange bulbs too. You can actually get orange bulbs that look clear, to avoid the 'fried egg' effect. Alternatively, get LED side repeaters.

Besides the various colour effects, side repeaters are available in many different shapes (triangular Focus-style side reps, for instance). But the standard ovals are recessed into the wings, so making other shapes fit properly may need a bit of bodywork.

Or how about ditching the repeaters altogether, and get some tasty Merc-style mirrors, with side reps built-in? You could smooth your front wings, then…

Side repeaters

01 Nothing too challenging here, in fact you don't even need to prise the old indicator out, just push the repeater a little to the front to disengage it from its recess in the

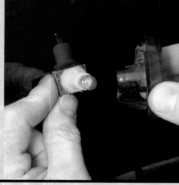

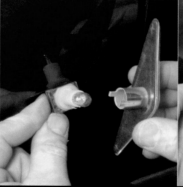

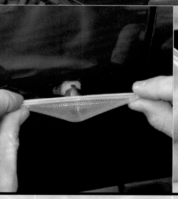

02 wing.
Turn the lens cover anti-clockwise by 90° to free

03 it from the bulbholder. Remove the backing paper from the new side repeater lens, and twist it

04 90° onto the bulbholder.
Now just line the new rep up, and stick it squarely onto the (freshly-cleaned) front wing. But wait! We've narrowly avoided disaster here - as we're fitting crystal clear side repeaters, we must also fit new orange bulbs. The MOT inspector will look for this, and will fail you, if you've forgotten to change the original clear bulbs for orange

05 ones.
Luckily, most kits will come with new orange bulbs (check before you buy – if they seem v. cheap, no bulbs supplied is probably the reason) and they're a simple

Rear lights

Fashions seem to be getting more and more extreme. The same can even be said in the world of aftermarket rear lights, and the designers at ABC Design are up there at the top, producing some really cool, unusual rear clusters. Techno rear lights? Yes please!

Light legality

Lots of 106 rear clusters there may be, but - often, they're not UK-legal (even lights which are E-marked sometimes have no rear fogs or reflectors). Mr. Plod is well-informed on this point, and those sexy rear lights are way too big a come-on for him to ignore.

You can buy stick-on reflectors, but these are about as sexy as NHS specs, so there's no easy answer on this. You'd have to be pretty unlucky to get pulled just for having no rear reflectors, but don't say we didn't warn you. And what happens if your car gets crunched, parked at night with no reflectors fitted? Will your insurance try and refuse to pay out? You betcha.

If you've got a rad rear bumper planned, why not cut a hole in your new rear bumper/mesh, and find a cool-looking rear fog to mount inside (the Peugeot 206 unit's pretty sweet). If you don't mind a bit extra work, source an exhaust tailpipe trim roughly the same size as your existing single pipe, mount it on the opposite side of the car, and fit a round foglight inside the end.

Any questions on light legality? Why not check out the ABC Design website tech tips page, at www.abcdesignltd.com - if you've any questions after that, you can e-mail them. We're so good to you.

Light tinting

Spraying your lights is a top idea if funds are too tight for replacements, or if you simply don't fancy paying loadsamoney for illegal lights which also don't fit very well. The first job before spraying is to get the old lights clean - we used meths, which works well enough to get off all the old silicone products and polish residue.

01

As with most spray-painting, the trick is to get the stuff on evenly, which means applying light coats. Blasting it on too thick will give you the runs, which is never pleasant. How thick is too thick? A couple of light coats might be too subtle a look for you, but don't go too mad if you want to avoid attention from the Law.

02

Rear light clusters

01 Before we get too excited about our new clusters, we gotta lose that old light unit, so start by opening the tailgate, and prising away the plastic trim panel from the rear of the light.

02 Next remove the securing screw and unclip the air extraction grille from the side of the luggage compartment.

03 Disconnect the wiring plug by depressing the retaining tabs around the sides of the plug.

04 Finally remove the two plastic retaining nuts and the unit is free to be lifted away from the car.

05 Before fitting your new lights, clean the area behind the unit, as no doubt it'll be pretty mucky. Check that the new light has a decent foam seal fitted, to keep the water out - if not, use a little silicone to seal it. Don't want water with our ICE, do we?

06 Pop the new light unit into place to check for size. A quality set of lights should slot straight into place.

07 Another bonus with fitting quality lights is they very often come all wired up, so it's just a case of plugging the new wiring into the existing plug. Fitting the new light unit is no harder than removing the old cluster – easy!

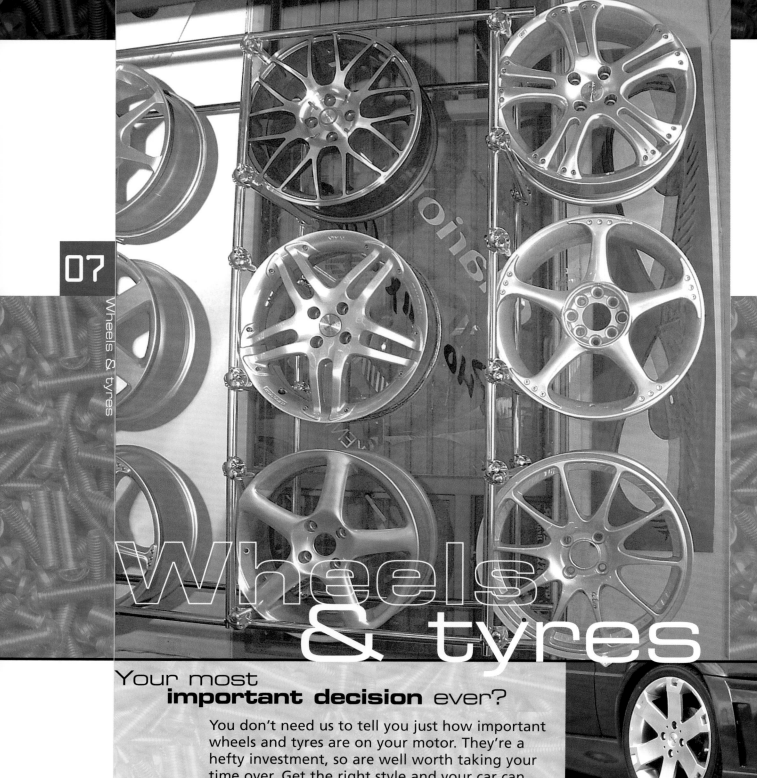

Wheels & tyres

Your most important decision ever?

You don't need us to tell you just how important wheels and tyres are on your motor. They're a hefty investment, so are well worth taking your time over. Get the right style and your car can turn from average to amazing in a matter of minutes. Get the selection wrong and not only will it affect the looks of the car, it can seriously hurt your finances.

For a change, some standard 106 alloys are quite tidy (GTI rims especially), but anything Peugeot is really a bit too common, and should be ditched when funds allow it. Advice on which particular wheels to buy would be a waste of space, since the choice is so huge, and everyone will have their own favourites. For what it's worth, though, it's gotta be something with a curvy kinda vibe on a 106, to look right, with plenty of people choosing Mille Miglia (Evo 5, Action), OZ Vela or Oxigin 1. This year's look is chrome (looks sweet on a 106 with the full set of crystal lights) and the US-based sites have plenty to see (MSI Online, for starters, and DM Tech America). Even Wolfrace have recently jumped on the chrome bandwagon - or try Cam chromes for a value choice.

One point not to overlook when choosing wheels is the wheel offset. Most normal cars fall somewhere in the mid-30s to early 40s. Unfortunately, the 106 is an oddball, at 16 (or 20, for an early three-stud rim). Going for a higher offset makes the wheel 'pull in' more, meaning a 40-offset rim may be clouting the brake calipers and rubbing on the inside edges (most likely, you won't even be able to bolt it on). Fitting wheels with the wrong offset may also do unpleasant things to the handling. When ordering, mention they're for a 106 at an early stage in negotiations. Many companies will supply you with spacers to make their wheels fit properly, but this is a bit of a pain (and a bit of a bodge, frankly). With spacers, you need longer wheel bolts, and changing wheels is much more fiddly. Only if your chosen wheels are a must-have.

Lead us not into temptation

Before we go any further into which wheels are right for you, a word about insurance and security. Fitting tasty alloys to your 106 is one of the first and best ways to make it look cool. It follows, therefore, that someone with dubious morals might very well want to unbolt them from your car while you're not around, and make their own car look cool instead (or simply sell them, to buy spot cream and drugs).

Since fitting a set of top alloys is one of the easiest bolt-on ways to trick up any car, it's no surprise that the market in stolen alloys is as alive and kicking as it currently is - your wheels will also look very nice on any number of other cars, and the owners of those cars would love to own them at a fraction of the price you paid... It's not unknown for a set of wheels to go missing just for the tyres - if you've just splashed out on a set of fat Yokohamas, your wheels look even more tempting, especially if you've got a common-size tyre.

Tell your insurance company what you're fitting. What will probably happen is that they'll ask for the exact details, and possibly a photo of the car with the wheels on. Provided you're happy to then accept that they won't cover the extra cost of the wheels if they get nicked (or if the whole car goes), you may find you're not charged a penny more, especially if you've responsibly fitted some locking wheel bolts. Not all companies are the same, though - some charge an admin fee, and yes, some will start loading your premium. If you want the rims covered, it's best to talk to a company specialising in modified cars, or you could be asked to pay out the wheel cost again in premiums. The daftest thing you can do is say nothing, and hope they don't find out - we don't want to go on about this, but there are plenty of documented cases where insurance companies have refused to pay out altogether, purely on the basis of undeclared alloy wheels.

How **cheap** are you?

Hopefully, you'll be deciding which wheels to go for based on how they look, not how much they cost, but inevitably (for most ordinary people at least), price does become a factor. Surely buying a cheaper wheel must have its pitfalls? Well, yes - and some of them may not be so obvious.

Inevitably, cheaper wheels = lower quality, but how does this show up? Cheap wheels are often made from alloys which are more 'porous' (a bit like a sponge, they contain microscopic holes and pockets of air). Being porous has two main disadvantages for a wheel, the main one being that it won't be able to retain air in the tyres. The days of tyres with inner tubes are long gone (and it's illegal to fit tubes to low-profile tyres), so the only thing keeping the air in are the three 'walls' of the tyre, with the fourth 'wall' being the inside of the wheel itself. If you like keeping fit by pumping up your tyres every morning, go ahead - the rest of us will rightly regard this as a pain, and potentially dangerous (running tyres at low pressure will also scrub them out very effectively - what was that about saving money?).

Porous wheels also have difficulty in retaining their paint, lacquer, or chrome finish, with flaking a known problem, sometimes after only a few months. This problem is made worse by the fact that porous wheels are much harder to clean (brake dust gets ingrained into the wheels more easily) - and the more you scrub, the more the lacquer comes off.

The final nail in the coffin for cheap wheels is that they tend to corrode (or 'fizz') more. This not only ruins the looks if visible from outside, but if you get corrosion between the wheel and the hub, you won't even be able to take the damn things off! Yes seriously, grown men with all the specialist tools in the world at their disposal will be scratching their heads when faced with wheels which simply **will not** come off.

Buying an established, popular make of wheel has another hidden benefit, too. Choosing a popular wheel will mean more suppliers will stock it, and the manufacturers themselves will make plenty of them. And if you're unlucky enough to have an accident (maybe a slide on a frosty road) which results in non-repairable damage to one wheel, you're going to need a replacement. If you've chosen the rarest wheels on the planet, you could be faced with having to replace a complete set of four, to get them all matching… A popular wheel, even if it's a few years old, might be easier to source, even second-hand.

The Sunday morning ritual

It's a small point maybe, but you'll obviously want your wheels to look as smart as possible, as often as possible - so how easy are they going to be to clean?

The real multi-spokers and BBS-style 'wires' are hell to clean - a fiddly toothbrush job - do you really want that much aggro every week? The simpler the design, the easier time you'll have. For those who like nothing better than counting their spokes, though, there are several really good products out there to make your life less of a cleaning nightmare.

Bolt from the blues

Don't forget about locking wheel bolts (see *"Hold on to your wheels"* further on) - bargain these into a wheel/tyre package if you're buying new.

A word of warning about re-using your existing wheel bolts, should you be upgrading from steel wheels. Most steel-wheel bolts are not suitable for use with alloy wheels (and vice-versa, incidentally). Make sure you ask about this when buying new wheels, and if necessary, bargain a set of bolts into the price. Most bolts for use with alloys will have a washer fitted, for two very good reasons - 1) the bolt will pull through the wheel hole without it, and 2) to protect the wheel finish.

Another point to watch for is that the new wheel bolts are the correct length for your fitment, taking into account whether you've fitted spacers or not. Bolts that are too short are obviously dangerous, and ones that are too long can foul on drum brakes, and generally get in the way of any turning activities. If in doubt ask the retailer for advice. Always check that the wheels turn freely once they've been put on, and investigate any strange noises before you go off for a pose.

Other options

If you're on a really tight budget, and perhaps own a real 'basic' model 106, don't overlook the possibility of fitting a discarded set of standard alloys (a set of 106 GTI rims would do). If you get offered a set of rims from another Peugeot entirely, the bolt pattern (PCD) will be right, but the offset probably won't – some later Pugs (such as the 206) have a higher offset, which means they probably won't fit. Try before you buy.

If the Peugeot range of wheels is too limiting, don't be too quick buying (for instance) alloys from other car makes altogether. For instance, some Ford alloys have the same bolt pattern (4x108), so they'll go on alright, but the offset's usually much higher on Ford rims (around 41), which will pull the wheel in too far. In the case of some alloys (VW, Vauxhall, or Renault, for example), the bolt pattern may be only fractionally different (4x100), but if you put these on, the strain on the wheel bolts is too great, and they can fracture…

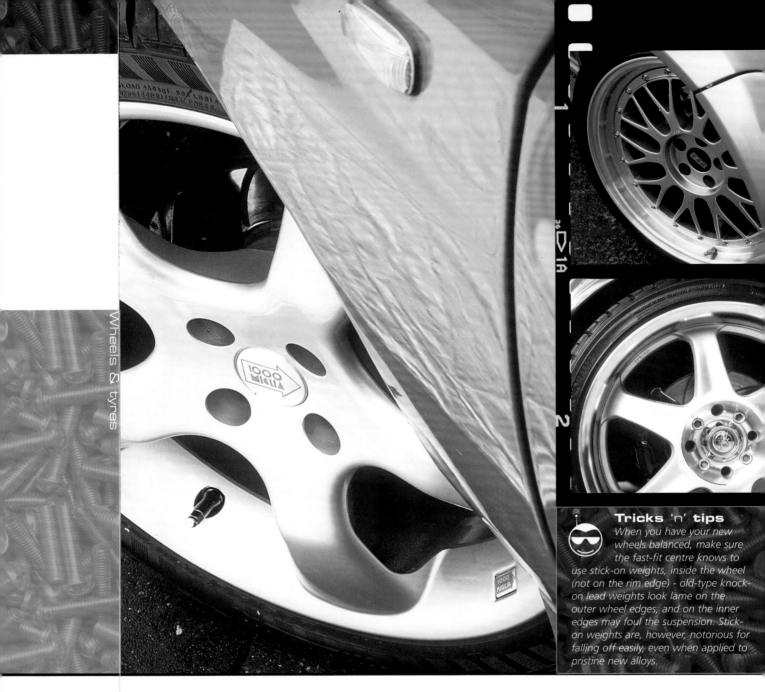

Tricks 'n' tips
When you have your new wheels balanced, make sure the fast-fit centre knows to use stick-on weights, inside the wheel (not on the rim edge) - old-type knock-on lead weights look lame on the outer wheel edges, and on the inner edges may foul the suspension. Stick-on weights are, however, notorious for falling off easily, even when applied to pristine new alloys.

Size **matters**

For us Brits, biggest is best - there are 106s out there on 17s and up. And yes, the mags all say you can't be seen with anything less than 17-inchers. In Europe, meanwhile, they're mad for the small-wheel look, still with seriously dropped suspension of course.

On 106s with 'wide arches' (GTI, Rallye, Quiksilver), you'll have a slightly easier time fitting big alloys – with these, 17s are possible, but it's a lot of bodywork. Unless you're planning a Dimma wide-arch kit, you'll be lucky to get anything like full steering lock on 17-inchers – that 3-point turn could be embarrassingly long-winded (but at least all those watching will get a good view of your ride). Seriously, not being able to steer very much

could be dangerous – think about it. And you risk ripping out the inner sidewalls of your tyres, which could give you a high-speed blowout. Better to aim for 16s, and have an easier life.

With standard arches (all non-sporty 106s), your realistic target is 15s, with 16s an outside bet. A little trimming of the plastic arch liners should be all that's needed, in the worst cases. Again, there's no need to get suckered into having huge alloys – getting 17s on a 106 with standard arches will be very, very expensive. Wait and buy a 306 instead?

Huge rims won't do wonders for the ride or handling. Which is a shame, as the 106 is pretty handy round corners. If you're bothered about how your 106 takes the bends, stick to 15s. Providing the rest of the car's up together, get the car low and you'll still get respect. According to one chat room expert, 195/45 x 15 tyres/wheels are probably the ideal set up for a 106. We're not arguing.

We like a challenge

To be honest, successfully fitting big wheels in combination with lowered suspension is one of life's major challenges. As much as anything, tyre width is what ultimately leads to problems, not so much the increased wheel diameter.

If the tyres are simply too wide (or with wheels the wrong offset), they will first of all rub on the suspension strut (ie on the inside edge of the tyre). Also, the inside edges may rub on the arches on full steering lock - check left and right. Rubbing on the inside edges can be cured by fitting offsets or spacers between the wheel and hub, which effectively pull the wheel outwards, 'spacing' it away from its normal position (this also has the effect of widening the car's track, which may improve the on-limit handling - or not). Fitting large offsets must be done using special longer wheel bolts, as the standard ones may only engage by a few threads, which is highly dangerous.

Rubbing on the outside edges is a simple case of wheelarch lip fouling, which must be cured by rolling up (or trimming off) the wheelarch return edge, and other mods. If you've gone for really wide tyres, or have already had to fit offsets, the outer edge of the tyre will probably be visible outside the wheelarch, and this is a no-no (it's illegal, and you must cover it up!). On models with arch extensions, you may need to remove the extensions, trim off the mounting lugs which poke through inside the arch, then bond the plastic bits back on with mastic.

The other trick with fitting big alloys is of course to avoid the '106 4x4 off-road' look, which you will achieve remarkably easily just by popping on a set of 17s with standard suspension. The massive increase in ground clearance is fine for Farmer Palmer, but your 'fistable' arches won't win much admiration at cruises. Overcoming this problem by lowering can be a matter almost of inspired guesswork, as much as anything (see 'Suspension').

Speedo error? Or not?

One side-effect of fitting large wheels is that your car will go slower. Yes, really - or at least - it will appear to go slower, due to the effects of the mechanical speedometer drive.

As the wheel diameter increases, so does its circumference (distance around the outside) - this means that, to travel say one mile, a large wheel will turn less than a smaller wheel. Because the speedometer is driven from the gearbox final drive, the apparent vehicle speed is actually based on the number of complete revolutions of the wheel. Therefore, for a given *actual* speed, since a larger-diameter wheel will be turning at a slower rate than a smaller wheel, and the method for measuring speed is the rate of wheel rotation, a car with larger wheels will produce a lower

speedo reading than one with smaller wheels - but it's NOT actually going any slower in reality. So don't worry if you think you've reduced your 106's performance somehow with the monster rims, 'cos you 'aven't.

With the ever-increasing number of those lovely grey/yellow roadside boxes with a nasty surprise inside, spare a thought to what this speedo error could mean in the real world. If (like most people) you tend to drive a wee bit over the posted 30s and 40s, your real speed on 17s could be a bit more than the bit more you thought you were doing already, and you could get an unexpected flash to ruin your day. What we're saying is, don't drive any faster, to compensate for the lower speedo reading. Actually, the speedo error effect on 17s really is tiny at around-town speeds, and only becomes a factor over 70. But then, Officer, you couldn't possibly have been going over 70, could you? Officer?

Jargon explained

Rolling Radius - You may have come across the term 'rolling radius', which is the distance from the wheel centre to the outer edge of the tyre, or effectively, half the overall diameter. The rolling radius obviously increases with wheel size, but up to a point, the effects are masked by fitting low-profile tyres, with 'shorter' sidewalls. Above 16-inch rims, however, even low-profiles can't compensate, and the rolling radius keeps going up.

PCD - this isn't a banned substance, it's your Pitch Circle Diameter, which relates to the spacing of your wheel holes, or 'bolt pattern'. It is expressed by the diameter of a notional circle which passes through the centre of your wheel bolts, and the number of bolts. Unlike the offset, the PCD often isn't stamped onto the wheels, so assessing it is really a matter of eyeing-up and trying the bolts - the wheel should go on easily, without binding, if the pattern is correct. On most 106s, the PCD is 108 mm with four bolts, which is given as 108/4, or 4 x 108 (some early cars had just three bolts, with a PCD of 3 x 98).

Offset - this is determined by the distance from the wheel mounting face in relation to its centre-line. The offset figure is denoted by ET (no, I mustn't), which stands for einpress tiefe in German, or pressed-in depth (now I KNOW you're asleep). The lower the offset, the more the wheels will stick out. Fitting wheels with the wrong offset might bring the wheel into too-close contact with the brake and suspension bits, or with the arches. Very specialised area - seek advice from the wheel manufacturers if you're going for a very radical size (or even if you're not). The correct offset for 106s with four wheel bolts is ET 16 (or ET 20 on three-bolt models).

Hold on to your wheels

The minute you bang on your wicked alloys, your car becomes a target. People see the big wheels, and automatically assume you've also got a major stereo, seats and other goodies - all very tempting, but that involves breaking in, and you could have an alarm. Pinching the wheels themselves, now that's a doddle - a few tools, some bricks or a couple of well-built mates to lift the car, and it's easy money

The trouble with fitting big wheels is that they're only screwed on, and are just as easily screwed off, if you don't make life difficult for 'em. If you're unlucky enough to have to park outside at night (ie no garage), you could wake up one morning to a car that's *literally* been slammed on the deck! Add to this the fact that your car isn't going anywhere without wheels, plus the damage which will be done to exhaust, fuel and brake pipes from dropping on its belly, and it's suddenly a lot worse than losing a grand's worth of wheels and tyres…

The market and demand for stolen alloys is huge, but since most people don't bother having them security-marked in any way, once a set of wheels disappears, they're almost impossible to trace. Thieves avoid security-marked (or 'tattooed') wheels (or at least it's a

pretty good deterrent) - and it needn't look hideous!

When choosing that car alarm, try and get one with an 'anti-jacking' feature, because thieves hate it. This is sometimes now called 'anti-tilt', to avoid confusion with anti-hijacking. Imagine a metal saucer, with a metal ball sitting on a small magnet in the centre. If the saucer tilts in any direction, the ball rolls off the magnet, and sets off the alarm. Highly sensitive, and death to anyone trying to lift your car up to remove the wheels - as we said, the crims are not fond of this feature at all. An alarm with anti-shock is not enough, because a careful villain might be able to avoid creating a strong enough vibration to trigger it - mind you, it's a whole lot better than nothing, especially if set to maximum sensitivity.

Locking nuts/bolts

Locking wheel bolts will be effective as a deterrent to the inexpert thief (kids, in other words), but will probably only slow down the pro.

Thieves want to work quickly, and will use large amounts of cunning and violence to deprive you of your stuff. If you fit a cheap set of locking bolts, they'll use a hammer and thin chisel to crack off the locking heads. Some bolts can easily be defeated by hammering a socket onto them, while some of the key-operated bolts are so pathetic they can be beaten using a small screwdriver. So - choose the best bolts you can, but don't assume they'll prevent your wheels from disappearing. Insurance companies seem to like 'em - perhaps it shows a responsible attitude, or something...

There's some debate whether it's okay to fit more than one set of locking bolts to a car - some people we know value their wheels so highly they've fitted four sets of lockers - completely replacing all the standards! Replacement locking bolts may not be made to the same standard as factory originals, and while one set is good for security, fitting more than that may be less good for safety (bolt could fail, wheel falls off, car in ditch, owner in hospital...).

Obviously, you must carry the special key or tool which came with your bolts with you at all times, in case of a puncture, or if you're having any other work done, such as new brakes or tyres. The best thing to do is rig this onto your keyring, so that it's with you, not left in the car. The number of people who fit locking bolts and then leave the tool to undo them cunningly 'hidden' in the glovebox or the boot... You don't leave a spare set of car keys in your glovebox as well, do you?

How to change a set of wheels

You might think you know all about this, but do you really?

Okay, so you know you need a jack and wheelbrace (or socket and ratchet), but where are the jacking points? If you want to take more than one wheel off at a time, have you got any axle stands, and where do they go? If you've only ever had wheels and tyres fitted by a garage, chances are you're actually a beginner at this. It's surprising just how much damage you can do to your car, and to yourself, if you don't know what you're doing - and the worst thing here is to think you know, when you don't...

What to use

If you don't already have one, invest in a decent hydraulic (trolley) jack. This is way more use than the standard car jack, which is really only for emergencies, and which isn't really stable enough to rely on. Lifting and lowering the car is much easier with a trolley jack, and you'll even look professional. Trolley jacks have a valve, usually at the rear, which must be fully tightened (using the end of the jack handle) before raising the jack, and which is carefully loosened to lower the car down - if it's opened fully, the car will not so much sink as plummet!

Axle stands are placed under the car, once it's been lifted using the jack. Stands are an important accessory to a trolley jack, because once they're in place, there's no way the car can come down on you - remember that even a brand new trolley jack could creep down (if you haven't tightened the valve), or could even fail completely under load (if it's a cheap one, or knackered, or both).

Under NO circumstances use bricks, wooden blocks or anything else which you have to pile up, to support the car - this is just plain stupid. A 106 may be a 'small' car, but it weighs quite enough to damage you convincingly if it lands on top of you - if you don't believe us, try crawling under it when it's resting on a few poxy bricks. The only place bricks can be used is in front of, and behind, any tyres which are staying on the ground (helps stop the car rolling away).

Where to use it

Only ever jack the car up on a solid, level surface (ideally, a concrete or tarmac driveway, or quiet car park). If there's even a slight slope, the car's likely to move (maybe even roll away) as the wheels are lifted off the ground. Jacking up on a rough or gravelled surface is not recommended, as the jack could slip at an awkward moment - such as when you've just got underneath…

How to do it - jacking up the front

Before jacking up the front of the car, pull the handbrake on firmly (you can also chock the rear wheels, if you don't trust your handbrake).

If you're taking the wheels off, loosen the wheel bolts before you start jacking up the car. It's easily forgotten, but you'll look pretty silly trying to undo the wheel bolts with the front wheels spinning in mid-air.

We'll assume you've got a trolley jack. The next question is - where to stick it? Up front, there's a chunky-looking pair of curved plates behind the engine, with the front suspension lower arms attached - as long as you don't jack under the arms, this should be fine, but put a flat offcut of wood on your jack head first, to spread the load. There's also a chunky box-section on the floorpan, running back from the lower arm pivots, which can be used for jacking, again with some wood on the jack head. You

can jack on the sill jacking points (indicated by arrowhead marks on the sill - there may be a plastic cover to remove first), but it's better to leave those for your axle stands.

Once you've got the car up, pop an axle stand or two under the front sill jacking points - this is the only part of the sill it's safe to jack under or rest the car on. With the stands in place, you can lower the jack so the car's weight rests on the stands. For maximum safety, spread the car's weight between the stands and the jack - don't lower the jack completely unless it's needed elsewhere.

I'm sure we don't need to tell you this, but don't jack up the car, or stick stands under the car, anywhere other than kosher jacking and support points. This means - not the floorpan or the sump (you'll cave it in), not the moveable suspension bits (not stable), and not under the brake/fuel pipes (ohmigawd).

How to do it - jacking up the rear

When jacking up the rear of the car, place wooden chocks in front of the front wheels to stop it rolling forwards, and engage first gear.

If you're taking the wheels off, you don't have to loosen the wheel bolts before lifting the car, but you'll be relying on your handbrake to hold the wheels while you wrestle with the bolts. Much cooler (and safer) to loosen the rear wheel bolts on the ground too.

Jacking and supporting the 106 back-end is a little trickier. Have a good look under there before making your choice. There's handbrake cables, brake pipes, torsion bars and a fuel tank to avoid – it's a bit of a minefield. The best places are the large mounting brackets bolted underneath the car, which support the rear axle – work the jack head in there without catching on the trailing arm (hangs down, where the wheel bolts on), and you'll be fine. For axle stands, it's the rear sill jacking point, again marked by the indent on the sill. Not so much need for a block of wood here, but still not a bad idea to use one if you can - saves your paint, spreads the load into the car.

Remember not to put your axle stands under any pipes, the spare wheel, or the fuel tank, and you should live to see another Christmas.

Finally…

As far as possible, don't leave the car unattended once it has been lifted, particularly if kids are playing nearby - football goes under your car, they go under to get it, knock the jack, car falls... it would almost certainly be your fault.

Changing
wheels

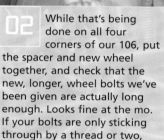

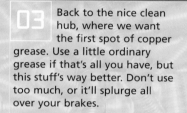

01 Our chosen Momo Fighter rims are one of those which come with spacers. Perhaps not what you'd choose for convenience, but we just liked the look of these wheels, so… With the old steels off, it's time first to clean off our hubs, or the new spacers might just rust on solid.

02 While that's being done on all four corners of our 106, put the spacer and new wheel together, and check that the new, longer, wheel bolts we've been given are actually long enough. Looks fine at the mo. If your bolts are only sticking through by a thread or two, that's not good.

03 Back to the nice clean hub, where we want the first spot of copper grease. Use a little ordinary grease if that's all you have, but this stuff's way better. Don't use too much, or it'll splurge all over your brakes.

04 Now offer on the new spacer (at least it's got a cool logo, to make you feel better about all this aggro) and line up the holes. If you're lucky, the grease we just applied will be enough to 'stick' the spacer in place while you get the wheel on. Some spacers are designed to be bolted on using the disc mounting bolts, but ours will be clamped on once the wheel bolts go in.

05 Have you got a nice ally/plastic ring inside the wheel hub? Make sure it's there, as it acts to centre the wheel properly, and may help to stop the wheel rusting on. Ever had a rusted-on wheel? Your local fast-fit centre will have, and they'll tell you it ain't funny.

06 This ring even has a spring clip to keep it in place. Nice touch.

07 Even with the ring of confidence, the metal bits can still corrode on. Equip yourself with some copper brake grease, and smear some on the hub. The pros 'paint' it on with a brush - the rest of us get messy. It's not a bad idea if some of that grease finds its way onto the wheel bolts, too.

08 Pop the wheel onto the hub, on with the bolts, and tighten up as far as possible by hand. With the wheel on the ground, tighten the wheel bolts securely (ideally, to the correct torque - 85 Nm). Use the car's wheel brace (clipped inside the boot?) to do them up – don't over-tighten, or you'll never get them off if you have a flat!

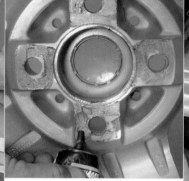

Always nice to see a good brand of tyre on a decent alloy. How cool do cheap tyres look?

Tyres

To some people, tyres are just round and black - oh, and they're nearly all expensive, and don't last long enough. When you're buying a new set of wheels, most centres will quote prices with different tyres - buying a tyred-up set of rims is convenient, and usually good value, too.

Some people try and save money by fitting 'remould' or 're-manufactured' tyres. These aren't always the bargain they appear to be - experience says there's no such thing as a good cheap tyre, with wheel balancing problems a well-known downside, for starters.

Choosing a known brand of tyre will prove to be one of your better decisions. Tyres are the only thing keeping you on the road, as in steering, braking and helping you round corners - what's the point of trying to improve the handling by sorting the suspension if you're going to throw the gains away by fitting naff tyres? Why beef up the brakes if the tyres won't bite? The combination of stiff suspension and cheap tyres is inherently dangerous - because the front end dives less with reduced suspension travel, the front tyres are far more likely to lock and skid under heavy braking.

Cheap tyres also equals more wheelspin - might be fun to disappear in a cloud of tyre smoke, but wouldn't you rather be disappearing up the road? Another problem with really wide tyres is aquaplaning - hit a big puddle at speed, and the tyre skates over the water without gripping - it's seriously scary when your car starts

Tricks 'n' tips
When buying tyres, look out for ones which feature a rubbing strip on the sidewall - these extend over the edge of the wheel rims, and the idea is that they protect the rim edges from damage by 'kerbing'. Any decent tyre has them - discreet and very practical, and much better than a chewed-up rim. But will they catch on your arches? Hmmm.

The size markings are obviously the most important, but take note of the directional marks too, if swapping wheels round. Most of the other markings are for anoraks only.

steering for you. Fitting good tyres won't prevent it, but it might increase your chances of staying in control. The sexiest modern low-profile tyres have a V-tread pattern, designed specifically to aid water dispersal, which is exactly what you need to prevent aquaplaning - try some, and feel the difference!

Finally, cheap tyres ruin the look - a no-name brand in big letters on your tyre sidewalls says you're a pikey loud and clear. If you're spending big dosh on wheels, you've gotta kit 'em out with some tasty V-tread tyres, or lose major points for style. Listen to friends and fellow modifiers - real-world opinions count for a lot when choosing tyres (how well do they grip, wet or dry? How many miles can you get out of them?) Just make sure, before you splash your cash on decent tyres, that you've cured any rubbing and scrubbing issues, as nothing will rip your new tyres out faster.

Marks on your sidewalls

Tyre sizes are expressed in a strange mixture of metric and imperial specs - we'll take a typical tyre size as an example:

205/40 R 17 V
for a 7-inch wide 17-inch rim
205 width of tyre in millimetres
40 this is the "aspect ratio" (or "profile") of the tyre, or the sidewall height in relation to tyre width, expressed as a percentage, in this case 40%. So - 40% of 205 mm = 82 mm, or the height of the tyre sidewall from the edge of the locating bead to the top of the tread.
R Radial.
17 Wheel diameter in inches.
V Speed rating (in this case, suitable for use up to 150 mph).

Pressure situation

Don't forget, when you're having your new tyres fitted, to ask what the recommended pressures should be, front and rear - it's unlikely that the Peugeot specs for this will be relevant to your new low-low profiles, but it's somewhere to start from. If the grease-monkey fitting your tyres is no help on this point, contact the tyre manufacturer - the big ones might even have a half-useful website. If you're really stuck, try 30 psi all round as a rough guide. Running the tyres at the wrong pressures is particularly stupid (you'll wear them out much faster) and can be very dangerous (too soft - heavy steering, tyre rolls off the rim; too hard - tyre slides, no grip).

Speed ratings

Besides the tyre size, tyres are marked with a maximum speed rating, expressed as a letter code:

T up to 190 km/h (118 mph)

U up to 200 km/h (124 mph)

H up to 210 km/h (130 mph)

V inside tyre size markings (225/50 VR 16) over 210 km/h (130 mph)

V outside tyre size markings (185/55 R 15 V) up to 240 km/h (150 mph)

Z inside tyre size markings (255/40 ZR 17) over 240 km/h (150 mph)

If you've got marks on your sidewalls like this, you're in trouble - this has almost certainly been caused by "kerbing".

08 Suspension

If your 106's still sitting on standard suspension, it's probably safe to say it doesn't cut it - yet. If you've decided you couldn't wait to fit your big rims, the chances are your 106 is now doing a passable impression of a tractor. An essential fitment, then - so how low do you go, and what nasty side-effects will lowering have?

The main reason for lowering is of course, to make your car look cool. Standard suspension is always set too soft and too high - a nicely lowered motor really stands out instantly. Lowering your car should also improve the handling. Dropping the car on its suspension brings the car's centre of gravity closer to its roll and pitch centres, which helps to pin it to the road in corners and under braking - combined with stiffer springs and shocks, this reduces body roll and increases the tyre contact patch on the road. But - if improving the handling is really important to you, choose your new suspension carefully. If you go the cheap route, or want extreme lowering, then you could end up with a car which don't handle at all...

As for what to buy, there are basically three main options when it comes to lowering, arranged in order of ascending cost below:

1 *Pair of front lowering springs.*

2 *Matched pair of front lowering springs and shock absorbers, and a pair of rear shocks.*

3 *Pair of front 'coilovers' (and rear shocks).*

How low to go?

Assuming you want to slam your suspension so that your arches just clear the tops of your wicked new rims, there's another small problem - it takes some inspired guesswork (or hours of careful measuring and head-scratching) to assess the required drop accurately, and avoid any nasty rubbing sounds and the smell of burning rubber. Lowering springs and suspension kits will only produce a fixed amount of drop - this can range from 20 mm to a more extreme drop of anything up to 80 mm. Take as many measurements as possible, and ask around your mates - suppliers and manufacturers may be your best source of help in special cases. Coilovers have a range of adjustment possible, which is far more satisfactory - at a price.

Torsion bars

Think you're a good mechanic? Here's where you get to prove it - or maybe not. If this is your first outing with the spanners, lowering the back-end of your 106 properly might be better left to a professional. The reason for this is the manufacturer's choice of rear suspension - the 106 is fitted with a torsion-bar rear axle (a favourite choice with the Frenchies).

For the uninitiated amongst you, torsion-bar rear suspension doesn't use coil springs, but instead uses hefty steel bars. The steel bars are splined at each end, and link each trailing arm to the centre of the axle crossmember. These steel bars twist as the suspension moves up and down throughout its travel, and it's the bars' resistance to this twisting (or torsional force) which provides the rear suspension springing.

Resetting the rear ride height is an involved procedure - not especially difficult or dangerous, but it can be damn fiddly (remember, anything sounds easy enough after a few pints, so trust us on this one). If you muck it up, you can lose the preload on the bars, which means the back will be lower, but floppy as hell. You'll need an unusual tool called a slide hammer, or else make up a susbstitute. On an older car, you could also be facing the possibility of rusted-in bits, and a really big slide-hammer is the only answer if you get into that. Even if you have the job done by a garage, you'll be doing everyone a favour if you give the torsion bars a blast with some WD-40, a week or two before. The positive side though, is that you can lower the rear ride height without purchasing any new springs - the only cost involved is the labour. It's worth treating the newly-lowered rear to some nice Spax or Koni dampers, though.

Lowering springs

The cheapest option by far, but with the most pitfalls and some unpleasant side-effects. Lowering springs are, effectively, shorter versions of the standard items fitted to your 106 at the factory. However, not only are they shorter (lower), they are also uprated (stiffer) - if lowering springs were simply shorter than standard and the same stiffness (the same 'rate'), you'd be hitting the bump-stops over every set of catseyes. With lowering springs, you just fit the new springs and keep the original shock absorbers ('dampers') - even if the originals aren't completely knackered, you're creating a problem caused by mis-matched components. The original dampers were carefully chosen to work in harmony with the original-rate springs - by increasing the spring rate without changing the dampers, you end up with a situation where the dampers will not be in full and effective control of the spring motion. What this usually does before long is wreck the dampers, because they simply can't cope with the new springs, so you really don't save any money in the end.

The mis-matched springs and dampers will have other entertaining side-effects, too. How would you like a 106 which rides like a brick, and which falls over itself at the first sign of a corner taken above walking pace? A very choppy ride and strange-feeling steering (much lighter, or much heavier, depending on your luck) are well-documented problems associated with taking the cheap option, and it doesn't even take much less time to fit, compared to a proper solution. Even if you're a hard man, who doesn't object to a hard ride if his car looks cool, think on this - how many corners do you know that are completely flat (ie without any bumps)? On dodgy lowering springs, you hit a mid-corner bump at speed, and it's anyone's guess where you'll end up.

If cost is a major consideration, and lowering springs the only option for now, at least try to buy branded items of decent quality - some cheap sets of springs will eat their way through several sets of dampers before you realise the springs themselves have lost the plot. Needless to say, if riding around on mis-matched springs and shocks is a bit iffy anyway, it's downright dangerous when they've worn out (some inside 18 months!).

Springs are generally only available in a very few sizes, expressed by the amount of drop they'll produce - most people go for 35 mm or so, but there's 55 mm springs too if you're brave (or you've gone for less-than-massive rims).

Suspension **kit**

A far better choice, Sir - matched springs and dampers are a genuine 'upgrade', and respect is due. There are several branded kits available, and Peugeot specialists may do their own. With a properly-sorted conversion, your 106 will handle even better, and you'll still be able to negotiate a set of roadworks without the risk of dental work afterwards. Actually, you may well be amazed how well the 106 will still ride, even though the springs are clearly lower and stiffer - the secret is in the damping.

Some of the kits are billed as 'adjustable', but this only applies to the damper rates, which can often be set to your own taste by a few minutes' work (don't mistake them for cheap coilovers). This Playstation feature can be quite a good fun thing to play around with, even if it is slightly less relevant to road use than for hillclimbs and sprints - but be careful you don't get carried away and set it too stiff, or you'll end up with an evil-handling car and a CD player that skips over every white line on the road!

Unfortunately, although you will undoubtedly end up with a fine-handling car at the end, there are problems with suspension kits, too. They too are guilty of causing changes to steering geometry (have it reset) and once again, you're into guesswork territory when it comes to assessing your required drop for big wheels. Generally, most suspension kits are only available with a fairly modest drop (typically, 25 to 35 mm).

Coilovers

If you've chosen coilovers, well done again. This is the most expensive option, and it offers one vital feature that the other two can't - true adjustability of ride height, meaning that you can make the finest of tweaks to hunker down on your new rims, or wind it back up when all your mates are on board. Coilovers are a variation on the suspension kit theme - a set of matched variable-rate springs (some have separate 'helper' springs too) and shocks, but their adjustability might not guarantee as good a ride/handling mix as a normal kit.

A coilover set replaces each spring and shock with a combined unit where the coil spring fits over the shocker (hence 'coil' 'over') - nothing too unusual in this, because so far, it's similar to a normal front strut. The difference lies in the adjustable spring lower seat, which can lower the spring (and car) to any desired height, within limits.

Unfortunately, making a car go super-low is not good for the ride or the handling. Coilover systems have very short, stiff springs, and this can lead to similar problems to those found with cheap lowering springs alone. If you go too far with coilovers, you can end up with a choppy ride, heavy steering and generally unpleasant handling. Combine a coilover-slammed car with big alloys, and while the visual effect may be stunning, the driving experience might well be very disappointing. At least a proper coilover kit will come with shock absorbers (dampers) which are matched to the springs, unlike a 'conversion' kit.

Coilover conversion

A better-value option is the 'coilover conversion'. If you really must have the lowest, baddest machine out there, and don't care what the ride will be like, these could be the answer. Offering as much potential for lowering as genuine coilovers (and at far less cost), these items could be described as a cross between coilovers and lowering springs, because the standard dampers are retained (this is one reason why the ride suffers). What you get is a new spring assembly, with adjustable top and bottom mounts - the whole thing slips over your standard damper. Two problems with this solution (how important these are is up to you):

1 Your standard dampers will not be able to cope with the uprated springs, so the car will almost certainly ride (and possibly handle) like a pig if you go for a really serious drop - and okay, why else would you be doing it?

2 The standard dampers are effectively being compressed, the lower you go. There is a limit to how far they will compress before being completely solid (and this could be the limit for your lowering activities). Needless to say, even a partly-compressed damper won't be able to do much actual damping - the results of this could be... interesting...

Suspension
kit

Attention!

Changing the damper cartridges presents another problem. The cartridge is retained by a nut which requires a special peg spanner to slacken/ tighten it. Without the special peg spanner, removing the nut will be tricky, since (yes, you guessed it) it's done up very tight.

01 Jack up the front of the car and remove both front roadwheels (see 'Wheels & tyres'). Using a hammer and pointed-nose chisel, relieve the staking on each driveshaft nut. Take note of how the nut is staked in place (this stops it coming undone, of course) - you'll need to stake the new nut in place the same way.

02 Before trying to undo the driveshaft nut, ask yourself one question: 'Do I feel lucky?'. Use decent-quality tools which fit the nut properly, AND support the car with a jack and axle stands, and luck won't enter into it. That driveshaft nut is really, really tight, and serious force will be needed to move it - don't take chances with dodgy equipment. Oh, and a new nut will be needed on refitting.

03 If the anti-roll bar is connected to the strut, unscrew the nut and washer and disconnect the anti-roll bar connecting link from the strut body. If the anti-roll bar is connected to the lower arm, unscrew the bolts and washers and remove the mounting clamp from the top of the lower arm. If necessary, also remove the rubber bush from the bar end.

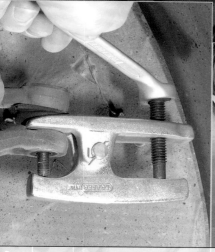

> **04** Unscrew the track rod balljoint nut and discard it (a new one should be used on refitting). Free the balljoint from the strut using a balljoint separator.

05 Unscrew the nut and remove the lower arm balljoint clamp bolt from the base of the hub carrier. Discard the nut (a new one should be used on refitting).

06 Lever down the lower arm, taking care not to damage the balljoint gaiter, just enough to release the balljoint from the hub carrier. As you can see we used a chain, block of wood and a metal bar to create a levering device. If the balljoint is a tight fit, open up the hub carrier clamp a little. Once the balljoint is free, position the strut clear then release the lower arm. Don't lose the protector plate from the lower arm balljoint.

07 Release the hub assembly from the driveshaft by pulling the strut/hub carrier outwards. If necessary, the driveshaft can be tapped out of the hub using a soft-faced hammer. Support the driveshaft by resting it on the lower arm or tying it to the car body. DON'T allow it to hang down, as this could damage the driveshaft joints and gaiters. Ensure the brake hose and any relevant wiring is released from the strut/hub carrier.

08 Slacken and remove the bolts securing the caliper/mounting bracket to the hub assembly (Peugeot recommend these bolts should be renewed every time they are removed). On models with solid brake discs, note the following: *a) On the ATE/Teves caliper, it will be necessary to remove the cap to gain access to the lower bolt; b) On the Bendix/Bosch caliper, note the correct fitted position of the retaining plate fitted to the mounting bolts.*

09 Slide the brake caliper off the disc, and tie it to the car body to support it. DON'T allow it to hang by the flexible hose as this will strain and damage the hose. On models with ABS, unscrew the nut and remove the protective shield from the sensor. Unscrew the sensor bolt, then free the sensor from the hub carrier and position it clear so it will not get damaged during strut removal.

>>

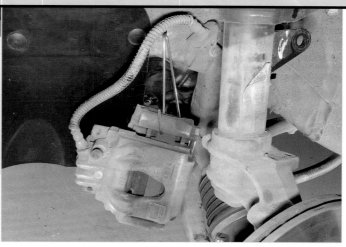

10 Note the correct location of the strut upper mounting nuts in relation to the body - it's essential that the struts are refitted to the same holes later (the position differs according to whether the car has power steering or not). Support the strut, then unscrew the upper mounting nuts.

11 With the nuts removed, manoeuvre the strut out from underneath the wing. Now repeat the procedure and remove the other strut.

12 Before dismantling the struts, make sure you have a decent set of spring compressors and obtain a new piston nut for each strut (the nut should be renewed every time it is removed). You'll also need the three-pronged special tool which will remove the damper nut. Fit the spring compressors and compress the coil spring until all spring pressure is relieved from the seats. Ensure the spring compressors are securely fitted and in no danger of slipping off before proceeding.

13 Remove the trim cap, then slacken and remove the piston nut and its collar. If necessary, retain the piston with a Torx/Allen key (ours was a T40 Torx) to prevent rotation whilst slackening the nut. Discard the nut (a new one should be fitted).

Respect
For the next bit, you MUST use coil spring compressors ('spring clamps'). Medical attention will be required if you don't. Do we have to draw you a diagram? The spring's under tension on the strut, even off the car - what do you think's gonna happen if you just undo it? The spring-embedded-in-the-forehead look is really OVER, too.

To remove the damper nut you need a special tool. If you do not have access to this tool, it might be worth taking your strut to your local dealer, and get them to undo it for you.

18 Remove the coil spring, complete with spring compressors.

19 Slide the rubber gaiter off the strut . . .

20 . . . along with the bump rubber and its collar - this will leave the brass-coloured damper nut in full view.

21

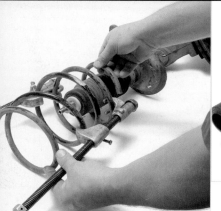

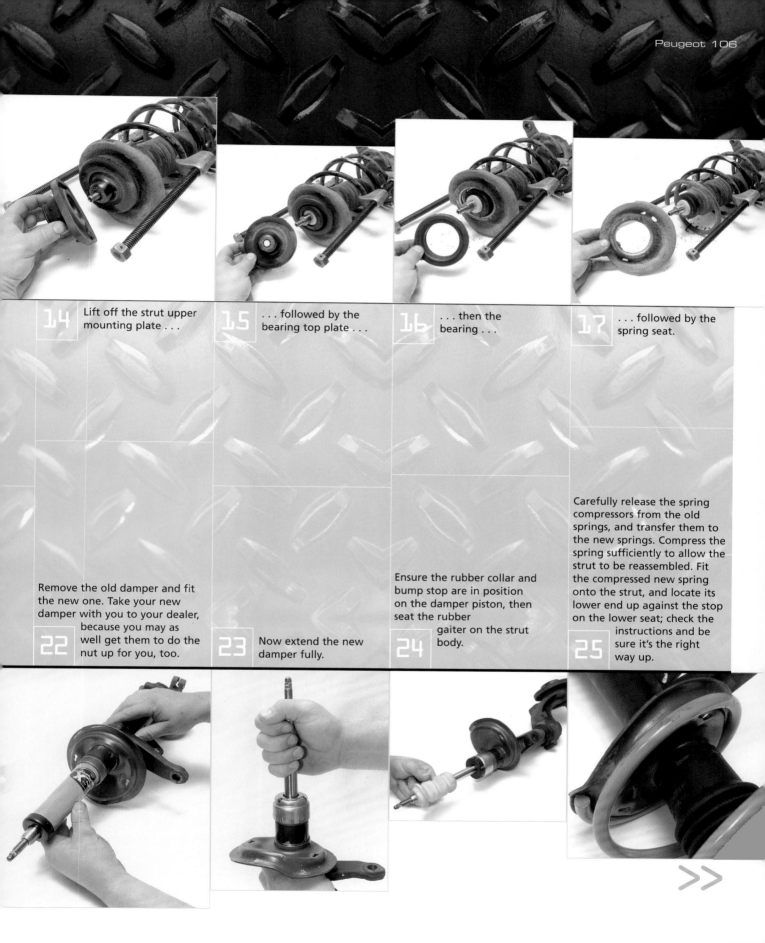

14 Lift off the strut upper mounting plate . . .

15 . . . followed by the bearing top plate . . .

16 . . . then the bearing . . .

17 . . . followed by the spring seat.

22 Remove the old damper and fit the new one. Take your new damper with you to your dealer, because you may as well get them to do the nut up for you, too.

23 Now extend the new damper fully.

24 Ensure the rubber collar and bump stop are in position on the damper piston, then seat the rubber gaiter on the strut body.

25 Carefully release the spring compressors from the old springs, and transfer them to the new springs. Compress the spring sufficiently to allow the strut to be reassembled. Fit the compressed new spring onto the strut, and locate its lower end up against the stop on the lower seat; check the instructions and be sure it's the right way up.

26 Fit the upper seat to the spring, positioning its stop against the spring upper end.

27 Fit the bearing to the centre of the upper seat.

28 Locate the bearing top plate on the top of the bearing . . .

29 . . . and fit the upper mounting plate.

30 Insert the dished collar, then screw the new nut onto the piston. Retain the piston and tighten the nut to 60 Nm. Fit the trim cap to the piston end

31 Ensure the spring upper and lower ends are correctly located against the stops on the seats, then carefully release the spring compressors. Remove the compressors and check that all components are correctly seated. Ensure the upper end of the rubber gaiter is pushed firmly up into the base of the lower seat, and the gaiter lower end is correctly seated on the strut body before fitting the strut to the car.

32 Refitting the strut is basically the reverse of removal, but listed below are the tightening torques for the various bits. After messing with your suspension, make sure that you get the wheel alignment checked - especially camber and tracking. If you don't, you may have curious handling, strange steering, and tyres which seem to disappear overnight (see 'Nasty side-effects').

Three strut mounting nuts	20 Nm
Lower arm balljoint clamp bolt	50 Nm
Track rod balljoint nut	45 Nm
Anti-roll bar to lower arm	25 Nm
Anti-roll bar to strut	30 Nm
Caliper bolts:	
Solid discs with ATE/Teves calipers:	
M8 bolt	32 Nm
M12 bolt	105 Nm
Solid disc with Bendix/Bosch calipers:	
M8 bolt	32 Nm
M12 bolt	120 Nm
Ventilated discs	120 Nm
Driveshaft nuts (stake in place when tight)	245 Nm

Nasty side-effects

Camber angle and tracking

With any lowering 'solution', it's likely that your suspension and steering geometry will be severely affected - this will be more of a problem the lower you go. This will manifest itself in steering which either becomes lighter or (more usually) heavier, and in tyres which scrub out their inner or outer edges in very short order - not funny, if you're running expensive low-profiles! Sometimes, even the rear tyres can be affected in this way, but that's usually only after some serious slammage. Whenever you've fitted a set of springs (and this applies to all types), have the geometry checked ASAP afterwards.

If you've dropped the car by 60 mm or more, chances are your camber angle will need adjusting. This is one reason why you might find the edges of your fat low-profiles wearing faster than you'd like (the other is your tracking being out). The camber angle is the angle the tyre makes with the road, seen from directly in front. You'll no doubt have seen race cars with the front wheels tilted in at the top, out at the bottom - this is extreme negative camber, and it helps to give more grip and stability in hard cornering (but if your car was set this extreme, you'd kill the front tyres very quickly!). Virtually all road cars have a touch of negative camber on the front, and it's important when lowering to keep as near to the factory setting as possible, to preserve the proper tyre contact patch on the road. Trouble is, there's not usually much scope for camber adjustment on standard suspension, which is why (for some cars) you can buy camber-adjustable top plates which fit to the strut tops. Setting the camber accurately is a job for a garage with experience of modified cars - so probably not your local fast-fit centre, then.

Rear brake pressure regulator

Some cars have a rear brake pressure limiting valve fitted, which is linked to the rear suspension - with 106s, the only ones which have this are those with ABS (standard on GTI models, optional on some others). If your 106 doesn't have ABS, you'll have limiting valves built into the rear brake lines, which simply restrict the flow of fluid to the rear brakes, regardless of how heavily loaded the car is - no worries here then.

On ABS models, when the car's lightly loaded over the rear wheels, the braking effort to the rear is limited, to prevent the wheels locking up. With the boot full of luggage, the back end sinks down, and the valve lets full braking pressure through to the rear. When you slam the suspension, the valve is fooled into thinking the car's loaded up, and you might find the rear brakes locking up unexpectedly - could be a nasty surprise on a wet roundabout!

The valves aren't generally intended to be easy to adjust, but they are quite simple devices - the best idea would be to get underneath and see how it looks when sat on its wheels unloaded (on standard suspension), and try to re-create the same condition once the car's been dropped. You're looking for a bracket bolted to the rear 'axle', with a small spring attached.

Strut brace

Another item inspired by racing, the strut brace is another underbonnet accessory which you shouldn't be without. The idea of the strut brace is that, once you've stiffened up your front suspension to the max, the car's 'flimsy' body shell (to which the front suspension struts are bolted) may not be able to cope with the 'immense' cornering forces being put through it, and will flex, leading to unsatisfactory handling.

The strut brace (in theory) does exactly what it says on the tin, by providing support between the strut tops, taking the load off the bodyshell. Where this falls down slightly is the 106 shell isn't exactly made out of tin foil. The strut brace may indeed have a slight effect, but the real reason to fit one is for show - and why not? Strut braces can be chromed, painted or anodised, and can be fitted with matching chromed/coloured strut top plates - a very tasty way to complement a detailed engine bay.

01 Our R & A Design strut brace came in red - but we didn't want that on our car, so we re-sprayed it. If you decide to do the same, remember to mask up the threaded adjuster section before you start.

02 Hanging the brace up by one of the mounting holes will make spraying it a whole lot easier.

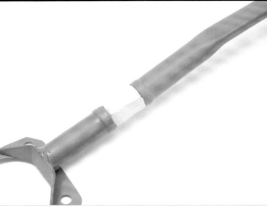

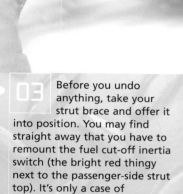

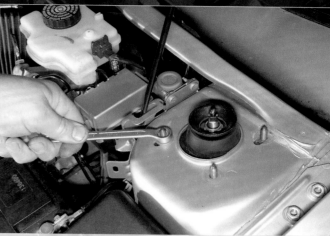

03 Before you undo anything, take your strut brace and offer it into position. You may find straight away that you have to remount the fuel cut-off inertia switch (the bright red thingy next to the passenger-side strut top). It's only a case of unbolting it, making up a new mounting bracket . . .

04 . . . and mounting it lower down, out of the way.

05 With the car resting on its wheels, remove the three suspension strut upper mounting nuts from each side of the engine compartment.

Place the strut brace into position, and refit the mounting nuts, leaving them loose at this stage.

Now tighten the strut brace itself, to set the 'tension' - don't try too hard with this, just take up the slack and a bit more. Use a screwdriver through the hole in the threaded section to hold it while the large nuts either side are done up. Now tighten the three nuts on each strut top mount - if you've got a torque wrench, set it to 20 Nm.

06

07

09 Brakes

The middle pedal

It's the one next to the throttle - some people don't use it much. Uprating the brakes is actually a very easy bolt-on upgrade, but there are some points to consider.

One of the strangest, given that improving the brakes should in theory also improve your chances of avoiding an accident, is that insurance companies do not like performance brakes. You should still tell them, but be prepared for bad news. To them, fitting sporty brakes means you drive like Jenson Button - if you need better brakes, you've either also uprated the engine (and not told them?), or you drive on the limit everywhere. Shame. We just like to know our cars will stop quickly. That, actually, might be another reason why they don't like better brakes - you stop better, but does the old dodderer behind you? Crunch.

Uprating the brakes will be a complete waste of time if you're a cheapskate on tyres. Cheap, no-name tyres (or ones with no tread left) won't always be able to translate extra braking power into car-stopping power - they'll give up their grip on the tarmac and skid everywhere. Something like 90% of braking is done by the front wheels - ie the ones you steer with. If you consider that locked-up wheels also don't tend to steer very well, you'll begin to see why top brakes and lame tyres are a well-dodgy mixture.

Groovy discs

Besides the various brands of performance brake pads that go with them, the main brake upgrade is to fit performance front brake discs and pads. Discs are available in two main types - grooved and cross-drilled (and combinations of both).

Grooved discs (which can be had with varying numbers of grooves) serve a dual purpose - the grooves provide a 'channel' to help the heat escape, and they also help to de-glaze the pad surface, cleaning up the pads every time they're used. Some of the discs are made from higher-friction metal than normal discs, too, and the fact that they seriously improve braking performance is well-documented.

Cross-drilled discs offer another route to heat dissipation, but one which can present some problems. Owners report that cross-drilled discs really eat brake pads, more so than the grooved types, but more serious is the fact that some of these discs can crack around the drilled holes, after heavy use. The trouble is that the heat 'migrates' to the drilled holes (as was intended), but the heat build-up can be extreme, and the constant heating/cooling cycle can stress the metal to the point where it will crack. Discs which have been damaged in this way are extremely dangerous to drive on, as they could break up completely at any time. Only fit discs of this type from established manufacturers offering a useful guarantee of quality, and check the discs regularly.

Performance discs also have a reputation for warping (nasty vibrations felt through the pedal). Justified, or not? Well, the harder you use your brakes (and we could be talking serious abuse), the greater the heat you'll generate. Okay, so these wicked discs are meant to be able to cope with this heat, but you can't expect miracles. Cheap discs, or ones which have had a mega-hard time over thousands of miles, will warp. So buy quality, and don't get over-heroic on the brakes.

Performance pads can be fitted to any brake discs, including the standard ones, but are of course designed to work best with heat-dissipating discs. Unless your 106 has something seriously meaty under the bonnet, don't be tempted to go much further than 'fast road' pads - anything more competition-orientated may take too long to come up to temperature on the road. Remember what pushbike brakes are like in the wet? Cold competition pads feel the same, and old dears always step off the pavement when your brakes are cold!

Lastly, fitting all the performance brake bits in the world is no use if your calipers have seized up. If, when you strip out your old pads, you find that one pad's worn more than the other, or that both pads have worn more on the left wheel than the right, your caliper pistons are sticking. Sometimes you can free them off by pushing them back into the caliper, but this could be a garage job to fix. If you drive around with sticking calipers, you'll eat pads and discs. You choose.

Big disc conversion

Fitting huge multi-spoke wheels makes your factory-fit discs look pretty puny, so many people's idea of impressive brakes is to go large. We can understand that. But it costs, and you might have quite a search to find a company doing the bits, to start with. Then it's got to be decent quality, and fitted properly - if you don't take your brakes seriously, the only mag feature you'll get is Crash of the Month.

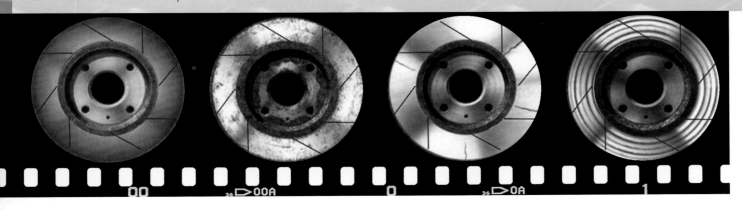

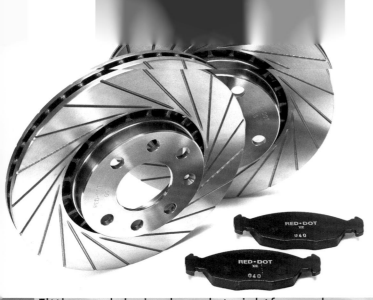

Front brake pads

Fitting pads is simple and straightforward operation; it doesn't matter what type of pads you buy, installation is the same for all makes. One area of confusion though, may be obtaining the correct type of pads; the 106 has three different types of front brake caliper. Make sure you state the exact make and model when purchasing pads, and check they are the right sort before wasting your time removing the originals. By the way, 'ventilated' discs are the ones with 'holes' in the edges - only fitted to 106s of the GTI / Rallye persuasion.

Remember 1 - *It's a good idea to have your brake mods MOT-tested once you've fitted new discs and pads, and you might even be able to 'blag' a free brake check at your local fast-fit centre if you're crafty! Brakes are a serious safety issue, and unless you're 100% confident that all is well, demo-ing your car's awesome new-found stopping ability could find you in the ditch...*

Remember 2 - *New pads of any sort need careful bedding-in before they'll work properly - when first fitted, the pad surface won't have worn exactly to the contours of the disc, so it won't actually be touching it, over its full area. Especially true when new pads are fitted to a worn discs. This will possibly result in very under-whelming brakes for the first few trips, so watch it - misplaced over-confidence in your brakes is a fast track to hospital...*

Bendix/Bosch caliper
solid discs

This caliper is generally only fitted to 106s up to 1.4 litres, without power steering - but hey - even our info could be wrong, so it's best to try and check before laying out on new bits.

01 Jack up the front of the car and remove both front roadwheels (see 'Wheels & tyres'). Before going any further, take a good look at the position of the pad springs, the retaining plate and spring clip, and memorise their correct fitted locations.

02 Using pliers, remove the spring clip from the pad retaining plate . . .

03 . . . then slide the plate out of position.

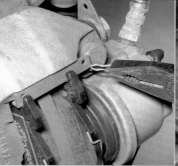

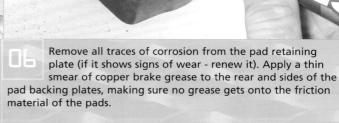

> **04** Slide the original pads complete with their pad springs out from the caliper. Remove the spring from each pad, noting its correct fitted location.

05 If the old pads are well worn, you'll need to push the piston back into the caliper to make room for your new pads. Do this either with a G-clamp or a pair of grips, or alternatively by levering the caliper outwards using a piece of wood. As you push the piston back in, watch the fluid level in the reservoir. If the fluid level rises above the 'MAXI' level line, siphon out the excess with a syringe. DON'T siphon it by mouth, as the fluid is poisonous!!

06 Remove all traces of corrosion from the pad retaining plate (if it shows signs of wear - renew it). Apply a thin smear of copper brake grease to the rear and sides of the pad backing plates, making sure no grease gets onto the friction material of the pads.

Attention!
Brake dust from old pads or shoes may contain asbestos. Wear a mask to avoid inhaling it.

Fit the pad springs correctly to the new pads. The springs must be fitted so that when the pads are installed in the caliper, they will be located at the opposite end to the retaining plate. Insert the pads, complete with pad springs, into the caliper, ensuring the friction material of each one is facing the brake disc.
07

Ensure the pads and spring are correctly located in the caliper . . .
08

. . . then slide the retaining plate into position (give this a little copper grease, too) and secure it in position with the spring clip.
09

Repeat the procedure (Steps 1 to 9) on the opposite side. With both sets of pads correctly fitted, repeatedly press the brake pedal to force the pads onto the discs. Refit the wheels then lower the car to the ground. Before driving the car, check the brake fluid level. Remember the pads will need to 'bed-in', so take it easy for the first 100 miles or so.
10

ATE/Teves
FN48 caliper
ventilated discs

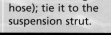

Attention!
Brake dust from old pads or shoes may contain asbestos. Wear a mask to avoid inhaling it.

01. Jack up the front of the car and remove both front roadwheels (see 'Wheels & tyres'). Note the correct fitted location of the pad spring then, using a flat-bladed screwdriver, carefully prise the spring out of position and remove it from the caliper.

02 Remove the two caps from the inner edge of the caliper to gain access to the guide pin bolts.

03 Unscrew both guide pin bolts.

04 Slide the caliper assembly off the brake disc, then unclip the inner pad from the caliper piston. Don't allow the caliper to hang from the brake hose (this will damage the hose); tie it to the suspension strut.

05 Remove the outer pad from the caliper mounting bracket.

06 If the originals are well worn, you'll need to push the piston back into the caliper to make room for all that extra friction material. Do this either with a G-clamp or a pair of grips or alternatively by levering it back using a piece of wood. As you're pushing the piston back in, keep an eye on the fluid level in the master cylinder reservoir. If the fluid level rises above the 'MAXI' level line, siphon out the excess with a syringe. DON'T siphon it by mouth, as the fluid is poisonous!!

07 Remove all traces of corrosion from the caliper mounting bracket, then apply a thin smear of copper-based brake grease to the rear and sides of the pad backing plates. Take care to make sure no grease gets onto the friction material of the pads. Also smear copper grease into the grooves where the pads rest. Where'd that new disc come from?

08 Clip the new inner pad into position in the caliper piston and fit the outer pad to the mounting bracket ensuring its friction material is facing the brake disc.

Repeat the procedure (Steps 1 to 11) on the opposite side. With both sets of pads correctly fitted, repeatedly press the brake pedal to force the pads onto the discs. Refit the wheels, then lower the car to the ground. Before driving the car, check the brake fluid level. Remember the pads will need to 'bed-in', so take it easy for the first 100 miles or so.

Slide the caliper and inner pad into position, and align it with the mounting bracket.

09

Lightly grease and refit the guide pin bolts, tighten them to the correct torque (32 Nm), then securely fit the bolt caps.

10

Fit the pad spring to the caliper, ensuring its ends are correctly hooked in the caliper holes.

11

12

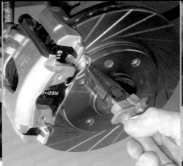

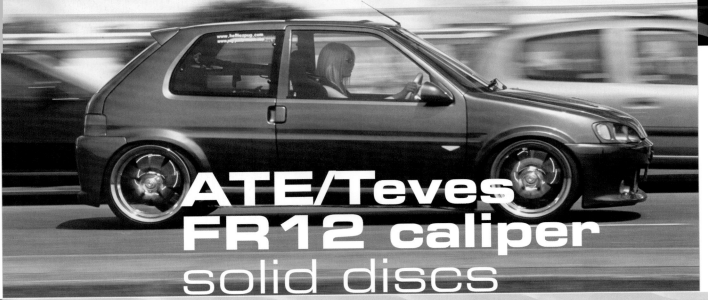

ATE/Teves
FR12 caliper
solid discs

We didn't actually see a 106 with this caliper, but we're sure they're out there. We want to believe. Just in case your car has these 'unpopular' calipers, we don't want you to be alienated, so here's the basic procedure. According to our files, this caliper's fitted to models up to 1.4 litres, with power steering - if that helps.

Jack up the front of the car and remove both front roadwheels (see 'Wheels & tyres'). Before going any further, take a good look at the position of the pad spring, and memorise its correct fitted location.

Using a hammer and pin punch, tap the pad retaining pins out from the caliper, and remove the pad spring. Slide the original pads and their backing shims (where fitted) out from the caliper.

If the old pads are well worn, you'll need to push the piston back into the caliper to make room for your all that extra friction material. Do this either with a G-clamp or a pair of grips, or alternatively by levering the caliper outwards using a piece of wood. As you're pushing the piston back in, watch the fluid level in the reservoir. If the fluid level rises above the 'MAXI' level line, siphon out the excess with a syringe. Don't siphon it by mouth, as the fluid is poisonous!!

Remove all traces of corrosion from the pad retaining pins (if they show signs of wear - renew them) then apply a thin smear of copper brake grease to each pin. Also apply a thin smear to the rear and sides of the pad backing plates. Take care to make sure no grease gets onto the friction material of the pads.

Insert the pads, complete with backing shims (where fitted), into the caliper ensuring the friction material of each one is facing the brake disc. Locate the pad spring on the top of the pads, and insert both retaining pins. Tap the lower pin into position, ensuring it passes through both pad holes and the centre of the spring. With the lower pin in position, tap in the upper pin through both pads and over the top of the spring ends.

Repeat the procedure on the opposite side. With both sets of pads correctly fitted, repeatedly press the brake pedal to force the pads onto the discs. Refit the wheels, then lower the car to the ground. Before driving the car, check the brake fluid level. Remember the pads will need to 'bed-in', so take it easy for the first 100 miles or so.

Painting
calipers

One downside to fitted big alloys is that it exposes your standard brakes. So why not paint some of the brake components so they look the biz, possibly to match with your chosen colour scheme (red is common, but isn't the only choice). Only the GTI (or the Mk2 Rallye) has rear discs, but painting the brake drums is acceptable under the circumstances.

Painting the calipers requires that they're really clean. Accessory stores sell aerosol brake cleaner, and some kits come complete with cleaner spray. Ideally, the calipers should also be removed completely for painting.

01 We know you won't necessarily want to hear this, but the best way to paint the calipers is to do some dismantling first. The kits say you don't have to, but trust me - you'll get a much better result from a few minutes' extra work. Remove the calipers as described in the brake pad section. You don't have to detach the brake hoses, but make sure that you support the calipers so that the hose is not under pressure. Clean the calipers using brake cleaner, making sure that you remove all the dirt and muck.

Attention!
Make sure when painting drums that you don't get paint anywhere near the wheel bolt holes.

02 Remove the caliper mounting bracket. Again, clean it thoroughly using brake cleaner, followed up with a wire brush.

03 Carefully paint the mounting bracket and the caliper body, making sure that you don't get the paint on any areas where the pads, discs or piston touch. Don't paint the caliper piston. Allow to dry, and apply a second coat if required. Refit all your bits.

Tricks 'n' tips
If you have trouble reassembling your brakes after painting, you probably got carried away and put on too much paint. We found that, once it was fully dry, the excess paint could be trimmed off with a knife.

Front brake discs

Besides the various brands of performance brake pads that go with them, the main brake upgrade is to fit performance front brake discs. Performance discs are available in two main types - grooved and cross-drilled (and a combination of both). The choice of which is up to you; both perform similarly and offer the same advantages, so the decision is probably down to which you think looks better.

Fitting discs is another simple and straightforward operation; it doesn't matter what type of discs you buy, installation is the same for all makes. Make sure you state the exact make and model when purchasing discs, and check they are the right diameter and have the correct amount of wheel bolt holes (yes, really) before wasting your time removing the originals. And always fit new pads at the same time.

01 Jack up the front of the car and remove both front roadwheels (see 'Wheels & tyres'). Remove the original brake pads as described earlier. On some models it is necessary to remove the caliper or mounting bracket; use new bolts on refitting.

02 All that holds the disc in place (apart from the wheel bolts, when the wheel's on) is one or two screws. Ah - but what if the screws are very tight, very rusty, or very chewed-up-so-you-can't-get-a-screwdriver-on? Then you're in trouble. A good clout with a hammer (and a soak with WD-40) might free off a rusted-in screw, but an impact driver or even a drill may be needed. Ours came off with no effort...

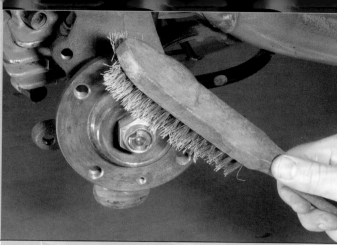

03 Ensure the new disc and the mating surface of the hub are perfectly clean. If the disc is covered with a preservative coating, degrease it thoroughly with brake cleaner.

04 Clean up the wheel hub by scrubbing it with a wire brush.

05 Locate the new disc on the hub, then fit the retaining screw(s) and tighten securely. When you first take out your two shiny new discs, you might think they're identical. Chances are, they're not, and they should only be fitted with the grooves facing a certain way (this is the left front). Check your paperwork.

06 If the new caliper/bracket bolts are not pre-coated with locking compound, apply a drop of locking compound to the threads of each one. Fit the caliper/bracket to the hub, and tighten its bolts to the correct torque - see the Haynes manual.

07 Fit the new brake pads (see 'Front brake pads'). Repeat the procedure (Steps 1 to 6) on the opposite side. With both discs and pads correctly fitted, repeatedly press the brake pedal to force the pads onto the discs. Refit the wheels, then lower the car to the ground. Before driving the car, check the brake fluid level. Remember the discs and pads will need to 'bed-in', so take it easy for the first 100 miles or so.

Rear disc brakes

This procedure covers changing the pads and discs together, so you won't have to do all this if you only want to change the pads. Read it all through before you start, though.

01 Jack up the rear of the car, and remove both rear roadwheels (see 'Wheels & tyres'). Extract the tiny little spring clip from the pad retaining plate. Apparently, you must fit a new spring clip when refitting - you'll probably need a new one anyway, once the original flies off and gets lost!

02 Slide the pad retaining plate out of the caliper.

Attention!
Brake dust from old pads or shoes may contain asbestos. Wear a mask to avoid inhaling it.

The brake pad with the lug on its backing plate is the inner pad. Refit the anti-rattle springs to the pads, so that when the pads are fitted in the caliper, the spring end will be located at the opposite end of the pad, in relation to the pad retaining plate. Smear a little copper grease onto the back of the brake pads.

Slide the inner pad into position in the caliper, ensuring that the lug on its backing plate is aligned with the slot in the caliper piston.

07 Clean up the wheel hub by scrubbing it with a wire brush.

08 Locate the new disc on the hub, then fit the retaining screw(s) and tighten securely. Bear in mind that the grooves should 'face' the same way as the front discs.

09

10

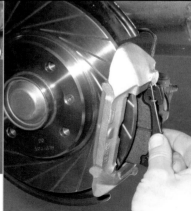

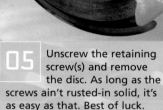

03 Using a pair of pliers, withdraw both the inner and outer pads from the caliper. Make a note of the correct fitted position of the anti-rattle springs, and remove the springs from each pad.

04 Make sure the caliper is clean, and free from dust and dirt - giving it a spray with some brake cleaner is a good move, but watch the fumes! Using a screwdriver in the notches provided, turn the caliper piston clockwise while pushing the piston back into its bore. Make sure that the piston is positioned like this (see picture) before you refit the pads. If you're just changing your pads, go to step 9.

05 Unscrew the retaining screw(s) and remove the disc. As long as the screws ain't rusted-in solid, it's as easy as that. Best of luck.

06 Ensure the new disc and the mating surface of the hub are perfectly clean. If the disc is covered with a preservative coating, degrease it thoroughly with brake cleaner.

Repeat the procedure (Steps 1 to 13) on the opposite side. With both discs and pads correctly fitted, repeatedly press the brake pedal to force the pads onto the discs. Refit the wheels, then lower the car to the ground. Before driving the car, check the brake fluid level. Remember the discs and pads will need to 'bed-in', so take it easy for the first 100 miles or so.

Locate the outer brake pad in the caliper body, ensuring that its friction material is against the brake disc. Duh-uh!

11

Ensure that the anti-rattle springs are correctly positioned, then slide the pad retaining plate into place.

12

Fit a new spring clip into the hole in the pad retaining plate (to stop it sliding out).

13

14

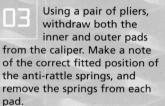

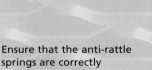

Interiors

The 106 dash is best described as functional. It does the job, but it's dull with a capital F (then it over-compensates, with some – er – 'lively' patterns on the seats). But you need suffer no longer, because the interior is one area where the goodies are pretty easy to fit, and provided you go for one particular 'theme' (rather than a mixture), the end result can certainly help you forget you're in a poverty model, if indeed you are…

To be fair to the 106, not many standard interiors are anything to shout about, particularly when you compare them with the sort of look that can easily be achieved with the huge range of product that's out there. As with the exterior styling, though, remember that fashions can change very quickly – so don't be afraid to experiment with a look you really like, because chances are, it'll be the next big thing anyway. Just don't do wood, ok? We've a feeling it's never coming in, never mind coming back…

Removing stuff

Take it easy and break less

Many of the procedures we're going to show involve removing interior trim panels (either for colouring or to fit other stuff), and this can be tricky. It's far too easy to break plastic trim, especially once it's had a chance to go a bit brittle with age. Another 'problem' with the 106 is that the designers have been very clever at hiding several vital screws, meaning that trim can be a pig to get off. We'll try and avoid the immortal words 'simply unclip the panel', and instead show you how properly, but inevitably at some stage, a piece of trim won't 'simply' anything.

The important lesson here is not to lose your temper, as this has a highly-destructive effect on plastic components, and may result in a panel which no amount of carbon film or colour spray can put right, or make fit again. Superglue may help, but not every time. So – take it steady, prise carefully, and think logically about how and where a plastic panel would have to be attached, to stay on. You'll encounter all sorts of trim clips (some more fragile than others) in your travels – when these break, as they usually do, many of them can be bought in packs from accessory shops, and rarer ones will be available from a Peugeot dealer, probably off the shelf. Even fully-trained Peugeot mechanics aren't immune to breaking a few trim clips!

Door trim panel

Tricks 'n' tips

Find something like an old ice-cream or margarine tub to keep all the little screws and bits in, as you take them off. This approach is far superior to the chuck-them-all-on-the-floor method most people use, until they lose something vital.

You'll find plenty of excuses for removing your door trim panels – fitting speakers, re-trimming the panel, de-locking, even window tinting, so we'd better tell you how …

01 Right from the off, the little Pug shows its quality build – first the window winder (if you've got one) just pulls off (with a plastic disc behind, which you may need again) . . .

02 . . . while next to be voted off is the door lock handle trim, which also puts up no resistance whatsoever.

03 If you're lucky enough to have a posh model, or just a later one, undo the screws round the edge of the door pocket, and take it off.

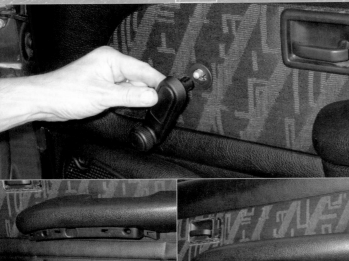
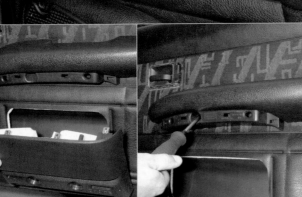

04 On Mk 2s, unclip the padded section under the armrest . . .

05 . . . then on all models, undo the two armrest screws and take the armrest off.

06 Mk 1 106s will have a small trim panel left in the centre of the door, which you just carefully prise off (don't scratch the on-display painted surfaces of the door). Mk 2 models have a larger door trim panel, with screws in the centre, and around the speaker, to remove . . .

07 . . . before the panel can be unclipped around the edges, and lifted off over the door lock button. So – is the door card being painted, or retrimmed? Should you wish to gain access to components inside the door, simply pull back the plastic membrane. Try not to tear it - if it wasn't important, Peugeot wouldn't fit it.

Wind-up windows?
No worries

01 These Richbrook door handles are going to look the business on our door cards, and they also take some of the non-electric-window pain out of things. Your first job will be to pull off the existing window handles. Which should take about two seconds.

02 The new handles come ready-assembled, but to fit them, they need to be dismantled first. Start by removing the four Allen-headed bolts.

03 Next, remove the chrome centre cap.

04 Now you're left with just the mounting disc, which has a grub screw fitted to its hub (on the back) to hold it onto the winder handle spindle. It's a simple case of slotting the disc onto the winder handle spindle, then tightening the grub screw behind. It's a bit of a tight fit behind there – don't poke any holes in your door trim with the Allen key!

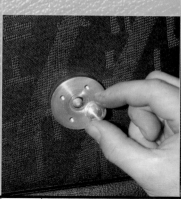

05 The chrome centre cap now slots onto the end of the spindle . . .

06 . . . followed swiftly by the anodised handle. Ensure that the holes in the handle are aligned with the holes in the mounting disc, then fit the Allen-headed bolts . . .

07 . . . and tighten with the Allen key supplied in the kit. They're so nice, you won't be able to keep your hands off 'em – which is more than could be said for the old ones!

Glovebox

Removing the glovebox is very straightforward, and shouldn't take more than a couple of minutes. First job is to remove the two plastic hinge pins at the base of the glovebox. You'll need a suitable tool (like a small screwdriver) to push these pins out (don't lose 'em). The glovebox can then be lifted out of the car.

Anything but black?

The interior trim on the 106 at least hides its age well, and doesn't rattle much. And that's about it - for a lover of goth-black or elephant-hide grey, it's heaven. For normal people, it's something else. Fortunately, there's plenty you can do to personalise it, and there are three main routes to take:

1) Spray paint - available in any colour you like, as long as it's… not black. This Folia Tec stuff actually dyes softer plastics and leather, and comes in a multi-stage treatment, to suit all plastic types. Don't try to save money just buying the top coat, because it won't work! Special harder-wearing spray is required for use on steering wheels. Ordinary spray paint for bodywork might damage some plastics, and won't be elastic - good primer is essential. Make sure you also buy lots of masking tape.

2) Adhesive or shrink-fit film - available in various wild colours, carbon, ally, and, er… walnut (would YOU?). Probably best used on flatter surfaces, or at least those without complex curves, or you'll have to cut and join - spray is arguably better here. Some companies will sell you sheets of genuine carbon-fibre, with peel-off backing - looks and feels the part (nice if you have touchy-feely passengers).

3) Replacement panels - the easiest option, as the panels are supplied pre-cut, ready to fit. Of course, you're limited then to styling just the panels supplied.

If you fancy something more posh, how about trimming your interior bits in leather? Very saucy. Available in various colours, and hardly any dearer than film, you also get that slight 'ruffled' effect on tighter curves.

Get the cans out

Any painting process is a *multi-stage* application. With the Folia Tec system (thanks to Eurostyling for supplying ours), many of you apparently think you can get away just buying the top coat, which then looks like a cheap option compared to film - wrong! Even the proper interior spray top coat won't stay on for long without the matching primer, and the finish won't be wear-resistant without the finishing sealer spray. You don't need the special foaming cleaner - you could get by with a general-purpose degreaser, such as meths. Just watch the grey/black plastic doesn't suddenly turn white - if it does, you're damaging the finish! This might not be too important to you, as it's being sprayed over anyway, but if you take out the grey too far on a part that's not being sprayed all over, you'll have to live with a cacky-looking white-grey finish to any non-painted surface…

Providing you're a dab hand with the masking tape, paint gives you the flexibility to be more creative. For instance, you could try colour-matching the exterior of the car - but will ordinary car body paint work on interior plastics? Course it will, as long as you prep the panels properly.

Choice of paint's one thing, but what to paint? Well, not everything - for instance, you might want to avoid high-wear areas like door handles. Just makes for an easier life. The glovebox lid and instrument panel surround are obvious first choices, as are the ashtray and fusebox lid. The centre console's not lighting anyone's fire in standard Peugeot grey, so hit it with some spray too. Any panels which just pop out are targets, in fact (lots less masking needed) - just make sure whatever you're dismantling was meant to come apart, or it'll be out with the superglue instead of the cans.

Don't be afraid to experiment with a combination of styles - as long as you're confident you can blend it all together, anything goes! Mix the painted bits with some tasteful carbon-fibre sheet or brushed-aluminium film, if you like - neutral colours like this, or chrome, can be used to give a lift to dash bits which are too tricky to spray.

Painting **trim**

01 Place your chosen item of interior trim on a clean, flat surface, and attack with sandpaper. The aim is to remove the nasty injection-moulded design that looks like elephant hide. Nice. In order to save total disintegration of your hands, it's best to wear gloves (well, you try telling our mechanic).

02 When you're satisfied that enough of the grain pattern has been removed by sandpaper (remember that you carry on the smoothing process by priming the area, rubbing the primer back and repeating the process), clean the area with a suitable degreaser. Try 'panel-wipe' from a bodyshop.

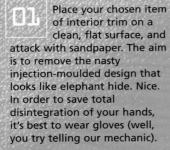

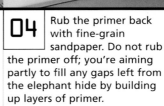

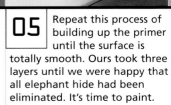

03 Plaster the surrounding area with newspaper (to avoid parental unrest), then add your first layer of plastic primer and leave to dry as per instructions on the can.

04 Rub the primer back with fine-grain sandpaper. Do not rub the primer off; you're aiming partly to fill any gaps left from the elephant hide by building up layers of primer.

05 Repeat this process of building up the primer until the surface is totally smooth. Ours took three layers until we were happy that all elephant hide had been eliminated. It's time to paint. We've chosen to paint our box that same colour as the car, but the possibilities are endless. One coat of paint should be enough – but use two coats if you feel it needs it. End by adding a nice layer of lacquer to make it really shiny!

Filming your **106**

If you fancy creating a look that's a bit more special than plain paint colours, film is the answer - but be warned - it's not the easiest stuff in the world to use.

01 The glovebox lid's an obvious choice for filming, as so much of the main dash is non-removable. You'll need to remove the glovebox first (see 'Removing stuff') and place it on a clean flat surface. Thoroughly clean the box using a suitable degreaser - methylated spirits will certainly strip away any polish or silicon on the plastic.

Now cut a section of film that completely covers the surface area, with some overlap for the edges. Cut a slit in the film to accommodate the handle. Peel off the backing, and position the film so that the lines of carbon fibre match up. Use a heat gun and cloth to smooth out any creases in the film. Trim

02 Applying film to curved surfaces is always tricky. The key to getting it right is to apply the film is sections. Firstly cut a piece of film to fit the handle recess . . .

Turn the glovebox over, and trim off the excess film around the edges – you may need to

. . . then peel off the backing paper and stick the film in place. Use a heat gun (or hairdryer set on a low heat) to warm the film, then stretch it to fit around the curved area of the recess, applying more heat as and when you need it. Don't melt the stuff – that's not

03 the idea. The heat will also kick-start the glue working.

04 Once you're happy with the results, take a craft knife and cut off the excess film.

05 the excess film around the handle recess, and fold the edges in.

06 apply some more heat to help the glue start working.

Bum notes
There are limitations to using film, and the quality of the film itself has a lot to do with that. We had major problems with one particular make of brushed-aluminium-look film - it was a nightmare to work with, and the edges had peeled the next day. Buying quality film will give you a long-lasting result to be proud of, with much less skill requirement and lots less swearing. But it still pays not to be too ambitious with it..

Dash Dynamics

A far easier route to the brushed-ally or carbon look, pre-finished ('here's some we did earlier') panels are available from suppliers. Dash kits are available for the 106 from companies like Dash Dynamics, and offer a simpler way of livening-up the dull 106 dash.

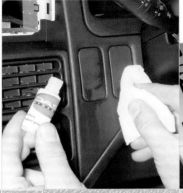

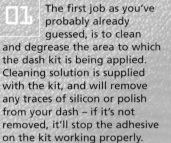

01 The first job as you've probably already guessed, is to clean and degrease the area to which the dash kit is being applied. Cleaning solution is supplied with the kit, and will remove any traces of silicon or polish from your dash – if it's not removed, it'll stop the adhesive on the kit working properly.

02 As you'll be fitting one piece of kit at a time, it is a good idea to cut out each individual section now.

03 Taking care not to touch the area you have cleaned so well, raise the temperature of the dash using a heat gun or hairdryer set on its lowest heat – don't melt the dash or burn yourself though! The low heat enables the glue on the back of the kit to stick to the dash quicker and more effectively.

04 Quickly apply the same low heat to the section of kit you're fitting – don't take too long doing this, or the dash will be stone-cold again. You have to be even more careful now that you don't burn/melt the dash kit, or the finished results will look pants.

05 Peel off the backing paper, then, without touching the adhesive on the back, position the section of kit on the dash (each section is labelled to show you where to fit it). At this stage, if you're not happy with the position of the kit, you're still able to peel the piece off and reposition it (though this isn't recommended – don't be too fussy, or it won't stick).

06 When you're happy with the positioning, use a cloth to press the kit firmly into place.

07 A little more heat will aid the first stages of adhesion, but the kit will still need 24 hours to be fully bonded in place. Over time, you may find that the corner edges may lift in certain areas – if this happens, simply apply some strong adhesive to the area to re-stick it.

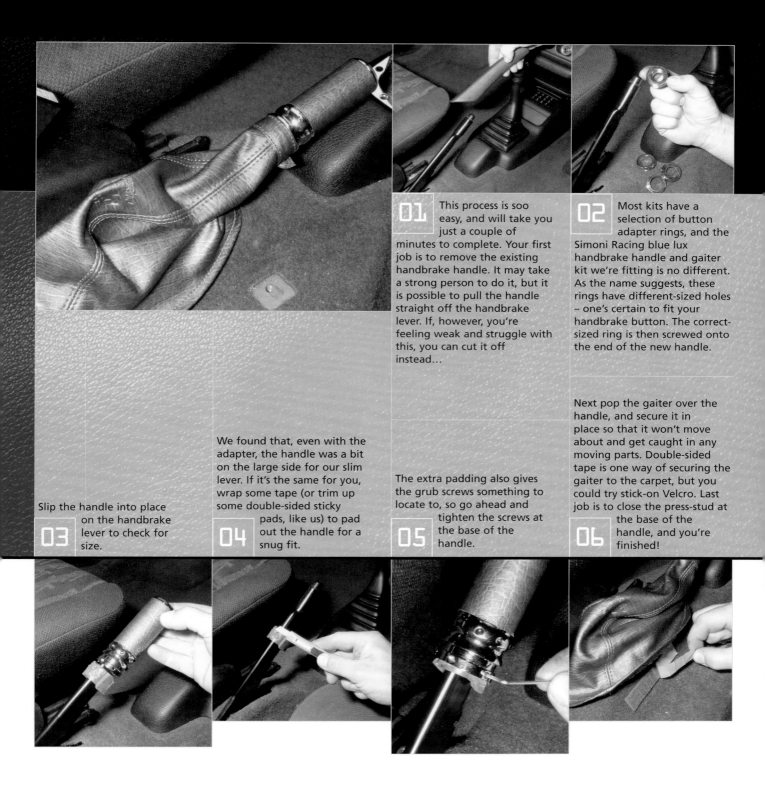

01 This process is soo easy, and will take you just a couple of minutes to complete. Your first job is to remove the existing handbrake handle. It may take a strong person to do it, but it is possible to pull the handle straight off the handbrake lever. If, however, you're feeling weak and struggle with this, you can cut it off instead...

02 Most kits have a selection of button adapter rings, and the Simoni Racing blue lux handbrake handle and gaiter kit we're fitting is no different. As the name suggests, these rings have different-sized holes – one's certain to fit your handbrake button. The correct-sized ring is then screwed onto the end of the new handle.

Next pop the gaiter over the handle, and secure it in place so that it won't move about and get caught in any moving parts. Double-sided tape is one way of securing the gaiter to the carpet, but you could try stick-on Velcro. Last job is to close the press-stud at the base of the handle, and you're finished!

03 Slip the handle into place on the handbrake lever to check for size.

04 We found that, even with the adapter, the handle was a bit on the large side for our slim lever. If it's the same for you, wrap some tape (or trim up some double-sided sticky pads, like us) to pad out the handle for a snug fit.

05 The extra padding also gives the grub screws something to locate to, so go ahead and tighten the screws at the base of the handle.

06

Gear knob jobs

Gear knobs and gaiters are a fairly inexpensive way of modifying the interior look of your car. You spend a lot of time in contact with that knob, so why not treat it to a new look?

01 As usual the first job will be to remove that standard plastic all-in-one gear knob and gaiter assembly. One screw at the base of the gear gaiter holds it all in place . . .

02 . . . don't believe us? Well, here's the whole assembly being lifted off the gear lever and away.

03 Those good guys at Simoni Racing have supplied a luxury blue leather gear gaiter to match our handbrake gaiter, so start by fitting this first. Most gaiters have elasticated bases, and that's great if it fits your centre console. However, if it won't fit properly, or you also want a chrome gear surround, the gaiter needs mods. Start by slicing the elastic at the base of the gaiter.

07 Onto the gear knob now. Start by threading the bottom collar of the new knob over the lever . . .

08 . . . then fit the rubber mounting sleeve that should be supplied with your gear knob. In fact there should be several, so find one that fits snugly to the end of the lever.

09 Time for the best bit – on goes the colour co-ordinated Poseidon blue leather gear knob. It's easier if you fit the knob-retaining little grub screws (by just a few turns) before you pop the knob in place – saves grovelling about in the centre console when you drop one.

04 Now the gaiter has extra slack, you can stretch each corner to meet the edges of the surround. On a 106, it's a good idea to fit a surround if you're going to remove the gaiter/knob assembly, as this gives you something to attach the gaiter to, plus you won't run the risk of the gaiter getting stuck in any moving parts.

05 Tuck the edges of the gaiter inside the surround (hold it in place temporarily with something like Blutac, if you must), and place it in position on the console.

06 Now it's a simple case of holding everything in place whilst you drill through the holes in the surround and on through the plastic of the centre console. Allen screws will then hold everything in place nicely.

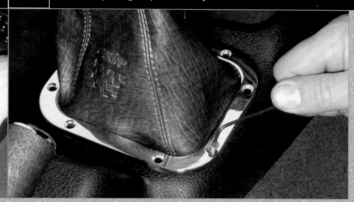

10 Yep, you guessed it – you can tighten the screws now using the Allen key supplied in the kit.

11 Lastly, screw the lower collar up to the gear knob and ensure the gaiter is sitting in the correct position at the base of the knob. To keep the gaiter in place, tighten the retaining laces (have them facing forwards, so they don't show as much). Et voilà – c'est tout!

Door sill plates

You can get these in any colour you like, but a new trick is getting trims which light up, preferably with the interior lights. We're keeping our Simoni Racing Blue Lux theme going here, though, with these wicked blue leather plates. Nice. One piece of advice, if you're planning major interior mods - fit the sill trims last. That way, there's less chance of scratching and scuffing 'em up during fitting the rest of the interior.

01 Sill plates are an inexpensive way of hiding scratched or damaged sills, and are easy to fit. Start by offering the sill into place to check for fitment.

02 Using some tape, mask up the area the sill plate will be fitted to. You can then use some Scotchbrite to roughen up the paint so the adhesive on the back of the sill plate will stick better. By masking the area off you don't attack paint that will be visible on the rest of the doorsill – bonus! Alternatively, just clean the sill with some meths.

03 You may have already noticed that the sill is stepped, but needs to be flat in order to fit the new plates properly. The easiest way round this problem is to stick on several layers of masking tape, to bring the level up. Try using some thick double-sided foam tape.

04 Then it's a case of removing the backing paper from the sill plate, taking a deep breath . . .

05 . . . and sticking the sill down firmly (straight, and in the right place, for preference).

The personal touch – re-trimming

Okay, so you're definitely not happy with how the inside of your 106 looks, but you're not sold on any of the off-the-shelf options for tricking it up, either. You know how you want it to look, though, so get creative!

There are any number of upholstery companies in Yellow Pages, who will be able to create any look you want (we got one in our own back yard, almost - Pipers of Sparkford, Somerset, and very helpful lads they are, too). If your idea of 106 heaven is an interior swathed in black and purple leather, these guys can help. Don't assume that you'll have to go to Carisma, to get a car interior re-trimmed - they might well be the daddies at this, but any upholsterer worth the name should be able to help, even if they normally only do sofas!

Of course, if you're even slightly handy with things like glue and scissors, you might be inspired to get brave and DIY. An upholsterers will still be a useful source for materials (and maybe advice too?).

Are your dials all white?

White dial kits aren't that difficult to fit, but you will need some skill and patience not to damage the delicate bits inside your instrument panel - the risk is definitely worth it, to liven up that dreary grey 106 dash, anyway.

Just make sure you get the right kit for your car, and don't start stripping anything until you're sure it's the right one - look carefully. Most dial kit makers, for instance, want to know exactly what markings you have on your speedo and rev counter. If they don't ask, be worried - the kit they send could well be wrong for your car, and might not even fit. When you receive your kit, before you even open the packet, ensure that the dials in the kit are an exact match of those in your car.

01 Safety and electrics go arm in arm, so begin by disconnecting the battery. Check your radio codes before you do, though – we don't want any tears when your stereo doesn't work! Next you need to remove the steering column lower shroud, held in place with three Allen-headed screws. The shroud slides off a metal bracket once the screws have gone.

02 Staying in the same area, remove the three steering column retaining nuts, as the column has to be dropped down so that the instrument cluster can be removed later.

03 Unclip and remove the steering column upper shroud.

>>

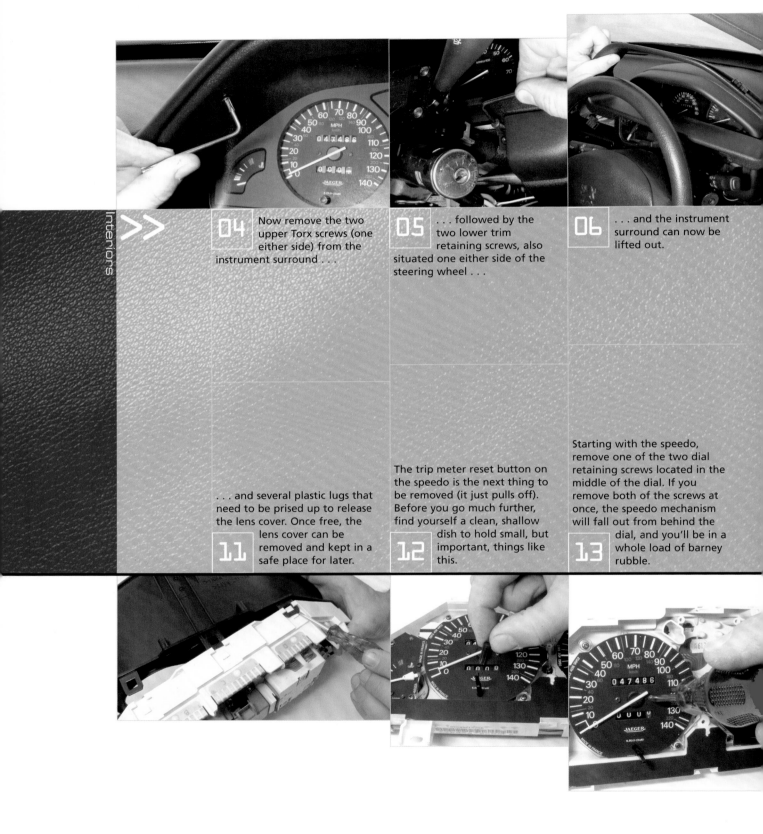

>>

04 Now remove the two upper Torx screws (one either side) from the instrument surround . . .

05 . . . followed by the two lower trim retaining screws, also situated one either side of the steering wheel . . .

06 . . . and the instrument surround can now be lifted out.

11 . . . and several plastic lugs that need to be prised up to release the lens cover. Once free, the lens cover can be removed and kept in a safe place for later.

12 The trip meter reset button on the speedo is the next thing to be removed (it just pulls off). Before you go much further, find yourself a clean, shallow dish to hold small, but important, things like this.

13 Starting with the speedo, remove one of the two dial retaining screws located in the middle of the dial. If you remove both of the screws at once, the speedo mechanism will fall out from behind the dial, and you'll be in a whole load of barney rubble.

07 Next, remove the three instrument cluster retaining screws (one at the top, two down below).

08 The unit can now be slid out from its recess so that the speedo cable and the four wiring plugs can be disconnected. Make a note of the order of the plugs as you disconnect them.

09 Now lower the column by pulling gently down on the steering wheel, and slide the cluster from the car.

10 Working on a clean flat surface, start by removing the lens cover from the cluster. This is held in place by three retaining screws located on the rear . . .

Once the dial's cut in half, it can be removed from the mounting plate. There will still be some glue to contend with when removing the dial, so gently prise it up bit by bit in order to remove it. Refit the second retaining screw afterwards.

Here comes the fun bit... Using a sharp blade, make a slit in the dial from the outside edge to the middle. Cut the dial on the side you removed the screw on.

14

Now refit the first screw, and remove the second screw. Repeat the process of cutting into the dial on the opposite side . . .

15

16

Using a suitable solvent (like meths), wipe the glue from the mounting plate.

17

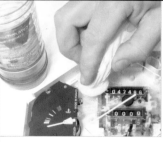

>>

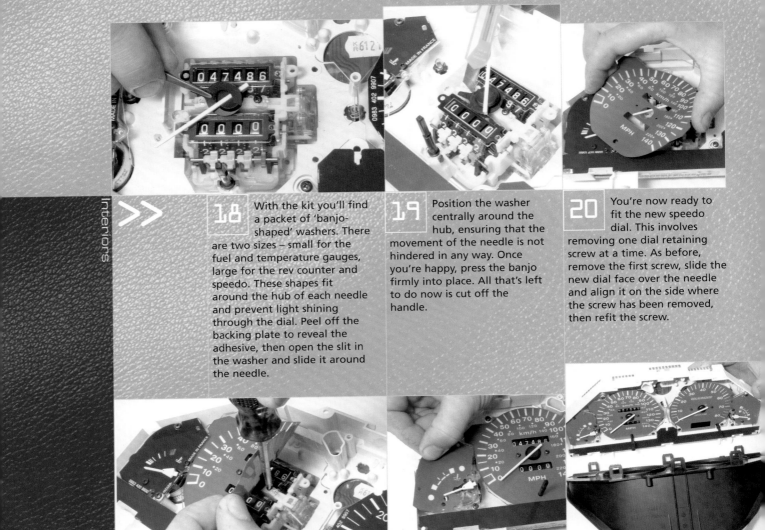

18 With the kit you'll find a packet of 'banjo-shaped' washers. There are two sizes – small for the fuel and temperature gauges, large for the rev counter and speedo. These shapes fit around the hub of each needle and prevent light shining through the dial. Peel off the backing plate to reveal the adhesive, then open the slit in the washer and slide it around the needle.

19 Position the washer centrally around the hub, ensuring that the movement of the needle is not hindered in any way. Once you're happy, press the banjo firmly into place. All that's left to do now is cut off the handle.

20 You're now ready to fit the new speedo dial. This involves removing one dial retaining screw at a time. As before, remove the first screw, slide the new dial face over the needle and align it on the side where the screw has been removed, then refit the screw.

21 Taking great care not to bend the needle (or crease the dial), lift the dial gently to remove the second screw from the mounting plate. Once removed, you can align the second half of the dial, then the screw can go back in.

22 Well, that's the trickiest of all the dials done, so you can relax. A bit. Go ahead and fit the new dial faces to the remaining three dials, following a similar process as above, ignoring the stuff about one screw at a time.

23 After this has been done, you should be left with something that looks a bit like this! All that's left to do now is refit the clocks to the car. PS – Clean the lens cover inside and out before refitting it, as there's a good chance you've got fingerprints all over it!

Attention!

This is one job where you'll be messing with big wires, carrying serious current - more than any other electrical job, don't rush it, and don't skimp on the insulating tape. Do it properly, as we're about to show you, and there's no worries. Otherwise, at best, you'll be stranded - at worst, it could be a fire.

01 First job is to find a suitable place to mount the starter button. We've chosen to fit ours in place of a blank switch in the main facia panel. Start as usual, by disconnecting the battery negative terminal . . .

02 . . . then, using a pair of pliers with card wrapped around the teeth to protect the plastic, pull off the heater blower knob.

Racing
starts

Like to have a racing-style starter button on your 106? Read on! A very cool piece of kit, and a great way to impress your passengers.

The idea of the racing starter button is the ignition key's made redundant, beyond switching on the ignition lights (it'd be a bit daft, security-wise, if you could start the engine without the key at all).

03 Pull off the two heater/ventilation control levers . . .

04 . . . and unscrew the Torx screw behind the heater blower knob.

05 Prise out the heater control panel . . .

06 . . . and pull the illumination bulbholder out from the rear.

>>

07 Next, remove the head unit as described in the ICE section.

08 Unscrew the two vent/switch trim panel Torx screws . . .

09 Withdraw the trim panel until you can see the wiring plug that needs to be disconnected before fully lifting the panel away.

>>

10 Now that you have the panel free, try the button for size in one of the blank switch holes. Secure the starter button into place with its retaining nut.

11 Won't be needing that blank switch now the cool starter button's in place, so lose it now.

12 To start the wiring-up process, undo the three screws holding the steering column shrouds together, from underneath.

13 Locate the relay supplied with the kit, and find a suitable mounting place for it. Maybe mount the relay using a DIY-store L-bracket in the driver's footwell under the facia panel – this gives easy access to the wiring, but it's still out of sight. The white wiring plug that connects to the relay can now be slotted into place.

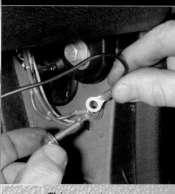
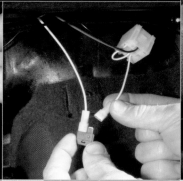

14 Now concentrate on the three wires (black, white and blue), from the relay. Start with the black wire first. This needs to be tidily routed to the starter button, where the end of the wire is bared, and a grub screw holds it in place.

15 This next stage requires a length of wire that will stretch from the other grub-screw terminal on the starter button to an earth point within the car. An ideal earth point is in the driver's footwell.

16 Back to the relay now, to pick up the white wire and connect it to the in-line fuse assembly supplied within the kit.

17 Pick up the white wire from the other side of the fuse, and the blue wire from the relay, and route them towards the ignition switch area.

Here you need to find a thick red wire that is the live feed to the ignition switch. Use a test light to find the correct thick red wire, as there are three of them in the same area – the one you want is live only when the ignition's on. Using a double bullet connector, join the white wire into the red.

Finally the little blue wire needs to find a home. The blue wire needs to be attached to a wire on the back of the ignition switch that activates the starter solenoid. On our 106 this was a thick blue wire (code 100), so it was a simple case of cutting through the thick blue wire before the plug . . .

. . . taping up the redundant end of the thick wire . . .

. . . and joining the other end of the thick blue to the thin blue from the relay. Crimp a female connector to the little blue wire, a bullet connector to the thick blue wire, and join the two together. Before refitting the column shrouds, give that pro start button a tickle, and feel very chuffed indeed when your 106 bursts into life. You are a wiring God.

18

19

20

21

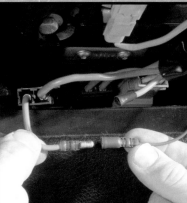

Under neon light...

So how much of a poser are you? How'd you like to show off all this shiny chequer floor and sexy pedals to full effect, in the midnight hour? You need some neons, baby! Yeah!

Interiors

Bum notes

It appears that interior neons have recently been declared ILLEGAL, and this means, in the first place, you're unlikely to find anywhere that even sells them any more. Exterior neons have been illegal from day one. If you fit interior neons, make sure they're at least easily switched off, should you get pulled. Remember that driving at night with a brightly-lit interior makes it even harder to see out. Neons are best used for show purposes.

01 There's not a great deal to this, really - decide where you want 'em, where you're going to get a live and an earth (and a switch, if necessary), then fit 'em. The first thing to do is offer one in place - remember, it would be sort-of useful if your feet don't hit them as you work the pedals...

05 Seeing as interior neons have recently been declared illegal, it's a good idea to have them on a switch. The Folia Tec kit comes with a switch, so it's kinda rude not to use it. Find somewhere easily accessible to mount the switch – this blank switch next to the wheel looks ideal.

06 Once the switch has been prised out of its hole, it's easy for you to remove any wiring plugs from behind. How come a blank switch has a wiring plug? Answers on a postcard...

07 Start by drilling a large-ish hole in the blank switch, then gradually enlarge and shape it so the new switch fits inside it like a glove. (Well, okay – gloves usually fit outside, but you get the idea).

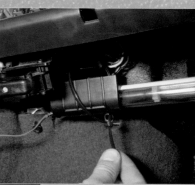

02 To mount the tubes, you can use the plastic securing clips supplied with the kit. Mark the holes for drilling, and get stuck in there with the cordless. Try not to drill through anything vital, like wiring. On the passenger side, it's best to remove the glovebox (which we tell you how to do in 'Removing stuff'").

03 A screw and nut will hold the clips in place, which in turn hold the tube up (well, they're not exactly heavy).

04 Because the bonnet pull's in the passenger footwell, it severely limits where you can actually drill a hole for tube securing clips. So instead, a cable-tie wrapped around the tube and secured under the dash will hold the other end of the tube up nicely. Mount the second tube in a similar way, depending on where you want the tube to go.

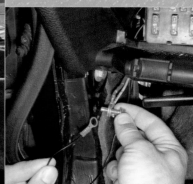

08 Once the switch is slotted into place, you can start routing the wires to it. Each tube has a red and black wire joined together, so start by separating the two. The red wire from each tube must then be routed under the dash, to the back of the switch, where they can be joined together into one connector and attached to a terminal on the back of the switch.

09 Next, a second wire is required to run from the back of switch, through an in-line fuse assembly to a live feed. The kit even provides a fuseholder for you, but if you've fitted an auxiliary fusebox (see 'Security') run the wire to that instead.

10 Finally, attach a ring connector to the black wire from each tube, and route it to a suitable earth point on each side of the car. Time to give your 106 that nightclub feel, without the bouncers.

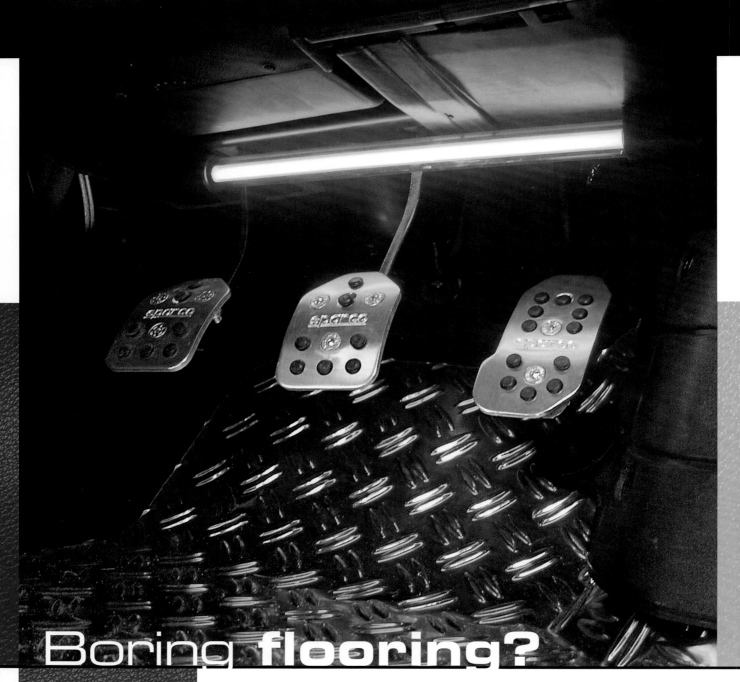

Boring flooring?

Alright, so carpets have always been a dull colour because they have to not show the dirt - when was the last time you heard of a car with white carpets? What goes on the floor needn't be entirely dull, though, and can still be easy to clean, if you're worried.

Ripping out the old carpets is actually quite a major undertaking - first, the seats have to come out (you might be fitting new ones anyway), but the carpets and underfelt fit right up under the dashboard, and under all the sill trims and centre console, etc. Carpet acts as sound-deadening, and is a useful thing to hide wiring under, too, so don't be in too great a hurry to ditch it completely. Unless, of course, your 106 is having a full-on race/rally style treatment, in which case - dump that rug!

Chequerplate is the current fashion in cool flooring, and it's easy to see why it'll probably have an enduring appeal - it's tough but flexible, fairly easy to cut and shape to fit, has a cool mirror finish, and it matches perfectly with the racing theme so often seen in the modified world, and with the ally trim that's widely used too.

Tips 'n' tricks

If you're completely replacing the carpet and felt with, say, chequerplate throughout, do this at a late stage, after the ICE install and any other electrical work's been done - that way, all the wiring can be neatly hidden underneath it.

Chequer mats

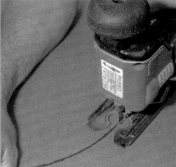

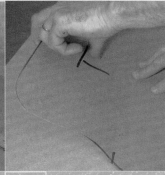

01 The halfway-house to a fully-plated interior is to make up your own tailored mats (hell, you can buy ready-mades if you're not allowed to play with sharp knives). Unless you buy real ally chequer, what you'll get is actually plastic, and must be supported by mounting it on hardboard. Take one of the lovely 'Granny' mats your car might have come with, and use it as a template to mark the shape onto the hardboard (you could always make a template from some thin card).

02 With the shape marked out, it's time for the jigsaw - next to a cordless drill, this has to be one of the most useful tools ever invented for the modder.

03 To make the hardboard fit better into the footwells, score it at the bend where it goes up under the pedals . . .

04 . . . then carefully 'fold' the hardboard back to the required shape - trust us, this will make your new chequer mats fit superbly.

05 Not unlike this in fact. Try your hardboard mat in place, and trim the corners and edges as necessary to get it fitting as flat as poss.

06 Now you can use your hardboard as a template, for cutting out the chequer. Try to make the chequer fractionally bigger overall than the hardboard, so you don't see the wood edge (you shouldn't anyway, if your board is a tidy fit). Stick the chequer to the board, using some decent glue - spray glue's convenient, but usually not quite up to the job. You can't beat good old brush-on Evo-Stik (and no, we're not being paid to say that).

07 Do it right, and you too can have a floor like this - looks sweet, and the mats don't slip. Sorted.

Wheely cool

A new steering wheel is an essential purchase in personalising your 106. It's one of the main points of contact between you and the car, it's sat right in front of you, and the standard ones are dull and massive!

Don't be tempted to fit too small a wheel - the smaller 106s never had power steering, and a tiny-rimmed steering wheel will make manoeuvring very difficult, especially with phat tyres.

One bit of good news is that, once you've shelled out for your wheel, it may be possible to fit it to your next car, too. When you buy a new wheel, you usually have to buy a boss (or mount) to go with it - the mounts are less pricey, so one wheel could be fitted to another completely different car, for minimum cost.

A trick feature worth investigating is the detachable wheel/boss. This feature comes in handy when you park up and would rather the car was still there when you come back (something most people find a bonus). It's all very well having a steering wheel immobiliser or steering lock, but I doubt many thieves will be driving off in your car if the steering wheel's completely missing! Also, removing the wheel may remove the temptation to break in and pinch… your wheel!

A word about **airbags**

Which 106s have airbags? If you've got a Mk 1, you're safe (or not, depending on your point of view) – they only came in on the Mk 2s, and not on all of those initially. So far, the market for replacement wheels with airbags hasn't materialised, so fitting your tasty new wheel means losing what some (old) people think is a valuable safety feature.

So just disconnect the damn thing, right? Wrong. Then your airbag warning light will be on permanently - not only is this irritating, your newly-modded motor will fail the MOT (having the airbag itself isn't compulsory, but if the warning light's on, it's a fail - at least at the time this was written). Two ways round this - either take out the clocks (see the section on fitting white dials) and remove the offending warning light bulb, or bridge the airbag connector plug pins with two lengths of wire soldered to either side of a 5A fuse. Bridging the pins this way 'fools' the test circuit (which fires up every time you switch on the ignition) into thinking the airbag's still there, and the warning light will go out as it should.

Disabling the airbag is yet another issue which will interest your insurance company, so don't do it without consulting them first. We're just telling you, that's all.

Warning: Airbags are expensive to replace (several £100s), and are classed as an explosive!!! Funny, that - for a safety item, there's any number of ways they can CAUSE injuries or damage if you're not careful - check this lot out:

a Before removing the airbag, the battery MUST be disconnected (don't whinge about it wiping out your stereo pre-sets). When the battery's off, don't start taking out the airbag for another 10 minutes or so. The airbag system stores an electrical charge - if you whip it out too quick, you might set it off, even with the battery disconnected. True.

b When the airbag's out, it must be stored the correct way up.

c The airbag is sensitive to impact - dropping it from sufficient height might set it off. Even if dropping it doesn't actually set it off, it probably won't work again, anyway. By the way, once an airbag's gone off, it's scrap. You can't stuff it back inside.

d If you're keeping the airbag to refit later (like when you sell the car), store it somewhere fairly cool, to start with. But what happens if it went off by accident? Sticking it under your bed might not be such a good idea. The loft, maybe?

e If you're not keeping the airbag, it must be disposed of correctly (don't just put it out for the bin men!). Take it to your local council tip or scrapyard, and let them deal with it.

f Airbags must not be subjected to temperatures in excess of 90°C (194°F) - just remember that bit about airbags being an explosive - you don't store dynamite in a furnace, now do you? Realistically in this country, the only time you'll get THAT hot is in a paint-drying oven.

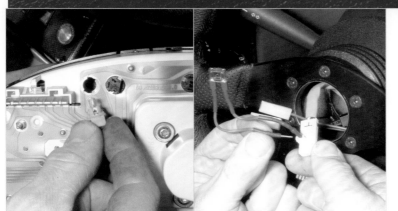

Removing a non-airbag wheel

If you're lucky enough not to have an airbag, removing the shonky old wheel is much easier - here's how. Start by prising off the centre pad (with the Peugeot lion logo), taking care not to gouge the plastic (if you're intending to refit the old wheel any time). Check you've got the front wheels set straight before undoing the steering wheel nut/bolt. Don't rely on the steering lock to stop the wheel turning while you unscrew the nut/bolt (you'll bust the lock) - use your other hand to hold the wheel rim. Unscrew the nut/bolt almost all the way off, then tap the wheel from behind to free it from its splines. When it's free, remove the nut/bolt completely, and the old wheel's just a bad memory.

Fitting a
sports wheel

01 Your first task will be to disconnect the battery negative lead (earth) and wait for 10 minutes before proceeding to remove the steering wheel. The two airbag Allen bolts are the first things to be removed, and they're 'round the back', on the rear of the wheel itself. To improve access to the bolts, turn the steering wheel a quarter of a turn either way.

02 Next, using your fingers, pull the airbag unit from the steering wheel, and disconnect its wiring plug (this is the plug you've got to bridge if you're using one of our airbag warning light dodges described earlier). Store the airbag in a safe place – on the pavement next to your car is not a safe place!

03 Ensure the front wheels are in the straight-ahead position and engage the steering lock. Hold the wheel with one hand (don't let the steering lock take the strain), and unscrew the steering wheel Torx bolt by a few turns. Don't take it right out yet.

04 Give the wheel a good pull to dislodge it from its splines. The bolt can now be removed and the wheel lifted away from the car. Ensure that, when removing the wheel, the horn wiring is carefully fed through the wheel so it doesn't get damaged.

05 The clock spring is the next thing to be removed, and it's held in place by three screws. If you haven't already guessed from the photos, the steering column upper and lower shrouds have to come off now – they're clipped together, and held on by three Allen bolts from underneath (see the white dials section for more info).

06 Disconnect the orange airbag wiring plug located underneath, at the top of the steering column.

07 To start fitting a new boss, it's necessary to remove the indicator stalk temporarily, as the self-cancelling indicator lug on the stalk gets in the way. Two screws hold the stalk in place, so lose them first, then gently pull the unit outwards.

08 Slot the new boss into place. Peugeot say that you should use a new steering wheel bolt (and we're not arguing) – if you have to re-use the old one, at least treat it to some thread-lock on the threads. A snap-off boss might be cool, but a self-loosening steering wheel definitely ain't. Tighten the bolt by hand for now.

09 Turning to our spanking new steering wheel at last, the horn button can be tried in place. Don't do too good a job of fitting this (you could even leave it off for now) – this will have to come off later, to fully tighten the steering wheel bolt.

10 Ensure the front wheels are still pointing straight-ahead, then put the new wheel in place on the boss. The holes in the steering wheel have to line up with one of the two sets of drilled holes on the boss – check that you're using the correct holes, and that the steering wheel looks as straight as possible. The gorgeous chrome ring can then slot into place on the wheel.

11 Now fit and tighten the six Allen bolts that hold the steering wheel to the boss, then pop out the horn button and tighten the centre steering wheel bolt to 40 Nm (or pretty darn tight). And there she is – a sexy Simoni Racing Bolide Lux wheel, courtesy of Auto Inparts Ltd. Now go and see how your new rim feels on the open road - what a difference a wheel makes!

Pedalling your 106

A tasty race-equipment touch to your modded machine, pedal extensions really look the part when combined with full chequerplate mats, or alloy footwells - available in several styles and (anodised) colours.

Not sure how well the anodising will wear, though… The only other issue with pedals is the clutch and brake must have rubbers fitted - this is first of all sensible (so your feet don't slip off them at an awkward moment) and it's also a legal requirement. Don't buy extensions without.

Attention!
Check your insurance company's position regarding pedal extensions. A while ago there was a big fuss after a couple of cars fitted with pedal extensions crashed, which resulted in pedal extensions being withdrawn from sale at a lot of places.

01 First job is to remove the rubber covers from each pedal. No worries so far. As you can see, we've already had a trial run at this with the clutch pedal!

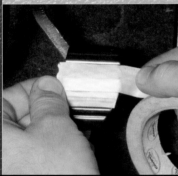

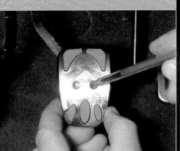

02 Stick some masking tape over the pedal . . .

03 . . . then offer the pedal into place and mark where to drill the mounting holes. Top tips – make sure the holes are at least 2 mm away from the outside edge of the pedal, don't try to drill through the pedal arm (you'll be there for ages), and check that you'll be able to fit a nut behind where your hole will be drilled.

04 Before finally getting busy with the drill, check the spacing of your new extensions. Having the brake and throttle too close together is obviously dangerous. Some embarrassment could result from the clutch and brake being in close proximity, too.

05 Time to drill some holes. Some newspaper or rags in the footwell will catch any swarf, making it easier to clean up after. A block of wood placed under the pedal is also a very good idea, as it stops the pedal from moving as you drill into it, whilst preventing any over-drill into the carpet! To stop the drill slipping when you start, use a hammer and punch to mark the hole.

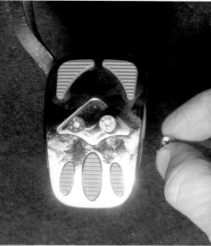
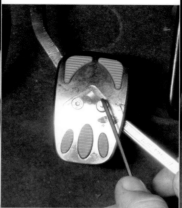

Attention!
These pedals have non-slip rubber sections built-in – other pedals have ones which you have to fit, and still others have no rubbers whatsoever. Rubber pads of some kind are essential – and they're an MoT requirement on the brake and clutch pedals at least. Not convinced? Well, just imagine the fun of having your foot slip off the brake at an awkward moment…

06 Next the Allen-headed bolt can be slipped into the hole, with the retaining nut on behind.

07 Tighten the nut with a spanner, while holding the bolt with an Allen key. Check these bolts regularly, to make sure they're still tight. Loose pedals could get you into all sorts of trouble…

08 Last job on the brake and clutch pedals is to peel off the backing paper on the sticker, and pop that into place to hide the bolts - another nice touch from Simoni Racing. Though it does make checking the tightness of those bolts a bit tricky…

09 Fitting the accelerator pedal extension is a tad more awkward. The standard pedal's too curved to sensibly fit the extension to, so it's got to come off for a little attention. To remove the pedal, firstly undo the two nuts holding the pedal and pivot to the bulkhead, then squeeze and release the white cable retaining clip at the top of the pedal.

10 The pedal's now free to be lifted from the car, and the plastic pivot cover can be removed too.

11 Now the pedal can be placed in a vice and bent flatter until the extension sits on the pedal nicely.

12 Once this has been done, you might as well put some masking tape over the pedal, then mark and drill the mounting holes while it's in the vice. As with the other pedals, keep the holes away from the edges, but also clear of the pedal arm

13 Now drill the holes, and in the same way as before once the holes are ready, pop the Allen bolt and nut into place and tighten. Refit the vital right pedal to the car, and the job's a winner. A cracking set of pedals now await some feet.

Well-heeled?

Simoni Racing have been at it again – designing cool new kit that allows the modifier to discover the true meaning of custom car interiors - custom made car mats! Call Auto Inparts for your Z1 heel pad, and read on so we can show you how to fit it.

01 Firstly you need a decent set of car mats – you don't want your spanking heel pad being mounted on any old rubbish. Put the heel pad on top of the mat, and move it around until you're happy with the position. You may prefer the heel pad to sit directly under the pedals, or slightly further back for maximum visual impact (posing).

02 Concentrate on the outer metal frame of the heel pad first, not the separate inner ones. Using Tipp-Ex or another suitable marker, highlight the holes ready for drilling.

03 Once the holes are marked, remove the heel pad and the mat from the car. Place the mat on a clean flat surface and drill the holes. Make sure you have some wood under the mat, to protect the surface you're drilling onto.

04 The kit supplies you with all the nuts and bolts you need. The nuts have a special black plastic holder to protect the carpet from any abrasion that may be caused by the metal nuts. All you have to do is pop the nut inside the plastic holder and squeeze the two together – do all of them at once, so you don't have to stop and do more later.

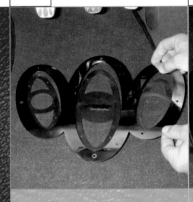   

05 Once the holes are drilled, fit the retaining bolt into place and tighten with an Allen key whilst holding the nut from behind. Repeat this for the remaining bolts around the edges of the pad.

06 One piece at time, offer the inner metal ovals into place. Hold the metal dead still, place the drill bit through the ready-drilled holes in the metal so they act as markers, then drill through the mat.

07 The mat is now all holey, so fit and tighten the retaining bolts, remembering to hold the plastic nut assembly still on the rear of the mat, or your efforts at tightening will be wasted.

08 Finally give the metal a quick polish to remove any fingerprints, and you're finished. Just add some neons, and your blinged-up footwell will be looking mighty fine.

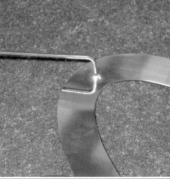   

Fitting harnesses

It's true that not everyone likes racing harnesses, but anyone like that's just boring, or should probably eat less pies. Besides, you don't fit sexy race seats and then not fit race belts, do you?

The only problem with harnesses is caused by where you have to mount them. Even with a three-point harness, you end up using one of the rear seat belt mounts, and it seriously reduces your ability to carry bodies in the back seats (webbing everywhere). The MOT crew say that, if you've got rear seats, you must have rear seat belts fitted, so you either 'double-up' on your rear belt mounts (use the same mounting bolts for your harnesses and rear belts), or you take the back seats out altogether. Removing the rear seats leaves the rear deck free for chequerplate, speakers, roll cages - whatever you like. It's just important to understand how fundamental harnesses can end up being, to the whole look of your car - there's almost no half-measures with race belts, so you've got to really want 'em.

One thing you must **not** do is to try making up your own seat belt/harness mounting points. Peugeot structural engineers spent plenty of time selecting mounting points and testing them for strength. Drilling your own holes and sticking bolts through is fine for mounting speakers and stuff, but you're heading for an interview with the Grim Reaper if you try it with seat belts. The forces in a big shunt are immense. We're not convinced either that the practice of slinging harnesses round a rear strut brace is kosher, from the safety angle - the poxy strut braces available are so flimsy (they're usually ally) you can bend them in your hands. Nuts to trusting my life to one of those!

01 To fit new harnesses, the old belts have to be unscrewed first. How far you go with this is up to you – we just unbolted the belts, and tucked the ends inside the trim panels, but you could remove them altogether (with a little help from a Haynes manual). First to go is the sliding rail next to the front seats, which just unbolts, then unhooks at the back.

02 Under the back seat cushion, you'll find more belts, and more mounting points waiting for your harnesses. Unbolt and remove. Keep hold of the old bolts and washers – we'll be needing them very soon.

03 Fitting a three-point harness, like this one, kindly supplied by Cobra, is easier than a four-point type, as you'll need one less mounting (d'uh). Your new harness just bolts in where the old belt came out . . .

04 . . . and it's the same story at the front, with one half of the harness being bolted to the old seat rail mounting. The correct torque for these bolts is 20 Nm, but do them up like your life depends on it – which it does, of course.

05 Our buckets have harness-friendly mountings provided on the seat subframes, but it's easiest to unbolt the mounting brackets from the seats first, to use them. That nut and bolt look sturdy enough . . .

06 . . . and by the time they're bolted back onto the subframe, you can be safe in the knowledge that you're... safe. Excellent.

 Attention!
The driver (that'll be you, then) should now carry out the strap adjustment process. Check out the instructions with your harnesses for the exact details on doing this, as it varies depending on harness style and manufacturer. Also observe their maintenance and safety advice - could save yer neck.

Are you **sitting stylishly?**

The perfect complement to your lovingly-sorted suspension, because you need something better than the standard seats to hold you in, now that you can corner so much faster... and they look brutal, by way of a bonus. Besides the seat itself, remember to price up the subframe to adapt it to the mounting points in your car. Most people also choose the three- or four-point harnesses to go with it (looks a bit daft to fit a racing seat without it), but make sure the harness you buy is EC-approved, or an eagle-eyed MOT tester might make you take 'em out.

Reclining seats are pricier than non-recliners, but are worth the extra. With non-adjustable seats, how are your mates meant to get in the back? Through the tailgate? Or maybe there is no back seat... You can get subframes which tilt, so that non-reclining seats can move forward. Non-reclining racing seats should be tried for fit before you buy.

An alternative to expensive racing seats would be to have your existing seats re-upholstered in your chosen colours/fabrics, to match your interior theme. You might be surprised what's possible, and the result could be something truly unique. If you've got a basic model, try sourcing seats from a breakers (haggle if the side bolsters are worn away - a common fault). A secondhand interior bought here will be a lot cheaper than buying new goodies, and you know it'll fit easily (all 106s are the same underneath) - but - it won't have that unique style. Specialist breakers may be able to supply something more rad, such as a leather interior from an old 205 1.9 GTI, newer 306, or top-spec 406 Coupé - might take some persuading to get it in, though!

Front **seats**

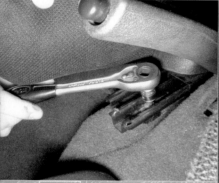

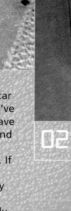

01 At some stage in transforming your car into something you've always dreamed of, you'll have to lose those sad old seats and accessorise your cabin with something sportier to sit on. If you're attached to your dull standard chairs, this is clearly going to be a difficult moment… Slide the seat fully backwards on its runners, and remove the two front seat runner bolts.

02 Next, slide the chair fully forwards on its runners, and remove the two rear seat runner bolts.

03 Squeeze yourself into the rear footwell, and tilt the front seat forwards to see if there's a bright orange wiring plug under the seat. If so, it's a seat belt pre-tensioner wiring plug (on Mk 2 models, mostly), which means the battery MUST be disconnected, and a wait of at least 10 minutes before unplugging. If you don't, you could trigger the airbag – not funny.

These very sexy new Cobra Misano recliners come with full subframes, pre-fitted with runners (usually, some dismantling of the old chairs is required). Sometimes you have to bolt the new subframes to the new seats, but that's hardly a challenge. There were four bolts altogether. With the front two done up, just release the seat sliding mechanism, and

Because the new subframes are designed for a 106, all the mounting bolt holes line up perfectly with the old holes in the floor. Just pop in your old bolts, and tighten securely (or to 25 Nm if you've got a torque wrench). There's even a mounting point on the

04 With the plug disconnected, the seat's free to be lifted out of the car and stored in a safe, dry place.

05 move the runners to get on the back two bolts.

06 Now the new seats can be offered into the car – and wow – what a transformation. If you're in the market for some new chairs, check these babies out.

07 subframe for your seat belt stalk (or race harnesses).

ICE
Headset

The cheaper your 106, the nastier your standard head unit's going to be. Course, by the time a 106 has passed through several owners, it's pretty unlikely to still have a standard set in anyway, but if all you've got is a hole, don't feel too bad. Standard sets are fine if all you want to do is aimlessly listen to the radio with your arm out the window, but not - definitely not - if you want to impress your mates with the depth and volume of your bass.

If you want to listen to CDs, it's got to go - and there's plenty of decent headsets out there which will give you a night-and-day difference in sound quality and features. The headset is the heart of your new install - always go for the best you can afford. Ask the experts which features matter most, if you're building a full system. And don't just go for the look!

Our new Kenwood KDC-W7027 headset is pretty typical of the current single-CD state of the art - decent looks, good sound, plenty of features.

01 First, the old set's got to be shifted. Resist the urge to just crowbar the thing out of the dash - you'll be needing two of the standard radio removal tools to do the job with less damage. And you could always sell it, or keep it, to stick back in when you sell the car? Our stock set won't fit anything except a 106, as it's got a moulded front panel (meant to discourage pikeys).

02 Another reason not to get too excited when removing the old set is that most of the wiring behind is fully 'recyclable' - ie we'll be using it again. One bonus on our 106 - it's got ISO plugs for power and speakers, meaning our new set should plug straight in.

03 The old cage has to go too - you can't use this with your new set, or the locking pins won't engage. Most DIY-fitted cages have absolutely every last locking tab bent over, which makes it a long job with a small screwdriver to remove it.

04 With the old cage out of the picture, now's a good time to introduce the new set's cage into the equation, and secure it by bending over just a few of the triangular lugs (not all of them!).

05 Having ISO plugs makes life much easier - one does power, the other speakers (the power one has red, yellow and black leads, among others). Here, we're plugging in the original speaker wiring plug to the new headset wiring . . .

06 . . . and now, we're cutting the original speaker wires. Why? We're running our 6x9s off the headset, so we'll be joining on some decent speaker wire to run to the back. By using the new headset's wiring instructions (these tell you which colour wires are front/rear, positive/negative), when you connect the original speaker plug, you can work out which of the original speaker wires did what. For more wiring info, see 'Wiring up' later in this section.

07 Virtually all headsets provide an output for remotely switching-on your amps (or for powering-up an electric aerial). Called the 'remote' or 'p-cont' wire, it's usually blue, and should be joined to your own wire which will run back to the amps. One of our RCA leads has a built-in p-cont, so we'd be pretty stupid not to use it.

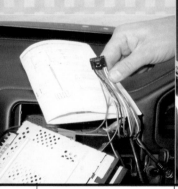

08 When you're confronted with a mass of wiring you can't sort out, don't forget the manual (the Kenwood one, in our case). Our man's got the right idea. Well, it's a lot better than blowing up the headset.

09 Feeling confident now, so we're bringing in the new headset for the first time - plugging in the new wiring is one of the simpler jobs. It's a bit vital to the plot, this plug, so make sure it clips in tight.

10 Those amps need a signal to work from, and that's what the RCA outputs on the headset provide. If the set's got more than one pair of connections (pre-outs), these may be marked 'front', 'rear' or 'sub'. Use whichever set makes sense for the system. Connect the red lead to the red socket - we think you can guess where the other one goes.

11 Don't forget to plug in the aerial lead if you plan on listening to Hip-Hop FM. Grrrreat. If the lead won't fit, you might need an adapter plug (should come with a good headset, but it might be a trip to the local auto accessory store), which fits into the original aerial lead . . .

12 . . . then lead and adapter can go straight into the back of the headset.

13 Test that everything's working at this point, before pushing the unit right into its cage. If all's well, push the headset home until it clicks. If it gets stuck, take the set out, and un-bunch all the wiring by hand (on our 106, this task took longest of all). Do not force it in, or you could end up having a very bad day. Success? Now get out the instruction manual again, and set those levels properly. Enjoy.

Front speakers

The standard items in the 106 speak volumes (hur-hur) about any car manufacturer's desire to build things down to a price - ie spend as little as poss. What does it cost Peugeot for the speakers in a 106? If it's more than a fiver a set, they're being robbed. Low on power, and with nasty paper cones which disintegrate after a few years, fitting any aftermarket speakers is going to be an upgrade.

So what are your options? Well, unless you've got plans for mahoosive door builds to take some 6x9s or the odd sub, you're limited to co-axial speakers (tweeter and woofer combined) or components (separate woofer and tweeter, with a crossover box). Components usually give the best sound, but you'll need space in your door for a tweeter, and the crossover also needs a home. Tricky. We're taking the easy option, with some quality Pioneer co-axials.

Tricks 'n' tips
When you're shopping for door speakers, check the quoted mounting depth for your chosen components. Based on our experience, the maximum depth you'll get in most front doors, without spacers, is 60 mm – if in doubt, check this before you buy, with the window glass wound right down .

01 Sorting the speakers on a 106 is so easy. On most models, you don't even have to remove the door trim panel first (but we did, to fully sound-deaden the door – see 'Removing stuff'). The speaker's held in by four screws . . .

02 . . . then it's off with the wiring plug. Those tattered paper cones should burn quite well . . .

03 Before actually fitting the speaker, sound-deaden that metal door panel, or it'll vibrate with all the kicking power of your new system. The leader in deadening is Dynamat - but - it comes at a price. What else is out there? Adhesive flashing for roofing repairs, from a DIY store. Use the real thing if you prefer, but this works. Besides, who'll see it? Cut off a decent-size length . . .

04 . . . then poke it in through the speaker hole. Don't get too carried away in your quest for sonic perfection, but don't skimp on it, either. Treat the large 'floppy' areas of the door, and some round the speaker hole will help too. Two things - use it warm (warm it up with a heat gun, on a cold day), and watch your fingers on the expensive stuff (the metal foil edges are sharp!).

05 Meanwhile, no-one's noticed we're cheating with the speaker wiring. Okay, for the ultimate in SPL, you should run oxygen-free (or better) right through into the door, to your speaker. In practice, even pro installers sometimes don't bother. Chop off the old plug . . .

06 . . . then use your Haynes manual wiring diagram to identify the pos and neg Peugeot wires, and crimp on suitable terminals. Our 106 had a red and a green wire to the speaker plug – as you'd expect, red was the positive, so it got the larger of the two terminals.

07 Now that's a sweet result. We've got a 150W door speaker in there, and it fits perfectly, even using the exact same holes as the original. Even with the skinny Peugeot wiring, it's gotta sound way better than before. Let's feed it some tunes, and find out.

Rear speakers

Stealth shelf 6x9s

01 First job with a new ready-made shelf is to mark the speaker positions. Not tricky.

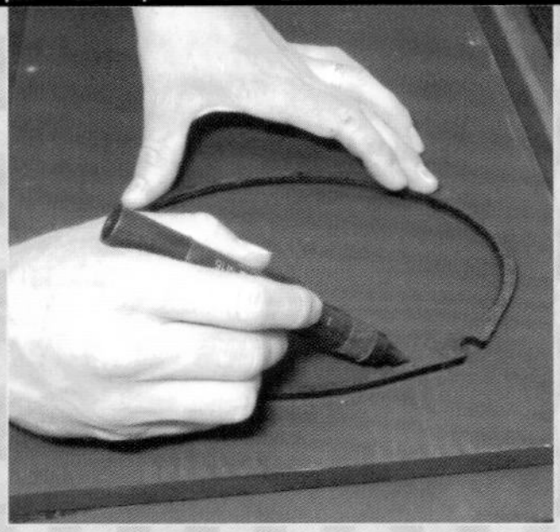

If we're talking about a set of 6x9s, rear shelf-mounting is the simplest option. If you don't want to butcher your standard shelf (always a flimsy item), either make a new one from MDF (using your stock shelf as a template), or buy a ready-made acoustic 'stealth' shelf. Either way, make hiding your new speakers a priority - tasty speakers on display in the back window could soon mean no rear window, and no speakers...

While shelf mounting has its advantages, 106s have another top spot for speakers - the rear side trim panels. Okay for speakers without huge, heavy magnets, you just cut a suitable-sized hole in the panel, and mount your speaker in from behind.

As we're ditching the rear seats on our 106, we've made up an MDF rear seat panel in place of the old seat backrest - firmly fixed in place, this makes an ideal home for some 6x9s. Maybe even two sets?

02 With a speaker outline marked, remove the wood from the rest of the shelf, and drill a nice big hole somewhere inside the outline... then get busy with the jigsaw.

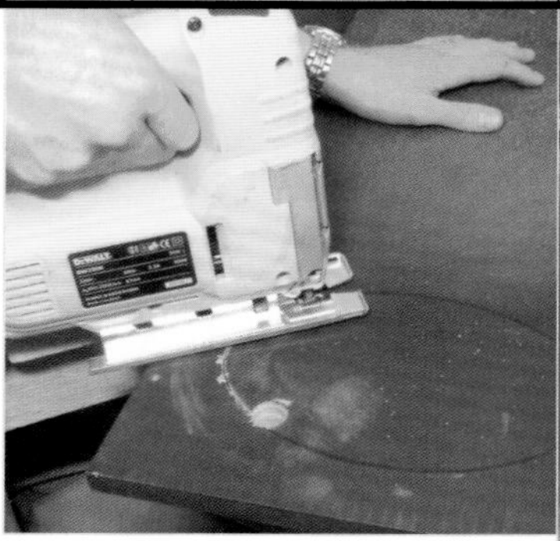

03 Use the speaker mounts (or even the speakers themselves) as a template to drill the mounting holes . . .

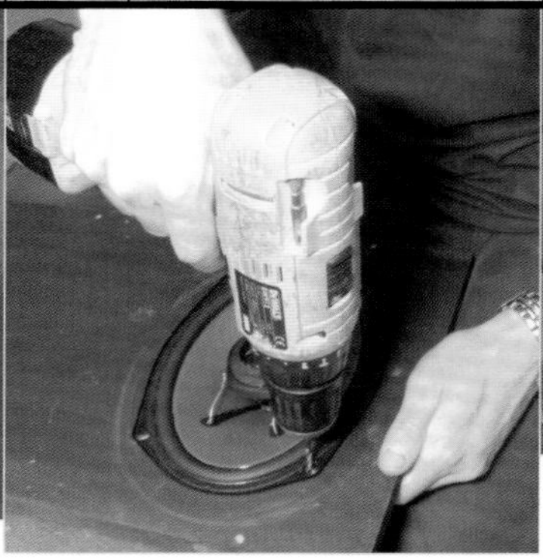

04 . . . then screw on the speakers themselves. Don't forget that 6x9s can be run off the headset, to provide a little 'rear fill' - if you have them amped-up, you might find that the sound's too biased to the back of the car.

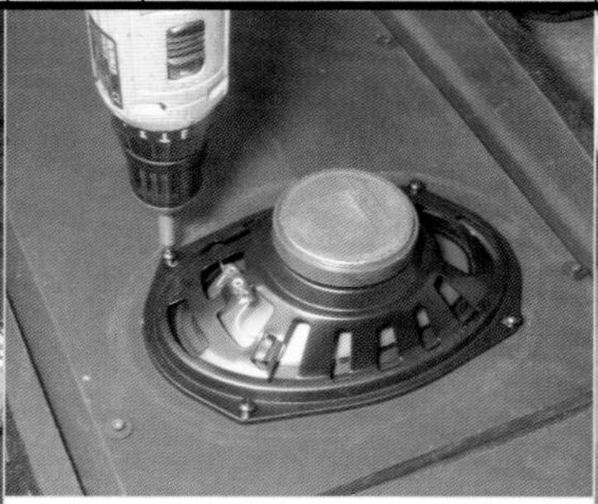

05 Remember that the length of wire to each speaker should be the same (as near as poss), or you might find the speakers run slightly out of phase. Crimp on the right terminals, and connect up your speakers. For max neatness, use P-clips screwed along the edge of the shelf. To remove the shelf more easily, fit some bullet connectors in the speaker wiring, or ask your ICE dealer for a Neutrik connector plug.

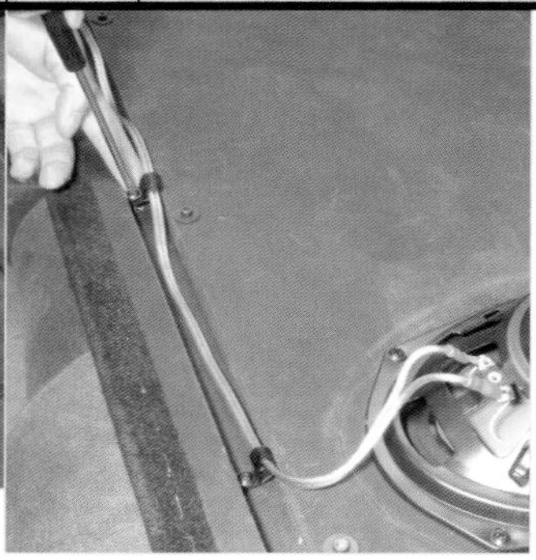

Attention!

MDF dust is nasty stuff to breathe in. Wear a mask when you're cutting, drilling or sanding it.

MDF back panel 6x9s

For those of you who've never noticed before (possibly because it's on the bit you throw away), speaker manufacturers usually provide a handy cardboard template for fitting their products. It's on the back of the box they come in. Just cut it out . . .

01

. . . and stick it onto your chosen piece of MDF. Drill a hole large enough to take your jigsaw blade, and you're all set. One speaker-sized hole, coming up.

02

Proper templates (like this Kenwood example) also give you guidance for drilling the speaker mounting holes.

03

So - the holes have been cut/drilled, and the panel's been neatly trimmed using spray glue and black carpet. Does the speaker fit? You betcha.

04

On this speaker, the bolts fit from the front . . .

05

. . . with a spring washer and nut on behind.

06

All that's left is the wiring - providing we remember it's large terminal and wire-with-writing on the pos side, we'll soon be hearing sweet, sweet music.

07

Subs & boxes

No system's complete without that essential deep bass boom and rumble. Don't muck about with bass tubes - get the real thing to avoid disappointment. So you lose some of your boot space - so what? Is getting the shopping in an issue? We think not.

Most people opt for the easy life when it comes to boxes, at least until they're ready for a full-on mental install. The 106 boot's not the biggest, but if you plan your install well, standard boxes will still fit easily. Making up your own box isn't hard though, especially if you were any good at maths and geometry. Oh, and woodwork. Most subs come with instructions telling you what volume of box they work best in, but ask an expert (or a mate) what they think - the standard boxes are just fine, and none are pricey. The only real reason to build your own is if you've got an odd-shaped boot (or want something that looks trick).

Importante!
MDF dust is nasty stuff to breathe in. Wear a mask when you're cutting, drilling or sanding it.

01 Take one standard sub box, and try the sub for size. Don't go fitting it yet, just make sure the hole's big enough for your needs. If not, have they sent you the wrong box? Minor trimmage can be accomplished using a file, or if it's a bit more than minor, use a jigsaw.

02 Once we're sure the sub's a good fit, it can come out again. Forgetting to wire up your sub before fitting it is a very common mistake, caused by being too keen. Most ready-made boxes come fitted with a terminal plate on the side of the box - with these, just run your speaker wire from the sub to the inside of the plate (keep the pos and neg wiring the right way round).

The terminal plates have either screw-type or spring-type terminals for connecting your speaker wire. You can just strip the end, twist it up and shove it in. Or you can 'tin' the end of your speaker wire, with solder, which makes it easier to fit your speaker wire, and removes the chance of any stray strands (which could touch, and blow a channel on your amp or headset). Keeping to our wiring convention, we're joining the writing-on wire to the positive (red) terminal.

Make sure the sub's logo is lined up correctly (this won't affect the sound, just the pose-value), then drill through the mounting holes round the edge of the sub.

03

04 Once the mounting holes are made, screw the sub down tight (unless you want bass all over the place).

05

Wiring-up

For most people, this is the scariest part of an install - just the thought of masses of multi-coloured spaghetti sticking out of your dash might have you running to the experts (or a knowledgeable mate). But - if you do everything in a logical order, and observe a few simple rules, wiring-up isn't half as brain-numbing as it seems.

Live feeds

Although a typical head unit can be powered off the standard Peugeot wiring (the stock wire is good for about 15 amps, tops) running amplifiers means you'll be needing a new live feed, taken straight off the battery. Or in our case, straight off the junction box we fitted as part of our fusebox install (see 'security').

Get some decent 'eight-gauge' (quite heavy) or 'four-gauge' (getting on for battery cable thickness - serious stuff) wire, and a matching fuseholder. If you're running more than one item off this feed wire, get a distribution block too, which splits the feed up, with a separate fuse for each item - who'd have thought electrical safety can look trick too?

Pub trivia

Hands up, who knows what 'RCA' stands for? We use it every day in ICE-speak, but WHAT does it really mean? Really Clever Amplifier lead? Remote Control Acoustic lead? Well, the answer's a strange one. RCA leads and connectors are also known as 'phono' connectors in the world of TV and hi-fi, and they've been around a long, long time. How long, exactly? We're talking back in the days when you could only get radios - big suckers with valves in them, and long before anyone thought of putting one in a car. RCA actually stands for Radio Corporation of America, who hold the patent on this type of connector and lead. Not a lot of people know that.

Speaker and RCA wiring

As with all wiring, the lesson here is to be neat and orderly - or - you'll be sorry! RCA leads and speaker wires are prone to picking up interference (from just about anywhere), so the first trick to learn when running ICE wiring is to keep it away from live feeds, and also if possible, away from the car's ECUs (the main one's right out of the way, under the bonnet). Another way to interference-hell is to loop up your wiring, when you find you've got too much (we've all been there). Finding a way to lose any excess lengths of wire without bunching can be an art - laying it out in a zig-zag, taping it to the floor as you go, is just one solution.

Another lesson in neatness is finding out what kinds of cable clips are available, and where to use them. There's various stick-on clips which can be used as an alternative to gaffer tape on floors, and then 'P-clips', which look exactly as their name suggests, and can be screwed down (to speaker shelves, for instance). 'Looming'

your wiring is another lesson well-learned - this just means wrapping short strips of tape around, particularly on pairs of speaker wires or RCAs. As we've already said, don't loom speaker wire with power cables (or even with earths).

The last point is also about tidiness - mental tidiness. When you're dealing with speaker wiring, keep two ideas in mind - positive and negative. Each speaker has a pos (+) and neg (-) terminal. Mixing these up is not an option, so work out a system of your own, for keeping positive and negative in the right places on your headset and amp connections. Decent speaker cable is always two wires joined together - look closely, and you'll see that one wire has writing (or a stripe) on, and the other is plain. Use the wire with writing or a stripe for pos connections throughout your system, and you'll never be confused again. While we're at it, RCA leads have red and white connector plugs - Red is for Right.

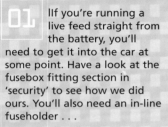

01 lIf you're running a live feed straight from the battery, you'll need to get it into the car at some point. Have a look at the fusebox fitting section in 'security' to see how we did ours. You'll also need an in-line fuseholder . . .

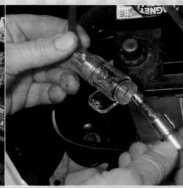

02 . . . containing a fuse that'll cover the total load for your system.

03 There's something really satisfying about this type of fuseholder - it's just made for the job. Pop the bared end of your eight-gauge wire in the other end, and clamp it with the Allen-headed grub screw. Now that's quality. Remember, though - as soon as the fuseholder's connected up, the other end of that wire is live (even if the ignition's off).

04 To do a proper job, any new cables should be run down the car as far from the Peugeot wiring as poss. Keep the power leads away from the RCAs and any speaker cable, for the best chance of avoiding interference. A few strips of gaffer tape keeps the wires where they should be.

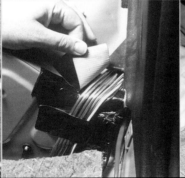

05 You'll often find with any install that there's a whole bunch of wires going through into the boot, close to the rear seat mountings. If the wires get squashed, and chafe through on the metal edges, this could be very dodgy to your system's long-term health. Gaffer tape has more than one use in your install – it sticks and protects.

06 The lazy option is to route the wires down the sides of the car. After unclipping the sill trim/door seal, you'll be surprised how much wire can be hidden this way. Keep the power feeds separate by running them down the other side. If your sill trims are secured using screws, be careful when refitting - a screw through the wiring is a good way to kill your system.

Amplifiers

01 First, we need power - masses of power. Here, we're splitting the main power feed from the front of the car into two, using this rather neat circuit-breaker instead of the more usual distribution block.

02 The all-important live supply is one amp connection you should really use a proper terminal on, rather than just stuffing a bare wire into the hole. And insulate any bare metal on the terminal - that live touches anything else, and the results won't be good.

So, how many amps do we want in our car? One school of thought says each pair of speakers, and each sub, should have an individual amp - by setting the output from each amp separately, you can control each aspect of the sound, before you even need to think about adding a graphic equaliser. You can also better match your speakers to the level of power they need, to work best. Trouble is, running several amps means doubling-up on wiring, and you could end up drawing a monster amount of power from that battery.

Any starter system can be made to seriously kick, using just one 400W four-channel amp - choose the right one carefully (and the components to go with it), and just one will do. With a 'tri-mode' amp, you could run your front components off one pair of channels, bridge the other two for a sub, and run some rear 6x9s off the head unit. Don't forget that decent modern headsets chuck out fifty-per-channel now, so don't assume you'll need separate amps for everything. Ideally, in any system, the sound shouldn't all come from behind you - ears were designed to work best with sound arriving from in front (and who are we to argue?).

Decide where you'll mount the amps carefully. Any amp must be adequately cooled - don't cover it up so there's no airflow, and don't hang it upside-down from your shelf.

Our system set-up uses two matching Sony Xplod amps - one 1000W beast for our sub, and a 480W two-channel for the front speakers. They've got the look, but how about the performance to back it up? Let's find out.

06 Don't use skinny wires for earths - ideally, it should be the same-thickness wire as you've used for your live feed. Connecting it to the amp's the easy bit (make sure it's done up tight).

07 Next up, it's the humble p-cont (remote) lead going on. This performs the vital function of carrying the 'switch-on' signal from your headset - without this, you won't hear much. The good news is, this is one time when size doesn't matter - it doesn't carry much current, so the wire can be as skinny as you like.

03 Before connecting up the earth, you'll need a decent earth point somewhere in the boot, to join your wire to. If you find a handy exisitng bolt, use it. You can make your own earth like this, if you have to – drill a hole in the rear of the boot . .

04 . . . slip in a nut and bolt, securely tightened . . .

05 . . . and now there's an earth point you can add any number of wires to, secured with a second nut. No dodgy self-tappers here, then.

08 Connecting up the RCAs shouldn't tax your brain too much. This amp has a pass-through facility, meaning you could run another RCA lead out of this amp, into another one. We just want the input connections for this install. Not all RCA leads are marked red and white, but there will be one colour on one lead, to avoid embarrassing mistakes.

09 Read the amp's instruction book carefully when connecting any wires, or you might regret it, especially for bridged or tri-mode. Identify your speaker pos and neg/left and right wires with a piece of tape, and get them screwed on. As with the lives and earths, it's also vital there's no stray bits of wire left poking out.

10 A good tip is to leave the amps loose until after you've set them up - if you can, leave good access to the gain adjustment (volume) screws after final fitting, too. Starting at normal listening volume, with the amp gain turned down, put on a kicking track, then turn the gain up until the speakers just start to distort. Turn the gain down a tad from there, and you've a good basic setting. Amp gain and headset faders can now be tweaked to give a good balanced sound - or whatever tickles your lugholes.

Tricks 'n' tips
Very few systems work 100%, first time. If the amp LEDs don't light up, for instance, are they getting power? Are the p-cont/remote wires connected properly? If the sub doesn't kick, is the amp switch set to bridged or tri-mode, not stereo? Are the low-pass switches in the correct position? RTFM.

Engines

Faster, faster!

So - does your car talk the talk (sounds fast), or does it walk the walk (actually is fast)? There's no shame in just having a fast-sounding car - not everyone can afford mega-performance, which is why bolt-on goodies like induction kits and big-bore exhausts are such big business. Serious engine tuning costs, and not just in the engine parts - your insurance company will throw a wobbly at a gas-flowed head, and might refuse to cover you altogether if you go for that supercharger conversion.

The induction kit and sports exhaust are an essential first choice, and usually it's as far as you can really go before your insurance company disowns you. Both mods help the engine to 'breathe' better, which helps when you go for the accelerator initially, improving the response you feel, while you also get a crowd-pleasing induction roar and rasp from the back box, so everyone's happy.

Now for the harsh and painful truth. On their own, an induction kit and back box may not gain you much extra 'real' power. Sorry, but it's a myth. Time and again, people fit induction kits and back boxes, expecting huge power gains, and those 'in the know' have a quiet chuckle. All these things really do is make the car sound sportier, and improve the response - accept this, and you won't be disappointed. Ask yourself why most insurance companies don't generally increase premiums for the likes of a performance rear box or induction kit. The answer is - because (on their own) they don't make enough difference!

The 'bolt-on' performance goodies have more effect as part of an engine 'makeover' package, and setting-up the engine properly after fitting these parts can make a huge difference. If you're halfway serious about increasing the go of your 106, talk to someone with access to a rolling road, so you can prove what's been done has actually made a useful gain. If you've spent time and a ton of money on your car, of course you're going to think it feels faster, but is it actually making more power?

Fitting all the performance goodies in the world will be pretty pointless if the engine's already knackered, but it might not be as bad as you think. One of the best ways to start on the performance road is simply to ensure that the car's serviced properly - new spark plugs, filters, and an oil change, are a good basis to begin from. Correct any obvious faults, such as hoses or wiring plugs hanging off, and look for any obviously-damaged or leaking components, too.

Breathe with me...

Replacement element

One of the simplest items to fit, the replacement air filter element has been around for years - of course, now the induction kit's the thing to have, but a replacement element is more discreet (if you're worried about such things).

While we're at it, don't listen to anyone who says just take out the air filter completely - this is a really naff idea. The fuel system's air intake acts like a mini vacuum cleaner, sucking in air from the front of the car, and it doesn't just suck in air, but also dust, dirt and leaves. Without a filter, all this muck would quickly end up in the sensitive parts of the fuel system, and will quickly make the car undriveable. Worse, if any of it makes it into the engine, this will lead to engine wear. Remember too, that cheaper performance filters can be of very suspect quality - if your new filter disintegrates completely inside six months, it'll do wonders for the airflow, but it'll also be letting in all sorts of rubbish!

Some performance filters have to be oiled before fitting - follow the instructions provided; don't ignore this part, or the filter won't be effective. If the filter won't fit, check whether you actually have the right one - don't force it in, and don't cut it to fit, as either of these will result in gaps, which would allow unfiltered air to get in.

Induction kit

You'd either have to be mad, or without a pulse, not to want more performance from your car, and freeing up your engine's breathing is one way to start.

Pipercross have been one of the top names in induction and air filtration for many years, because they have a great reputation for producing quality goods. What the increased cool air flow from a complete induction kit will do is tell the engine ECU that it needs to add more fuel, which it will do (in small amounts). This will result in a quick-revving, throaty-sounding engine, with (maybe) more power and more torque. So, you're waiting for what exactly?

01 In order to fit the new kit, the old air filter housing must be removed (excellent – that's the whole point), so start by disconnecting the air intake pipe.

02 Next, if you have one, disconnect the air temperature sensor wiring plug.

03 Using a small screwdriver, un-hinge and remove the retaining clips on the cam cover-to-air filter housing breather hose. These clips really are pathetic – you can't re-use them, so get some new Jubilee clips for refitting.

>>

04 Another of these excellent clips is used on the second breather hose that locates in the top of the air filter housing.

05 At last – a Jubilee clip! This connects the air duct from the old air cleaner to the throttle housing, and yes, it can be re-used.

06 On our car, the brake servo pipe was in the way, sitting over the top of the air intake trunking/pipes. Which meant we had to slacken another clip and disconnect it from the servo itself – you might not have to. Take care, as this pipe is vital to the operation of your brakes (which is another way of saying – don't forget to reconnect it afterwards!).

07 Finally, turn this quick-release fastener to free up the air intake pipe . . .

08 . . . and the whole assembly is now free to be lifted away.

09 Park the old air cleaner on a clean, flat surface, then use a spanner to remove the air temperature sensor itself. This sensor's needed for refitting to the new filter cone.

10 Unpack your spanking new induction kit, and check that all the parts are present and correct. Looking good so far – as usual, another quality piece of kit. Before we start fitting, spray the cone with a good dose of the filter oil supplied.

11 Now it's time to fit the air temperature sensor you removed in step 9 to the cone. Tighten it securely.

12 Our kit contained a rubber sleeve, which fits over the end of the throttle housing . . .

13 . . . before sliding on the new filter cone. Remember to have a suitably-sized Jubilee clip in place on the metal pipe, then tighten it to secure the cone to the throttle body – we don't want any air leaks.

14 The rest of fitting is just tidying-up, really. If you had to disconnect the servo pipe, reconnect it and tighten the clip firmly – any leaks here, and your brakes won't work too well. Plug in the air temperature sensor . . .

15 . . . and connect the two breather hoses to the ports provided on the new filter. Those nice Pipercross lads have thought of everything – they even supply two new hose clips. Cheers! Now bark up the engine, and blip that throttle. Impressed?

Finally...

Once you've fitted your new filter or induction kit, even if you don't take the car to a rolling road for setting up, at least take it to a garage and have the emissions checked - any minor adjustments should ensure that the engine will, if nothing else, still tick over okay, and should ensure an MOT emissions pass.

Adjustable fuel
pressure regulator
(power boost valve)

These valves allow the fuel system pressure to be increased over the standard regulator valve. Contrary to what you might think, they don't actually provide much more fuel (this is regulated separately by the injection ECU). The effect of increasing the injection pressure is to improve the injector spray pattern, which helps the fuel to burn more efficiently, and has the effect of increasing engine power while actually reducing emission levels.

To see the true effect of these valves, they must be set up using emission test gear and ideally a rolling road - merely turning the pressure up to the maximum level might not produce the desired effect. Fitting one of these valves involves breaking into the high-pressure fuel line, which is potentially dangerous for the inexperienced - also, if the valve is poorly fitted (or the fuel lines are in poor condition), you could end up with fuel spraying out under pressure onto a hot engine. Make sure you know what you're doing - anything involving petrol requires talent - and watch carefully for any sign of fuel leakage after fitting, even if this is done by a professional.

No quicker but it
looks nice

Looks are just as important as performance. No hot hatch is 'finished' without making it look sweet. Details to the engine bay as well as your interior and exterior mods are an important factor, especially if you were thinking about getting your motor featured in top magazines. Everyone does it, and you're next.

First up - try cleaning the engine, for flip's sake! How do you expect to emulate the show-stopping cars if your gearbox is covered in grot? Get busy with the degreaser (Gunk's a good bet), then get the hosepipe out. You can take it down to the local jetwash if you like, but remember your mobile - if you get carried away with the high-power spray, you might find the car won't start afterwards!

When it's all dry (and running again), you can start in. Get the polish to all the painted surfaces you reasonably can, and don't be afraid to unbolt a few of the simpler items to gain better access. We're assuming you've already fitted your induction kit, but if not, these nicely do away with a load of ugly plastic airbox/air cleaner and trunking, and that rusted-out exhaust manifold cover, in favour of decent-looking product. Take off the rocker cover, and paint it to match your chosen scheme (heat-resistant paint is a must, really, such as brake caliper paint), set off with a funky oil filler cap. A strut brace is a tasty underbonnet feature, especially chromed. Braided hose covers (or coloured hose sets), ally battery covers and bottles, mirror panels - all give the underbonnet a touch of glamour.

You's a hose

Attention!
The engine must be completely cold before you start. Even if you've only done a quick lap, it would be dangerous to attempt doing anything with a remotely warm engine, as the fluids inside the pipe are often a lot hotter than they appear. Be warned!

01 There are many ways to add detail and colour to otherwise boring components. Spraying your hoses is just one of those ways. Only apply paint that is suitable for engine bay use, as temperatures get very high under the hood. The good folk from ABC Design supplied our Tube-It hose paint.

02 Choose the most visible hoses first, and be careful undoing the hose clips - there could be coolant or fuel in there. Don't even think about spraying the hoses in place - do you really want to colour-code the entire underbonnet area? Give the pipe a good clean to thoroughly degrease it - any oil or silicone-slippery stuff, and the paint won't stick.

03 A preferred way of spraying, to ensure maximum coverage, is to hang the pipe from above. Use a stiff piece of wire inserted into the end of the hose (not poked through the hose) to hold onto.

04 Apply the paint in three or four light layers until pipe is evenly covered. You'll also have to wait a while (ideally, leave overnight) before that hose can go back on.

05 Given enough time to dry, this hose paint's really good stuff - doesn't crack or flake off. But we wouldn't advise going ballistic with the pressure washer, once the hose is back on - the paint might not be quite that good.

06 Tighten all hose clips securely - coolant leaks are not cool, and fuel leaks could be deadly. If you've lost any coolant, the system will need topping-up once you're done - you'll want a 50-50 mix of antifreeze and water, not just plain water.

Braiding hoses

Engines

First step is to remove your chosen hose. If supplies of braiding are limited, go for the hoses at the top of the engine first, then the ones underneath you can't see won't matter so much. You'll either find spring-type clips, best released using pliers, or one-shot clips which you destroy during removal. Make sure you've got a supply of new Jubilee clips available, just in case.

01

If the hose is stuck, be careful how you free it, or you could snap the pipe stub underneath (some are only plastic). This sort of thing can really ruin your day. Careful prising with a screwdriver is usually enough to loosen a stubborn hose end.

02

Unroll your braiding, check the length against your freshly-removed hose . . .

03

08 . . . before trimming off the excess braiding (and not the hose).

09 Slide a new Jubilee clip over the braiding at one end, then slip one of the coloured end fittings over the clip.

10 Repeat this process at the other end of your chosen hose, and it'll be ready to fit back on.

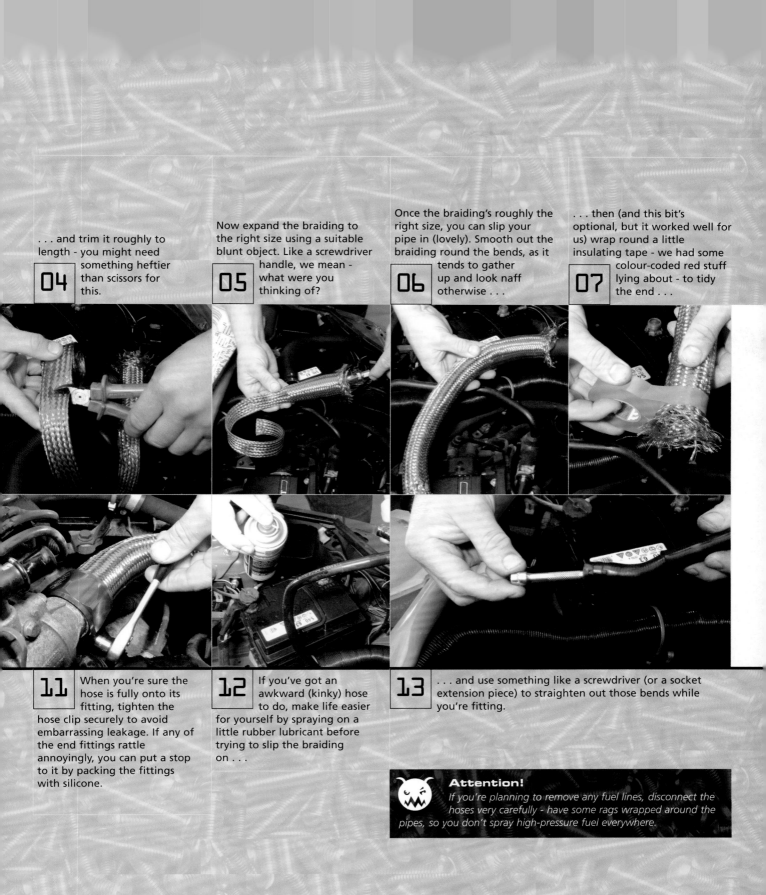

04 . . . and trim it roughly to length - you might need something heftier than scissors for this.

05 Now expand the braiding to the right size using a suitable blunt object. Like a screwdriver handle, we mean - what were you thinking of?

06 Once the braiding's roughly the right size, you can slip your pipe in (lovely). Smooth out the braiding round the bends, as it tends to gather up and look naff otherwise . . .

07 . . . then (and this bit's optional, but it worked well for us) wrap round a little insulating tape - we had some colour-coded red stuff lying about - to tidy the end . . .

11 When you're sure the hose is fully onto its fitting, tighten the hose clip securely to avoid embarrassing leakage. If any of the end fittings rattle annoyingly, you can put a stop to it by packing the fittings with silicone.

12 If you've got an awkward (kinky) hose to do, make life easier for yourself by spraying on a little rubber lubricant before trying to slip the braiding on . . .

13 . . . and use something like a screwdriver (or a socket extension piece) to straighten out those bends while you're fitting.

Attention!
If you're planning to remove any fuel lines, disconnect the hoses very carefully - have some rags wrapped around the pipes, so you don't spray high-pressure fuel everywhere.

Silicon **heaven**

All fuel-injected 106s have an engine management system with a 'computer' at its heart, known as the ECU, or Electronic Control Unit. The ECU contains several computer chips, at least one of which has programmed onto it the preferred fuel/air mixture and ignition advance setting for any given engine speed or load - this information is known as a computer 'map', and the system refers to it constantly while the car's being driven. Obviously, with the current trend towards fuel economy and reducing harmful exhaust emissions, the values in this 'map' are set, well, conservatively, let's say (read 'boring'). With a little tweaking - like richening-up the mixture, say - the engine can be made to produce more power, or response will be improved, or both. At the expense of the environment. Whatever.

Companies like Superchips offer replacement computer chips which feature a computer map where driveability and performance are given priority over outright economy (although the company claims that, under certain conditions, even fuel economy can be better, with their products). While a chip like this does offer proven power gains on its own, it's obviously best to combine a chip with other enhancements, and to have the whole lot set up at the same time. By the time you've fitted an induction kit, four-branch manifold, big-bore pipe, and maybe even a fast-road cam, adding a chip is the icing on the cake - chipping an already-modified motor will liberate even more horses, or at least combine it with

majorly-improved response. Peugeot tuning specialists are best placed to advise you on the most effective tuning mods.

Another feature programmed into the ECU is a rev limiter, which cuts the ignition (or fuel) progressively when the pre-set rev limit is reached. Most replacement chips have the rev limiter reset higher, or removed altogether. Not totally sure this is a good thing - if the engine's not maintained properly (low oil level, cambelt changes neglected), removing the rev limiter and running beyond the red line would be a quick way to kill it. But a well-maintained engine with rally cam(s) fitted could rev off the clock, if the ECU would let it, so maybe not a bad thing after all…

Now the bad news

Chipping is often thought of as an easy, 'no-tell' route to increased performance and driveability - usually, the ECU is well-buried inside the car, so who's gonna know?* Needless to say, the insurance companies have been wise to this trick for a long time. A sure way to tell whether any 'performance' product does what it says on the tin is to see what it'll do to your premium - telling them you're fitting a sports ROM chip will cost. Big-time. But, in the event of a claim, if they suspect your car's been 'chipped', rest assured, they will make efforts to find out, because if you haven't told them about it, it means they save on paying out. What's an insurance assessor's salary for one day, compared to the thousands you could be claiming in case of an accident or theft? Do it by all means, but at least be honest.

*This isn't so on the 106 - the ECU's clearly on display under the bonnet.

Engine tuning

So you've done the filter/induction kit and exhaust box - what's next, short of going for a complete engine swap?

If you've got a sports back box, try a performance exhaust manifold up front - or better still, a full 'cat-back' system for the best gains. Your 1993-onwards 106 is, of course, being strangled all the time you're driving. By a cat - how embarrassing is that? There's the option of a de-cat pipe, which does away with the power-sapping catalytic converter at a stroke, freeing-up as many as 10 or 15 horses on the way (but remember the car's not MOT-able with one of these fitted, so isn't strictly legal for use on the road).

A new camshaft's often a juicy way to pep up a standard motor. Standard cams are pretty good these days, but a fast road cam will still give you more top-end (possibly, right at the very top-end, with nothing much below that). Once the ECU rev limiter's been disabled (by chipping), swap the cam(s) and you should see more power further up the rev range. Treat your 106 to a skimmed, gas-flowed, big-valve cylinder head as well, and it'll really start to percolate.

The Rallye and XSI / GTI are obviously the most tuneable 106s, with chipping a favourite first mod. Otherwise, what you can do to a Saxo, you can do just as well to a 106. Which means there's turbo and even supercharger conversions to save up for.

Engine **swaps**

Most young 106 owners wait 'til they've built up some no-claims bonus on their insurance, and go for a bigger Peugeot engine. Why throw shedloads of cash modding a weenie Peugeot engine, when lots less money spent on fitting a new motor could buy you the same power, with room left for tuning?

If you've "only" got a 1.1 litre lump, even a swap for the 1.3 engine from the Mk 1 Rallye will make a useful difference, as would transplanting any of the 1.6 engines on offer (stick to the 90-brake 1.6 from the XS or XT for half-sensible insurance quotes). The ultimate 106 motor, of course, is the 16-valve GTI, with 120 bhp. But why stop there? Anyone tried swapping in a 2.0 litre? Like the 206 GTI 180, for instance?

And finally

And finally tonight - the bad news. Any major engine mods means telling those nice suits who work for your insurance company, and it's likely they'll insist on a full engineer's report (these aren't especially expensive - look one up in the Yellow Pages, under *'Garage Services'* or *'Vehicle Inspection'*).

Exhausts

It's gotta be done, hasn't it? Your rusty old exhaust lacks the girth to impress, and doesn't so much growl as miaow. Don't be a wimp and fit an exhaust trim - they'll fool nobody who really knows, and they certainly won't add to your aural pleasure (oo-er). Sort yourself out a decent back box upgrade, and even a timid 1.0 litre 106 can begin to cut it at the cruise.

What a back box won't do on its own is increase engine power - although it'll certainly sound like it has, provided you choose the right one, and fit it properly. Check when you're buying that it can be fitted to a standard system - you'll probably need something called a reducing sleeve for a decent fit, which is a section of pipe designed to bridge the difference between your small-diameter pipe and the larger-diameter silencer. Try and measure your standard pipe as accurately as possible, or you'll have major problems trying to get a decent seal between the old and new bits - don't assume that exhaust paste will sort everything out, because it won't.

Fashion has even entered the aftermarket exhaust scene, with different rear pipe designs going in and out of style. Everyone's done the upswept twin-pipe 'DTM' style pipes, while currently the trend in single pipes is massive Jap-style round exits, or fat oval (or twin-oval) designs. If you must have the phattest 106 on the block, you

Know your enemy - this is what your cat looks like inside. Is it any wonder they restrict gas flow?

can't beat a twin-exit system (from someone like Powerflow or Milltek), even though it'll probably mean losing your spare wheel in the fitting process. Well, when was the last time you had a puncture? And what are mobiles and breakdown cover for, anyway?

You might need to lightly modify even your standard rear bodywork/bumper to accommodate a bigger rear pipe; if you're going for a bodykit later, your back box will have to come off again, so it can be poked through your rear valance/mesh.

You'll see some useful power gains if you go for the complete performance exhaust system (cat-back system), rather than just the back box. Like the factory-fit system, the sports silencer works best combined with the front pipe and manifold it was designed for! Performance four-branch manifolds alone can give very useful power gains. Watch what you buy, though - cheap exhaust manifolds which crack for a pastime are not unknown, and many aftermarket systems need careful fitting and fettling before you'll stop it resonating or banging away underneath. A sports rear box alone shouldn't attract an increased insurance premium, but a full system probably will.

All 106s (even the GTI) are lumbered with a catalytic converter (or 'cat'), which acts like a restrictor in the exhaust, inhibiting the gas flow and sapping some engine power (maybe 5 to 10%). Various specialist exhaust companies market replacement sections which do away with the cat (a 'de-cat pipe'), and get you your power back. Unfortunately, by taking off or disabling the cat, your car won't be able to pass the emissions test at MOT time, so you'll have to 're-convert' the car every 12 months. This means the car's illegal on the road with a de-cat pipe fitted - you'd have no defence for this, if questions were asked at the roadside, and potentially no insurance if the unthinkable happens. Sorry, but we have to say it…

If your 106 has been slammed to the floor, will your big new sports system be leaving behind a trail of sparks as it scrapes along the deck? Shouldn't do, if it's been properly fitted, but will the local multi-storey be out-of-bounds for your 106, from now on? And - pub trivia moment - you can actually be done for causing damage to the highway, if your exhaust's dragging. Well, great.

You probably couldn't give a stuff if your loud system's a very loud major public nuisance, but will that loud pipe start interfering with your sound system? If you rack up many motorway miles, you might find the constant drone of a loud pipe gets to be a real pain on a long trip, too…

Fitting a sports back box

01 Before even thinking about fitting a new back box, the standard box (aka rusty old silencer) has to come off first. To make life a little easier, spray the exhaust clamp and rubber mountings with some WD-40. Removing the rear bumper (see 'body styling') is also a good idea.

02 Undo the nut and bolt securing the tailpipe clamping ring. Sounds easy when you say it quickly – in reality, you may have a seizure on your hands. Luckily, this is one time when it doesn't matter if the bolt shears, as you can easily get another clamp. Another way round is to get the hacksaw to it. Just try not to damage the exhaust centre section, if violence is required.

03 The clamping ring (or what's left of it?) can now be levered off the tailpipe using a flat-bladed screwdriver.

04 Unhook the exhaust from the two rubber mountings, and drop it out from under the car. Looks a bit on the pristine side, this 'rusty old silencer' we're throwing away. Damn.

05 Take a little time to clean up the centre section joint – ours seems pretty solid, but if yours isn't, you'll need to take care here. Seriously, if there's nothing left of the pipe you're joining to, a new centre section (or a complete cat-back performance system) is the only answer.

06 A squirt of exhaust paste will help the joint seal nicely, so apply a good bead of it to the pipe.

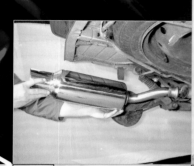

07 Offer the shiny new back box into place on the car and check for size. Our Peco box fits nicely (no surprise there) so there's no extra work for us – we like!

08 Unless you have the luxury of a helper on hand, you'll need something holding up the new box in place while you fit the clamp. We suggest you use a jack for this – it's nearly as good as a person, and doesn't moan half as much.

09 With the jack taking the strain, slip the clamp into place and loosely fit the retaining bolt and nut. Don't tighten the clamp fully until you've aligned the box on the rubber mountings.

10 The bracket for one of the rubber mountings comes ready-welded to the box, and simply requires you to slide the metal bracket into the rubber. At this point, the jack (or the helper) has served its purpose and can be moved out of the way.

11 Our box also came with a wrap-around support bracket, which you slide onto the box. This support bracket is designed to hook onto the remaining rubber mounting. For it to work, the clamp nut has to be done up tight.

12 Adjusting the position of the back box is still possible by undoing the clamp and support bracket and moving the box by hand. Once you're happy with the way the exhaust hangs, go back and tighten the nuts on the clamp and bracket.

13 Refit the rear bumper and check to see if the new back box fouls the bumper. If like us things seem a little too close for comfort, you'll have to mask up the offending area and mark exactly where the bumper needs to be trimmed. A hacksaw blade will cut through that bumper in no time!

14 If no bumper trimming is required, and your exhaust install has gone as smoothly as ours, why not advertise what a great system you've got fitted? Not sure how long the sticker here would last, but you could always stick it on your windows instead.

Safety and tools

Safety

We all know that working on your car can be dangerous - and we're not talking about the danger of losing your street cred by fitting naff alloys or furry dice! Okay, so you'd be hard-pushed to injure yourself fitting some cool floor mats or a tax disc holder, but tackle more-serious mods, and you could be treading dangerous ground. Let's be honest - we have to put this safety section in to cover ourselves, but now it's in, it would be nice if you read it…

Burning/scalding

The only way you'll really burn yourself is if your car's just been running - avoid this, and you won't get burned. Easy, eh? Otherwise, you risk burns from any hot parts of the engine (and especially the exhaust - if you've got one, the cat runs very hot), or from spilling hot coolant if you undo the radiator hoses or filler cap, as you might when you're braiding hoses.

Fire

Sadly, there's several ways your car could catch fire, when you think about it. You've got a big tank full of fuel (and other flammable liquids about, like brake fluid), together with electrics - some of which run to very high voltages. If you smoke too, this could be even worse for your health than you thought.

a Liquid fuel is flammable. Fuel vapour can explode - don't smoke, or create any kind of spark, if there's fuel vapour (fuel smell) about.

b Letting fuel spill onto a hot engine is dangerous, but brake fluid spills go up even more readily. Respect is due with brake fluid, which also attacks paintwork and plastics - wash off with water.

c Fires can also be started by careless modding involving the electrical system. It's possible to overload (and overheat) existing wiring by tapping off too many times for new live feeds. Not insulating bare wires or connections can lead to short-circuits, and the sparks or overheated wiring which results can start a fire. Always investigate any newly-wired-in kit which stops working, or which keeps blowing fuses - those wires could already be smouldering…

Crushing

Having your car land on top of you is no laughing matter, and it's a nasty accident waiting to happen if you risk using dodgy old jacks, bricks, and other means of lifting/supporting your car. Please don't.

Your standard vehicle jack is for emergency roadside use only - a proper trolley jack and a set of axle stands won't break the overdraft, and might save broken bones. Don't buy a cheap trolley jack, and don't expect a well-used secondhand one to be perfect, either - when the hydraulic seals start to fail, a trolley jack will drop very fast; this is why you should always have decent stands in place under the car as well.

Steering, suspension & brakes

Screwing up any one of these on your car, through badly-fitted mods, could land you and others in hospital or worse. Nuff said? It's always worth getting a mate, or a friendly garage, to check over what you've just fitted (or even what you've just had fitted, in some cases - not all "pro" fitters are perfect!). Pay attention to tightening vital nuts and bolts properly - buy or borrow a torque wrench.

To be absolutely sure, take your newly-modded machine to a friendly MOT tester (if there is such a thing) - this man's your ultimate authority on safety, after all. Even if he's normally a pain once a year, he could save your life. Think it over.

Even properly-fitted mods can radically alter the car's handling - and not always for the better. Take a few days getting used to how the car feels before showing off.

Wheels

Don't take liberties fitting wheels. Make sure the wheels have the right stud/bolt hole pattern for your car, and that the wheel nuts/bolts are doing their job. Bolts which are too long might catch on your brakes (especially rear drums) - too short, and, well, the wheels are just waiting to fall off. Not nice. Also pay attention to the bolt heads or wheel nuts - some are supposed to have large tapered washers fitted, to locate properly in the wheel. If the nuts/bolts "pull through" the wheel when tightened, the wheel's gonna fall off, isn't it?

Asbestos

Only likely to be a major worry when working on, or near, your brakes. That black dust that gets all over your alloys comes from your brake pads, and it may contain asbestos. Breathing in asbestos dust can lead to a disease called asbestosis (inflammation of the lungs - very nasty indeed), so try not to inhale brake dust when you're changing your pads or discs.

Airbags

Unless you run into something at high speed, the only time an airbag will enter your life is when you change your steering wheel for something more sexy, and have to disable the airbag in the process. Pay attention to all the precautionary advice given in our text, and you'll have no problems.

One more thing - don't tap into the airbag wiring to run any extra electrical kit. Any mods to the airbag circuit could set it off unexpectedly.

Exhaust gases

Even on cars with cats, exhaust fumes are still potentially lethal. Don't work in an unventilated garage with the engine running. When fitting new exhaust bits, be sure that there's no gas leakage from the joints. When modifying in the tailgate area, note that exhaust gas can get sucked into the car through badly-fitting tailgate seals/joints (or even through your rear arches, if they've been trimmed so much there's holes into the car).

Tools

In writing this book, we've assumed you already have a selection of basic tools - screwdrivers, socket set, spanners, hammer, sharp knife, power drill. Any unusual extra tools you might need are mentioned in the relevant text. Torx and Allen screws are often found on trim panels, so a set of keys of each type is a wise purchase.

From a safety angle, always buy the best tools you can afford - or if you must use cheap ones, remember that they can break under stress or unusual usage (and we've all got the busted screwdrivers to prove it!).

DO Wear goggles when using power tools.

DO Keep loose clothing/long hair away from moving engine parts.

DO Take off watches and jewellery when working on electrics.

DO Keep the work area tidy - stops accidents and losing parts.

DON'T Rush a job, or take stupid short-cuts.

DON'T Use the wrong tools for the job, or ones which don't fit.

DON'T Let kids or pets play around your car when you're working.

DON'T Work entirely alone under a car that's been jacked up.

Legal modding?
No such thing!!

The harsh & painful truth

The minute you start down the road to a modified motor, you stand a good chance of being in trouble with the Man. It seems like there's almost nothing worthwhile you can do to your car, without breaking some sort of law. So the answer's not to do it at all, then? Well, no, but let's keep it real.

There's this bunch of vehicle-related regulations called Construction & Use. It's a huge set of books, used by the car manufacturers and the Department of Transport among others, and it sets out in black and white all the legal issues that could land you in trouble. It's the ultimate authority for modifying, in theory. But few people (and even fewer policemen) know all of it inside-out, and it's forever being updated and revised, so it's not often enforced to the letter at the roadside - just in court. Despite the existence of C & U, in trying to put together any guide to the law and modifying, it quickly becomes clear that almost everything's a "grey area", with no-one prepared to go on record and say what is okay to modify and what's not. Well, brilliant. So if there's no fixed rules (in the real world), how are you meant to live by them? In the circumstances, all we can promise to do is help to make sense of nonsense…

Avoiding roadside interviews

Why do some people get pulled all the time, and others hardly ever? It's often all about attitude. We'd all like to be free to drive around "in yer face", windows down, system full up, loud exhaust bellowing, sparks striking, tyres squealing - but - nothing is a bigger "come-on" to the boys in blue than "irresponsible" driving like this. Rest assured,

if your motor's anywhere near fully sorted, the coppers will find something they can nick you for, when they pull you over - it's a dead cert. Trying not to wind them up too much before this happens (and certainly not once you're stopped) will make for an easier life. There's showing off, and then there's taking the pee. Save it for the next cruise.

The worst thing from your point of view is that, once you've been stopped, it's down to that particular copper's judgement as to whether your car's illegal. If he/she's having a bad day anyway, smart-mouthing-off isn't gonna help your case at all. If you can persuade him/her that you're at least taking on board what's being said, you might be let off with a warning. If it goes further, you'll be reported for an offence - while this doesn't mean you'll end up being prosecuted for it, it ain't good. Some defects (like worn tyres) will result in a so-called "seven-day wonder", which usually means you have to fix whatever's deemed wrong, maybe get the car inspected, and present yourself with the proof at a police station, inside seven days, or face prosecution.

If you can manage to drive reasonably sensibly when the law's about, and can ideally show that you've tried to keep your car legal when you get questioned, you stand a much better chance of enjoying your relationship with your modded beast. This guide is intended to help you steer clear of the more obvious things you could get pulled for. By reading it, you might even be able to have an informed, well-mannered discussion about things legal with the next officer of the law you meet at the side of the road. As in: "Oh really, officer? I was not aware of that. Thank you for pointing it out." Just don't argue with them, that's all…

Documents

The first thing you'll be asked to produce. If you're driving around without tax, MOT or insurance, we might as well stop now, as you won't be doing much more driving of anything after just one pull.

Okay, so you don't normally carry all your car-related documents with you - for safety, you've got them stashed carefully at home, haven't you? But carrying photocopies of your licence, MOT and insurance certificate is a good idea. While they're not legally-binding absolute proof, producing these in a roadside check might mean you don't have to produce the real things at a copshop later in the week. Shows a certain responsibility, and confidence in your own legality on the road, too. In some parts of the country, it's even said to be a good idea to carry copies of any receipts for your stereo gear - if there's any suspicion about it being stolen (surely not), some coppers have been known to confiscate it (or the car it's in) on the spot!

Number plates

One of the simplest mods, and one of the easiest to spot (and prove) if you're a copper. Nowadays, any changes made to the standard approved character font (such as italics or fancy type), spacing, or size of the plate constitutes an offence. Remember too that if you've moved the rear plate from its original spot (like from the tailgate recess, during smoothing) it still has to be properly lit at night. You're unlikely to even buy an illegal plate now, as the companies making them are also liable for prosecution if you get stopped. It's all just something else to blame on speed cameras - plates have to be easy for them to shoot, and modding yours suggests you're trying to escape a speeding conviction (well, who isn't?).

Getting pulled for an illegal plate is for suckers - you're making it too easy for them. While this offence only entails a small fine and confiscation of the plates, you're drawing unwelcome police attention to the rest of your car. Not smart. At all.

Sunstrips and tints

The sunstrip is now an essential item for any modded motor, but telling Mr Plod you had to fit one is no defence if you've gone a bit too far. The sunstrip should not be so low down the screen that it interferes with your ability to see out. Is this obvious? Apparently not. As a guide, if the strip's so low your wiper(s) touch it, it's too low. Don't try fitting short wiper blades to get round this - the police aren't as stupid as that, and you could get done for wipers that don't clear a sufficient area of the screen. Push it so far, and no further!

Window tinting is a trickier area. It seems you can have up to a 25% tint on a windscreen, and up to 30% on all other glass - but how do you measure this? Er. And what do you do if your glass is tinted to start with? Er, probably nothing. Of course you can buy window film in various "darknesses", from not-very-dark to "ambulance-black", but being able to buy it does not make it legal for road use (most companies cover themselves by saying "for show use only"). Go for just a light smoke on the side and rear glass, and you'd have to be unlucky to get done for it. If you must fit really dark tints, you're safest doing the rear side windows only.

Some forces now have a light meter to test light transmission through glass at the roadside - fail this, and it's a big on-the-spot fine.

Single wiper conversion

Not usually a problem, and certainly not worth a pull on its own, but combine a big sunstrip with a short wiper blade, and you're just asking for trouble. Insufficient view of the road ahead. There's also the question of whether it's legal to have the arm parking vertically, in the centre of the screen, as it obscures your vision. Probably not legal, then - even if it looks cool. Unfortunately, the Man doesn't do cool.

Lights

Lights of all kinds have to be one of the single biggest problem areas in modifying, and the police are depressingly well-informed. Most people make light mods a priority, whether it's Morette conversions for headlights or Lexus-style rear clusters. If they fit alright, and work, what's the problem?

First off, don't bother with any lights which aren't fully UK-legal - it's just too much hassle. Being "E-marked" only makes them legal in Europe, and most of our Euro-chums drive on the right. One of our project cars ended up with left-hand-drive rear clusters, and as a result, had no rear reflectors and a rear foglight on the wrong side (should be on the right). Getting stopped for not having rear reflectors would be a bit harsh, but why risk it, even to save a few quid?

Once you've had any headlight mods done (other than light brows) always have the beam alignment checked - it's part of the MOT, after all. The same applies to any front fogs or spots you've fitted (the various points of law involved here are too many to mention - light colour, height, spacing, operation with main/dipped headlights - ask at an MOT centre before fitting, and have them checked out after fitting).

If Plod's really having a bad day, he might even question the legality of your new blue headlight bulbs - are they too powerful? Keeping the bulb packaging in the glovebox might be a neat solution here (60/55W max).

Many modders favour spraying rear light clusters to make them look trick, as opposed to replacing them - but there's trouble in store here, too. One of the greyest of grey areas is - how much light tinting is too much? The much-talked-about but not-often-seen "common sense" comes into play here. Making your lights so dim that they're reduced to a feeble red/orange glow is pretty dim itself. If you're spraying, only use proper light-tinting spray, and not too many coats of that. Colour-coding lights with ordinary spray paint is best left to a pro sprayer or bodyshop (it can be done by mixing lots of lacquer with not much paint, for instance). Tinted lights are actually more of a problem in daylight than at night, so check yours while the sun's out.

Lastly, two words about neons. Oh, dear. It seems that neons of all kinds have now been deemed illegal for road use (and that's

interior ones as well as exteriors, which have pretty much always been a no-no). If you fit neons inside, make sure you rig in a switch so you can easily turn them off when the law arrives - or don't drive around with them on (save it for when you're parked up). Distracts other road users, apparently.

ICE

Jungle massive, or massive public nuisance? The two sides of the ICE argument in a nutshell. If you've been around the modding scene for any length of time, you'll already know stories of people who've been done for playing car stereos too loud. Seems some local authorities now have by-laws concerning "music audible from outside a vehicle", and hefty fines if you're caught. Even where this isn't the case, and assuming a dB meter isn't on hand to prove the offence of "excessive noise", the police can still prosecute for "disturbing the peace" - on the basis of one officer's judgement of the noise level. If a case is proved, you could lose your gear. Whoops. Seems we're back to "do it - but don't over-do it" again. If you really want to demo your system, pick somewhere a bit less public (like a quiet trading estate, after dark) or go for safety in numbers (at a cruise).

Big alloys/tyres

One of the first things to go on any lad's car, sexy alloys are right at the heart of car modifying. So what'll interest the law?

Well, the first thing every copper's going to wonder is - are the wheels nicked? He'd need a good reason to accuse you, but this is another instance where having copies of receipts might prove useful.

Otherwise, the wheels mustn't rub on, or stick out from, the arches - either of these will prove to be a problem if you get stopped. And you don't need to drive a modded motor to get done for having bald tyres…

Lowered suspension

Of course you have to lower your car, to have any hope of street cred. But did you know it's actually an offence to cause damage to the road surface, if your car's so low (or your mates so lardy) that it grounds out? Apparently so! Never mind what damage it might be doing to your exhaust, or the brake/fuel lines under the car - you can actually get done for risking damage to the road. Well, great. What's the answer? Once you've lowered the car, load it up with your biggest mates, and test it over roads you normally use - or else find a route into town that avoids all speed bumps. If you've got coilovers, you'll have an easier time tuning out the scraping noises.

Remember that your new big-bore exhaust or backbox must be hung up well enough that it doesn't hit the deck, even if you

haven't absolutely slammed your car on the floor. At night, leaving a trail of sparks behind is a bit of a giveaway…

Exhausts

One of the easiest-to-fit performance upgrades, and another essential item if you want to be taken seriously on the street. Unless your chosen pipe/system is just too damn loud, you'd be very unlucky to get stopped for it, but if you will draw attention this way, you could be kicking yourself later.

For instance - have you in fact fitted a home-made straight-through pipe, to a car which used to have a "cat"? By drawing Plod's attention with that extra-loud system, he could then ask you to get the car's emissions tested - worse, you could get pulled for a "random" roadside emissions check. Fail this (and you surely will), and you could be right in the brown stuff. Even if you re-convert the car back to stock for the MOT, you'll be illegal on the road (and therefore without insurance) whenever your loud pipe's on. Still sound like fun, or would you be happier with just a back box?

It's also worth mentioning that your tailpipe mustn't stick out beyond the very back of the car, or in any other way which might be dangerous to pedestrians. Come on - you were a ped once!

Bodykits

The popular bodykits for the UK market have all passed the relevant tests, and are fully-approved for use on the specific vehicles they're intended for. As long as you haven't messed up fitting a standard kit, you should be fine, legally-speaking. The trouble starts when you do your own little mods and tweaks, such as bodging on that huge whale-tail spoiler or front air dam/splitter - it can be argued in some cases that these aren't appropriate on safety grounds, and you can get prosecuted. If any bodywork is fitted so it obscured your lights, or so badly attached that a strong breeze might blow it off, you can see their point. At least there's no such thing as Style Police. Not yet, anyway.

Seats and harnesses

Have to meet the UK safety standards, and must be securely bolted in. That's about it. It should be possible to fasten and release any seat belt or harness with one hand. Given that seat belts are pretty important safety features, it's understandable then that the police don't like to see flimsy alloy rear strut braces used as seat harness mounting points. Any other signs of bodging will also spell trouble. It's unlikely they'd bother with a full safety inspection at the roadside, but they could insist on a full MOT test/engineer's report inside 7 days. It's your life.

While we're on the subject of crash safety, the police also don't like to see sub boxes and amps just lying on the carpet, where the back seat used to be - if it's not anchored down, where are these items gonna end up, in a big shunt? Embedded in you, possibly?

Other mods

We'll never cover everything else here, and the law's always changing anyway, so we're fighting a losing battle in a book like this, but here goes with some other legalistic points we've noted on the way:

a It's illegal to remove side repeaters from front wings, unless they're "replaced" with Merc-style side repeater mirrors. Nice.

b All except the most prehistoric cars must have at least one rear foglight. If there's only one, it must be fitted on the right. We've never heard of anyone getting stopped for it, but you must also have a pair of rear reflectors. If your rear clusters ain't got 'em, can you get trendy ones? Er, no.

c Fuel filler caps have to be fitted so there's no danger of fuel spillage, or of excess fumes leaking from the top of the filler neck. This means using an appropriate petrol-resistant sealer (should be supplied in the kit). Oh, and not bodging the job in general seems a good idea. Unlikely to attract a pull, though.

d Front doors have to retain a manual means of opening from outside, even if they've been de-locked for remote locking. This means you can't take off the front door handles, usually. It seems that rear door handles can be removed if you like.

e Tailgates have to have some means of opening, even if it's only from inside, once the lock/handle's been removed. We think it's another safety thing - means of escape in a crash, and all that.

f You have to have at least one exterior mirror, and it must be capable of being adjusted somehow.

g If you fit new fog and spotlights, they actually have to work. No-one fits new lights just for show (or do they?), but if they stop working later when a fuse blows, relay packs up, or the wiring connectors rust up, you'd better fix 'em or remove 'em.

h Pedal extensions must have rubbers fitted on the brake and clutch pedals, and must be spaced sufficiently so there's no chance of hitting two pedals at once. This last bit sounds obvious, but lots of extension sets out there are so hard to fit that achieving this can be rather difficult. Don't get caught out.

i On cars with airbags, if you fit a sports wheel and disconnect the airbag in the process, the airbag warning light will be on permanently. Apart from being annoying, this is also illegal.

j Pace-car strobe lights (or any other flashing lights, apart from indicators) are illegal for road use. Of course.

k Anything else we didn't think of - is probably illegal too. Sorry.

Any questions? Try the MOT Helpline (0845 6005977). Yes, really.

Thanks to Andrew Dare of the Vehicle Inspectorate, Exeter, for his help in steering us through this minefield!

Thanks to:

We gratefully acknowledge all the help and advice offered from the following suppliers, without whom, etc, etc. Many of those credited below went way beyond the call of duty to help us produce this book - you know who you are. Cheers, guys! Roll the credits...

ABC Design Autostyling
(AutoArt & MHW)
www.abcdesignltd.c

Auto Inparts Lt
(accessories)
01525 382713

Brown & Geeson
(Momo accessories)
01268 764411
www.brownandgeeson.com

Cobra Seats
(seats and harnesses)
01952 684020
www.cobraseats.com

Cooper Avon Tyres
01225 703101
www.coopertire.com

Dash Dynamics
(dash kit)
0870 127 0003
www.dashdynamics.co.uk

Demon Tweeks
(accessories)
www.demon-tweeks.co.uk

Draper Tools
(tools)
023 8026 6355
www.draper.co.uk

Ecosse Peugeot Specialists
(body kit)
01506 516106
www.ecosse-peugeot.co.uk

urostyling (Folia tec)
0870 162 4448
www.eurostyling.com

Halfords
www.halfords.com

Microscan Alarms
www.microscanalarms.co.uk

A & I Peco
(exhaust box)
0151 647 6041
www.peco.co.uk

Pipercross
(induction systems)
01604 707750
www.pipercross.com

Red Dot Racing
(brake discs & pads)
0870 300 2354
www.reddotracing.co.uk

Richbrook
(sport auto accessories)
01328 862387
www.richbrook.co.uk

Ripspeed at Halfords
www.halfords.com

SPAX
01869 244771
www.spaxperformance.com

SW Autodesign
(Momo wheels)
0161 366 8536
www.swautodesign.com

A special thank you to:
Bryn Musselwhite

Editorial Director	Matthew Minter
Designer	Simon Larkin
Page Build	James Robertson
Workshop	Paul Buckland Pete Trott
Editor	Ian Barnes
Project Co-ordinator	Carole Turk
Production Control	Charles Seaton